MW00811221

"This kind of book is both long overdue, and, for that reason, deeply needed. Generations of research on theological education (Farley, Kelsey, Foster) have pointed to the dis-integrating character of traditional patterns of theological education. This book offers a rich (and integrated!) discussion of how to change these patterns. Staff, faculty, administration, trustees, and church leaders involved in forming faith leaders should read, discuss, and enact changes based upon this energetic, collaborative book."

—**Christian Scharen**, The Center for the Study of Theological Education, Auburn Theological Seminary

Integrating Work in
Theological Education

Integrating Work in Theological Education

EDITED BY

Kathleen A. Cahalan,
Edward Foley,

AND

Gordon S. Mikoski

FOREWORD BY

Stephen R. Graham

PICKWICK *Publications* · Eugene, Oregon

Pickwick Publications
An Imprint of Wipf and Stock Publishers
199 W. 8th Ave., Suite 3
Eugene, OR 97401

www.wipfandstock.com

PAPERBACK ISBN: 978-1-4982-7879-9
HARDCOVER ISBN: 978-1-4982-7881-2
EBOOK ISBN: 978-1-4982-7880-5

Cataloguing-in-Publication data:

Names: Cahalan, Kathleen A., editor | Foley, Edward, editor | Mikoski, Gordon S., editor | Graham, Stephen R., foreword.

Title: Integrating work in theological education / edited by Kathleen A. Cahalan, Edward Foley, and Gordon S. Mikoski ; foreword by Stephen R. Graham.

Description: Eugene, OR: Pickwick Publications, 2017 | Includes bibliographical references and index.

Identifiers: ISBN 978-1-4982-7879-9 (paperback) | ISBN 978-1-4982-7881-2 (hardcover) | ISBN 978-1-4982-7880-5 (ebook)

Subjects: Theology—Study and teaching. | Seminarians—Religious life. | Spiritual formation.

Classification: BV4020 I558 2017 (print) | BV4020 (ebook)

Manufactured in the U.S.A.   03/06/17

Contents

Foreword

For the three decades of my involvement with theological schools, the question of integration regularly has been identified as a challenge and discussed. Integration implies unity, and in this era of growing diversities integrative unity is as difficult to achieve as it ever has been. Theological schools face a range of pressures toward divergence related to students, faculty, and institutions. Glenn Miller's third volume of his comprehensive study of theological education in the United States bears the title *Piety and Plurality*, and describes the growing divergence.[1] In their energetic work to address a growing number of issues and to serve an ever greater variety of constituencies, theological schools can lose focus, and their work can feel fragmented without a clear center and the stability and stillness needed to listen to the voice of the Spirit. As one author in this volume put it, religious leaders need "the ability to slow down and contemplate what God is doing."[2]

Students bring a richness of diversities to theological schools that makes them exciting places to be, but those diversities also contribute to the complex challenge of integration. The authors identify a range of student diversities in their essays: the remarkably varied experiences students bring to their theological studies, for example; a wide spectrum of ages; different vocational goals; and racial and ethnic differences. Theological educators regularly lament that, compared to years past, today's students

1. Miller, *Piety and Plurality: Theological Education since 1960*. The first study is *Piety and Intellect* and the second is *Piety and Profession*.

2. See chapter 19, "Integrative Knowing and Practical Wisdom," 216, in this volume.

frequently bring less experience in communities of faith to their theological study and fewer are prepared through completing undergraduate degrees in the humanities. The Association of Theological Schools Standards of Accreditation once identified areas of liberal arts study as preferable for those pursuing graduate theological studies. Whether it was ever carefully followed, that list disappeared some time ago, and many students come to seminary with undergraduate degrees that do not include courses in history, philosophy, or literature, and many lack experience in public speaking or the level of writing that is needed for graduate theological studies.

Faculty serving in theological schools also represent a greater variety of demographics, perspectives, and preparation than in the past. In its faculty development programming the Association of Theological Schools (ATS) emphasizes the work of faculty as "theological educators" serving within a theological faculty to form religious leaders rather than guild specialists. Seeking to create new knowledge, the doctoral programs that train faculty hired by graduate theological schools encourage ever-narrower topics of research. Guilds (and many theological schools) reward focused research, yet theological schools normally need faculty to teach broadly within their disciplines and provide a wide range of services to the schools and their students. ATS studies of faculty have identified the greatest strength of doctoral programs is, not surprisingly, to prepare the graduates as researchers. Research remains important in the work theological faculty do in their schools, but they identify teaching as their most important work. They also spend a significant amount of time in the formation of students and the work of administration, neither of which receives attention in their doctoral programs. According to faculty studies by the Auburn Center for the Study of Theological Education, fewer faculty come to theological schools with either the master of divinity degree or significant leadership experience in communities of faith.[3] Chapters in this volume note the challenges faced by faculty to develop the skills needed for more integrative work. And the authors expand the definition of who sits at the faculty table and why. Faculty members in theological schools are remarkably gifted and dedicated to the work, but relatively few have been trained in ways that facilitate integrative thinking and work.

External pressures also mitigate against integration on the institutional level. At the same time that institutions need to do *more* educationally,

---

3. Wheeler, "True and False"; Wheeler and Wilhelm, "Tending Talents"; and Wheeler, Miller, and Schuth, "Signs of the Times.

since many students are less fully prepared for graduate theological education than in previous generations, financial and missional pressures push schools to provide shorter and less expensive degree programs. Because of budget constraints, schools work to decrease expenditures, but a number of integrative practices require additional personnel (team teaching, pastoral mentors, spiritual directors), travel, and collaborations (with congregations and other institutions), all of which can add pressure to the institution's budget.

Together, these forces and circumstances make integration both necessary and very challenging.

That is why this book is so timely and important.

The editors and authors have provided an extraordinary service to their colleagues in theological schools and the students they serve by unpacking and illustrating the range of meanings and applications of integration in graduate theological studies. The book's four main parts—schools, curriculums, courses, and frameworks—capture the breadth of integrating needed within theological schools. The first three parts begin with an introductory section that frames the section, followed by case studies that illustrate it, concluding by "harvesting insights" on what has been learned. The volume effectively represents the diversities present in graduate theological schools—sizes and types of schools, ecclesial families, approaches, models, and examples—and the book effectively illustrates integrative work through its structure.

Some approaches to integration are rather narrow, seeking integration in curricula for example, by attempting to bridge the disciplinary gap in a few courses by team teaching. In contrast, this book takes a very broad view of integration, using the term in three ways: making connections between bodies of knowledge, overcoming the divide between theory and practice, and enhancing what is called the "professional" model by integrating intellectual, practical, and moral and professional aspects of theological education. The result is that virtually every facet of the enterprise of theological education is presented for examination of how it contributes, or fails to contribute, to integration: from curriculum to persons to the uses of time and space. One author summarizes, "Integrating is a long-term process that is the proper work of entire institutions—and not just students."[4]

The editors and authors review work already being done in their schools through illustrative case studies, describe frameworks as a means to

---

4. See chapter 5, "Harvesting Insights," 71, in this volume.

examine the integrating process, and seek to understand integrative work theologically within the various ecclesial traditions. They hope to "advance the conversation" through attention to *who* does the integrating, examining the roles of the larger community and not just students who are normally identified as those most in need of learning the skills of integration. They approach integrating as a dynamic process that evolves over time. And they want to be "attentive to theory and theology." As one author puts it, "The theological affirmation of God as triune suggests that all integrating work finally takes its cues from the mystery of God as revealed in Jesus Christ by the power of the Holy Spirit."[5]

Lack of integration is certainly an educational problem. The work of this volume illustrates that it is also a *theological* problem. The Holy Trinity models perfect integration in diversity, creation displays astonishing diversity while all is sustained by the same life-giving Spirit, and the Incarnation draws together human and divine in perfect unity. To what extent do our theological schools and theological education reflect (or reject) the integrating character of God?

This timely volume makes an important contribution to the ongoing processes of exploration and assessment of educational models and practices in theological education and leads us on a remarkably fruitful journey toward integrating that is wise, theologically informed, and effective.

—Stephen R. Graham

Senior Director of Programs and Services
The Association of Theological Schools
and the Commission on Accrediting

5. See chapter 18, "Models of Integrating Work," 201, in this volume.

Bibliography

Miller, Glenn T. *Piety and Intellect: The Aims and Purposes of Ante-Bellum Theological Education.* Scholars Press Studies in Theological Education. Atlanta: Scholars, 1990.

——. *Piety and Plurality: Theological Education since 1960.* Eugene, OR: Cascade Books, 2014.

——. *Piety and Profession: American Protestant Theological Education, 1870–1970.* Grand Rapids: Eerdmans, 2007.

Wheeler, Barbara G. "True and False: The First in a Series of Reports from a Study of Theological School Faculty." *Auburn Studies* 4 (January 1996) 7–9.

Wheeler, Barbara G., and Mark N. Wilhelm, eds. "Tending Talents: The Second in a Series of Reports from a Study of Theological School Faculty." Special issue, *Auburn Studies* 5 (March 1997).

Wheeler, Barbara G., Sharon L. Miller, and Katarina Schuth. "Signs of the Times: Present and Future Theological Faculty." *Auburn Studies* 10 (February 2005).

Contributors

Kathleen A. Cahalan is professor of practical theology at Saint John's School of Theology and Seminary and project director of the Collegeville Institute Seminars in Collegeville, Minnesota. She is co-author of *Christian Practical Wisdom: What It Is, Why It Matters* with Dorothy C. Bass, Bonnie J. Miller-McLemore, James N. Nieman, and Christian Scharen.

Emily Click is assistant dean for ministry studies and field education and Lecturer on Ministry at Harvard Divinity School. She is author of "Practical Theology in Contextual Education," in *The Blackwell Companion to Practical Theology*.

Edward Foley is the Duns Scotus Professor of Spirituality and ordinary professor of liturgy and music at Catholic Theological Union in Chicago, where he was the founding director of the Ecumenical Doctor of Ministry Program. His most recent book is *Theological Reflection across Faith Traditions: The Turn to Reflective Believing*.

David O. Jenkins is associate professor in the practice of practical theology at Candler School of Theology. He is coauthor and coeditor of *Equipping the Saints: Best Practices in Contextual Theological Education*.

Jeffrey D. Jones taught at Andover Newton Theological Seminary, retiring in June 2015 as an associate professor of ministerial leadership and director of ministry studies. He is author most recently of *Facing Decline, Finding Hope: New Possibilities for Faithful Churches.*

Gordon S. Mikoski is associate professor of Christian education and director of PhD studies, Princeton Theological Seminary. He serves as the editor of *Theology Today* and is coeditor of *Opening the Field of Practical Theology*, with Kathleen A. Cahalan.

David Rylaarsdam is professor of the history of Christianity at Calvin Theological Seminary. He is author of *John Chrysostom on Divine Pedagogy: The Coherence of His Theology and Preaching.*

Rebecca Slough is academic dean and associate professor of worship and the arts at Anabaptist Mennonite Biblical Seminary. She is author, most recently, of *Nurturing Spirit through Song: The Life of Mary K. Oyer.*

Jeffery L. Tribble, Sr. is associate professor of ministry at Columbia Theological Seminary and presiding elder of the Atlanta District of the Georgia Annual Conference of the African Methodist Episcopal Zion Church. He is author of *Transformative Pastoral Leadership in the Black Church.*

Introducing Integrating Work

KATHLEEN A. CAHALAN

Jeremy, an associate pastor of a large suburban church, is baffled about how to move the worship committee to embrace a wider repertoire of music. Doris has coordinated a local homeless shelter for ten years but realizes that the church needs also to advocate low-income housing for the people who use the shelter. Jose has been hired to rejuvenate a congregation's youth program that once had seventy-five youth but has dwindled to fifteen. Bryan is a hospital chaplain in a large suburban area to which Muslim immigrants have recently moved. In the span of twenty-four hours, Leslie led a morning Bible devotion, visited two church members in the hospital, attended a finance committee meeting about budget cuts, welcomed youth from a weekend mission outing, discussed the possibility of a new parking lot with the town's zoning commissioner, and glanced (too quickly) at the upcoming Sunday readings to begin sermon preparation.

At graduation I watch these MDiv students receive their diplomas and wonder about their readiness to enter ministry as they graduate: Does Jeremy know how to negotiate worship tensions in a parish? Can Doris take the long view of justice work in the nonprofit organization for which she serves as director? Will Jose be able to improve his skills in this first-time position? Is Bryan ready to do ministry in a multifaith context? Are these graduates formed in their vocation and can they sustain spiritual practices in positions, like Leslie's, that demand more and more of them?

I look around at my colleagues too. Do we have any clue about the challenges these students face? What makes our teaching, or for that matter the entire curriculum, attuned to what effective ministers need to know and do in the varied contexts they enter? We have mastered our academic disciplines and can speak to their competence in our curricular area. Yet I fear we have left it to the students to connect the dots between study, calling, and ministry.

When beginning ministers lack meaningful integration, results can be disappointing, even disastrous, for them and their communities. Jeremy, who learned little about the tradition of hymn singing, disregards the music sung by his new congregation. Doris, without experience in community organizing, fails to build partnerships with other groups and ends up trying to reinvent the wheel on her own. Bryan has read the latest books and attended a conference on multifaith ministry, but blunders his way through a conversation with a Muslim family about end-of-life treatment. Leslie is on the verge of burnout. What theological education needs, many will say, is to be more *integrative*.[1] Jeremy does not understand enough history, Bryan has to move from book theory into real time, and Leslie needs a spiritual director.

The lack of integration in theological education and ministerial practice comes at a high price. It reverberates through the personal, ecclesial, and systemic messes we see every day in the church. It can leave ministers depleted, disconnected from their vocation, feeling inadequate, or on the verge of dishonesty with herself and others. Lack of integration also has negative consequences for contexts of ministry. A community of faith can become unmoored from its tradition or lack the critical lens by which to reform it. Systems become imbued with arrogance, self-seeking power, even corruption.

Theological educators do not have to look at their graduates, the churches, or denominations for evidence of such fragmentation. We have only to look at ourselves. Our theological schools are marked by these same realities: we work in isolation, in areas beyond our competence, in conflict, and with far too many tasks.

Theological educators' desire to make ministry preparation more integrative is fueled by concerns both internal and external to the seminary. Internally, theological knowledge is increasing and becoming highly specialized. Our disciplines remain in silos, disconnected from each other; we

---

1. In fact, integration is a concern across education. In primary education, see Nagel, *Learning through Real-World Problem Solving*. In higher education, see Brownell and Swaner, "Integrated Approaches," and Palmer and Zajonc, *Heart of Higher Education*.

are unsure how to embark on the long and hard task of skill building and competent practice; increasingly the moral and spiritual formation, which the church once performed and for which most faculty are unprepared, is now left to the school; and seminary structures are quickly unraveling as enrollments, finances, and church support dwindles.

Externally, the challenges are numerous as well. We must demonstrate, with sufficient empirical evidence, to accreditors that our education is integrative.[2] Theological educators have to show that we are preparing graduates competent to minister in a wide array of contexts (campus ministries, hospitals, hospices, denominational offices, social service agencies, and retreat centers). Congregational ministry has become so complex that industrial and organizational behavior psychologist Richard DeShon, who studied work patterns of United Methodist pastors, was surprised at "the breadth of tasks performed by local church pastors coupled with the rapid switching between task clusters and roles . . . I have never encountered such a fast-paced job with such varied and impactful responsibilities."[3] The sheer number and variety of discrete tasks undertaken by ministerial practitioners in any one day brings into sharp focus the demands of integrating work. Leslie's day, then, is not that unusual for a church pastor. And, finally, the culture's secularizing reach makes religious belonging unappealing for many people, and the relevance of preaching the word, caring for the poor, or gathering on Sunday mornings is not so obvious. A social environment that does not support the demanding work of leading a community of faith can erode a minister's sense of purpose.

Frameworks for Integrating Work

When integration is identified as the solution to the problems besetting much (not all) of theological education and ministry, educators ordinarily use the term in three ways: as making connections between bodies of knowledge; overcoming the theory and practice divide; and enhancing the professional model. First, calls for integrating areas of disciplinary knowledge that remain largely disconnected from each other is widespread across education. As noted above, theological educators are concerned with bridging the gulf between areas of theological study, be it Bible and postmodern ethics, or theology and other disciplines, such as pastoral care

2. See *Standards of Accreditation*.

3. DeShon and Quinn, "Job Analysis Generalizability Study."

and neuroscience. Most theological educators believe at some level that if students were able to make meaningful connections across areas of knowledge, their learning would be enriched and their ministries more effective.

Second, integration is posed as the solution to overcoming the split between theory and practice. We have long heard that students need to be better prepared to draw upon theology, social science theory, biblical studies, or homiletic methods in their day-to-day practice; if they cannot connect what they know with what they are doing, their ministries often falter. In the field of practical theology alone, people have debated this issue since the Association of Seminary Professors in the Practical Fields was established in 1950. One purpose of the organization was "to discover the principles which can integrate the practical fields with other fields of theological study." Integration was the theme at five biennial meetings up to 1984.[4] Scholars compared ministry to other professions,[5] examined supervised ministry as the primary context in which practice and theory meet, and explored the relationship between the disciplines in practical fields and between the practical and classical fields. Yet, integration was rarely defined beyond the need to bring knowledge and practice together.[6] In the 1980s theological educators from across the disciplines participated in the Basic Issues in Theological Education project, which generated considerable discussion about the long-standing split between the conceptual and the practical.[7]

A third understanding of integration, the professional model, was rearticulated in the mid-2000s through the Carnegie Foundation's

4. For example, the 1966 meeting was entitled "Professional Training in Theological Education"; in 1972, "Integrating the Disciplines in Theological Education"; in 1980, "Integration: Objective Studies and Practical Theology"; and in 1982, "Seminary and Congregation: Integrating Learning, Ministry, and Mission."

5. At its first meeting in 1950, Elliott Dunlap Smith, professor of engineering at the Carnegie Institute of Technology, addressed the topic "Re-Designing Professional Education for the Ministry," comparing divinity education to engineering, law, and medicine.

6. A definition was offered in a 1972 address: "By integration I refer to systematic attempts to synthesize, intermesh, and coordinate the major learning experiences appropriate to the formation and education of priests and ministers. Simplistically, without resorting to a naïve faculty-psychology (body-mind-spirit), these main experiences involve the life of the reflective scholarly mind; the tensions of personality growth; the prayerful, liturgical disciplines; and the practice of ordained ministry in local situations and . . . these main experience areas, woven together, do comprise the proper curriculum of a seminary." Wagoner, "Theological Education," 1.

7. Farley, *Theologia*; Browning, *Practical Theology*; Wheeler and Farley, *Shifting Boundaries*.

Preparation for the Professions Program. Lee Shulman, then Carnegie's president, noted that "all the professions suffer when it comes to providing sufficient attention to the challenges of integration across the intellectual, practical, and moral/professional domains."[8] Authors of five studies on professional education argued that professional schools that train practitioners should "aim for an increasingly integrated approach to the formation of students' analytical reasoning, practical skills, and professional judgment."[9]

In the Carnegie study *Educating Clergy: Teaching Practices and Pastoral Imagination*, Charles Foster and colleagues interviewed, surveyed, and observed numerous theological teachers who "consistently identified integration as a highly desired outcome of their teaching."[10] What they meant was "pulling it all together." When the researchers probed further, however, they found several meanings: a kind of "theological thinking" demonstrated in the "confluence of knowledge and skills"; the "vertical" movement from basic to more sophisticated and complex understandings; and "horizontal" connections made across courses and disciplines. Foster and associates argued for something more in relationship to the professional model: "At the heart of clergy education is a still more complex integrative challenge—one that embraces, to some extent, all of these expectations. This integrative challenge emphasizes linking, in student learning, the knowledge, skills, and priestly, rabbinic, or pastoral identity typically identified with the educational tasks of the cognitive, practical, and normative apprenticeships."[11]

Others have articulated the professional ideal using various descriptors. At the outset of my research on the topic, I used the language of knowing, being, and doing.[12] My coeditor Edward Foley takes up the metaphor of juggling to capture the movement of keeping three or four things in play; he develops an approach that is "the triangulation of head, hand, and heart" also known as orthodoxy (right believing), orthopraxy (right acting), and orthopathy (right feeling).[13]

In a recent longitudinal study of learning pastoral imagination, the first finding identified by Christian A. B. Scharen and Eileen R. Campbell-Reed

8. Sheppard et al., *Educating Engineers*, 6.

9. Ibid., 2.

10. Foster et al., *Educating Clergy*, 330.

11. Ibid.

12. See Cahalan, "Reframing Knowing, Being, and Doing in the Seminary Classroom," and "Integration in Theological Education."

13. Foley, *Theological Reflection across Religious Traditions*, 68–69.

is that "learning pastoral imagination happens best in formation for ministry that is integrative, embodied, and relational."[14] Ministers in their study experienced a "lack of alignment" between the various parts of theological education: "teaching, spiritual formation, curricular pacing, denominational requirements, student intentions, and cultural expectations." Interviewees reported that the most integrative learning took place in immersion into a ministry context (field education or clinical pastoral education) and in classrooms where "the horizon of ministry" was clearly in view.[15] Integrative and embodied learning happened when three characteristics were present: "*an experience of the clash of abstract, decontextualized knowledge with lived situations, a sense of overwhelming which comes from dealing with multiple variables in these situations, and a sense of responsibility for the risk entailed in choosing a course of action.*"[16]

In *Integrating Work in Theological Education*, the authors draw on all these models—integrating across disciplines, theory and practice, and the professional ideal—and expand them. These nine theological educators from a variety of denominations, settings (divinity schools and freestanding and university-based seminaries), and academic fields began work in the fall of 2011 as the Collegeville Institute Seminar on Integration in Theological Education and Ministry.[17]

Our research into the nature of the integrating process involved several modes of inquiry. First, we started with the assumption that integrative work is happening in our schools in multiple ways, but many theological educators fail to go beyond naming the problem. To better understand where and how integrative teaching and learning occurs, we began with describing integrative efforts in our schools, curriculums, and classrooms. We wrote case studies as a form of narrating the particulars of our situations; we also interviewed colleagues and talked with our students. We attempted to articulate the assumptive worlds behind the integration speech in our contexts.

Second, we sought to build constructive and strategic frameworks for understanding the integrating process. To do so, like earlier generations of theological educators, we looked to other professions and read widely in learning theory, expertise studies, and pedagogy. Third, we sought to

14. Scharen and Campbell-Reed, "Learning Pastoral Imagination," 14.

15. Ibid., 18.

16. Ibid., 21; emphasis original.

17. See Collegeville Institute, "Research Seminars."

interpret theologically what we mean by integrating work—both what it looks like within our various ecclesial traditions and what difference our faith perspectives might make in broader conversations about professional education.

Our seminar has been a collaborative, interdisciplinary, and ecumenical approach to theological inquiry, which included worshipping together. We formed a learning community, meeting twice a year for four years. We could not have seen or understood the complexity of integrating, and changed our thinking about it, without such a commitment of time and study.

We hope to advance the conversation about integrating work with particular attention to three issues. First, we are attentive to *who* does the integrating. Students are the primary focus in most conversations, as the examples at the beginning of this introduction illustrate.[18] Yet the burden has disproportionately been placed on learners as individual agents of the integrating process. Such understanding of the human person is inadequate, one centered on a modernist egocentric perspective rather than a sociocentric one. Persons are social creatures and integrating is a communal process; we don't integrate on our own. A social and communal view of persons shifts the weight of integrating solely from students to include the school community, its context, practices, and traditions. Central to the school is its faculty and the work they do in creating curriculums and courses. Integrating work becomes as much a part of what staff, faculty, and administrators do as what students carry out.

Second, we are attentive to language. As much of this work shows, integrating is not easily defined or described but, in general, refers to making things that are apart into something whole, complete, or entire. *Integration* is often used as a noun, in which integrating appears as an achievable end point, something that is attainable.[19] We decided to replace the noun with more dynamic language, either the verb *integrate* or a modifier *integrating* or *integrative*. Shifting the language more closely captures integrating as a process with a trajectory that fluctuates and modifies over time, and is not

18. Foley, *Theological Reflection across Religious Traditions*, 67.

19. Klimoski describes integration in three ways: as a "benchmark" or "global outcome of the curriculum," "a process that moves at different rates for different individuals," and an "educational strategy that engages teachers and learners in purposeful action." Klimoski et al., *Educating Leaders for Ministry*, 52–53.

static.[20] Integrating work is dynamic rather than linear and, as discussed throughout the book, includes disintegrating and reorienting experiences.

The authors generated multiple metaphors and images to capture integrating work: an act of the natural world (rhizomes, crab grass, streams, tides, ecosystems, food chains); chemical models or reactions (DNA, catalysts); human work (cultivating, gardening, building, laying bricks or bricolage, hosting a potluck); handiwork (weaving, knitting, patchwork, quilting); artistic work (sculpting, scavenging, connecting the dots); playing (juggling, Lego building, games, puzzles, betting); trajectories (pathways, itineraries, routes, trails, tracks); improvisation (jazz, comedy); and warning signs ("Mind the Gap," "Caution," "Danger Ahead"). Such metaphors brought much laughter to our conversation and, in the end, we decided not to use one for a catchy title, since no one image fully captures what we mean by integrating. Like images of God, we needed multiple metaphors to open out this complex human dynamic.

Third, we are attentive to theory and theology. We found in the field of theological education little theorizing about integrating work—what it is and how it happens—and virtually no theology of integrating. Granted, the terms *integrate*, *integrating*, and *integration* are not biblical nor are they found in the theological tradition. To gain more clarity about a theology of integrating work, we turned to biblical sources and each of our theological traditions, where we found integrating work an important divine and human venture.

Theological Characteristics of Integrating Work

At first glance, the Bible seems to have a lot more to say about work than it does about integrating, and yet, on closer examination, integrating work appears to be both a crucial human effort and a crucial divine effort. At the outset of the book of Genesis, God is at work to create the natural world, animals, and human beings. The Creator breathes life into all the earth, calls upon human persons to care for it so that all might flourish (Gen 2:15), and rests on the Sabbath as time apart from this work (Gen 2:1–4). By this holy power, the natural and human world are interrelated and interdependent, emerging from divine blessing, wholeness, and goodness.

We might say that God's creative work is integrative insofar as all that is emerges from the same life-giving breath, or *ruach*, as evidenced in our

20. Foley, *Theological Reflection across Religious Traditions*, 68.

genetic structure, much of which we share with all living things, even stardust. We can see from pictures generated by the Hubble Space Telescope that planet earth is but a small abode in the ancient, enormous, expanding, and dynamic reality we call a universe, some fourteen billion years old. The unfinished cosmos continues to expand, becoming more complex and distinctive, yet interrelated with each new breath.

How can we not be curious about this Creator and the ongoing work God is about? In the creation stories, human persons share with God a propensity to be curious. God gives Adam and Eve a garden to "till it and keep it" (Gen 2:15) and animals to name; it seems God is curious "to see what he [Adam] would call them" (Gen 2:19). Human curiosity combines desire with understanding—we are created as inquisitive creatures. Naming animals, plants, and galaxies allows persons to differentiate, organize, categorize, and systematize, all part of mature cognitive processes.[21]

Learning is fueled by such curiosity. Cognitive psychologist Robert Kegan argues that we create new cognitive structures well into adulthood through meaning making. To create new understandings, existing structures of knowledge must be dismantled, reconceived, and disembarked and new configurations established. By making meaning out of new experiences and information, Kegan says, we are "hatched-out" again and again.[22] Learning entails integrating and disintegrating momentums as part of the creative dynamic of human development, knowing, and learning.

The biblical narrative points to another aspect of our curiosity. Adam and Eve's banishment from the garden is not due to just being curious about the tree of the knowledge of good and evil but due to their disobedience in touching it. Their sin against God alienates them from the very thing that bound them to the Creator from the beginning—work as creation making. From this time on, the ground from which persons came is cursed and human work is difficult and a struggle (Gen 3:16–19); relationships between creatures is marked by fear and division (Gen 3:14–15). We reject God's gracious gift of creation and strive to make a world in our own image. We end up destroying relationships due to enmity and jealousy (Gen 4:1–16), and we harm the natural order by way of domination rather than

---

21. Human development theorists view development as a system of systems "envisioned as a series of patterns evolving and dissolving over time and, at any point in time, possessing particular degrees of stability." Stevens-Long and Michaud, "Theory in Adult Development," 6.

22. Kegan, *Evolving Self*, 80.

stewardship. From this perspective sin can be viewed as the disintegration and alienation of things and beings that belong together.

God's integrating work in the Bible is one of making and remaking covenants. When the Israelites cry out from their enslavement, work has become a primary form of human exploitation and injustice. God remembers the promise made to Abraham and Sarah and is compelled to save them (Exod 3:23–24). He establishes the covenant through his servant Moses—the community is to be a holy people in service to Yahweh. Even when the disrupting and disintegrating power of sin and corruption devastate the community as it wanders through the desert, makes a nation, and then is cast into exile, the people of God do not lose sight of the covenant. They hold on to the promise to be saved, redeemed, and made whole, as the prophets' visions of restored communion and the interrelatedness of all creatures attest (Isa 65:17–25).

God's integrating work continues in the Incarnation story—the drawing together in one person both the human and the divine. The Spirit of Life that hovers over creation is the dynamic power that overshadows Mary and brings forth the Word of Life (Luke 1:35). That same power is at work in Jesus's ministry, through which God's integrating work is made known in his teachings, table fellowship, and healings. God's power (*dýnamus*) working through Jesus makes known God's purposes for the world—captives are set free, the blind see, the poor are filled with good things, the deaf hear, and the mute speak (Luke 4:18–19). Jesus confronts the sinful powers of the world and finally is brought to death by them. The cross paradoxically is at the heart of God's integrating work for humanity. For through the crucified one, God's power is made known by the resurrection, in which the divine integrating work overcomes all evil, even death itself, and makes of Jesus, and his followers, a new creation.

The Spirit breathes new life into the community of witnesses who together set forth to continue Jesus's work through proclamation and sacrament, service and justice tending, healing and reconciliation. The Spirit of the risen Lord constitutes the church and empowers the disciples to embody and enact the integrating power of love demonstrated by Christ. The church participates in God's mission of integrating work for world transformation and awaits with hope the eschatological promise that all things will be whole and complete again.

Integrating work, then, is integral to the triune God as creator, liberator, savior, redeemer, and sanctifier—a power that liberates the oppressed, saves the crucified, forgives the sinner, heals the sick, and makes all things new. Our integrating work is good and blessed when our curiosity honors and participates in God's purposes for the world; disintegrating is as much a part of learning and creation as putting things together. Yet curiosity can also turn us to our own purposes, be it pride or the lack of self-construction or disobedience. Our desire to categorize or systematize also excludes and colonizes; we become disintegrated creatures opposed to ourselves and others. We are utterly dependent, then, on the Spirit's gracious power at work within and among us if we are to have any hope that our work participates in God's work.

An Invitation

What we have to say here about integrating work is certainly not the last word on the subject. We offer some glimpses from our contexts, test our hypotheses, and gain greater clarity in conversation with other theological educators. Theological education taken as a whole refers to a broad array of masters' and doctoral degrees in which integrating is an educational goal and challenge; however, our focus is ministry education, primarily the master of divinity (MDiv) or other graduate ministerial degrees.

We hope to reach several groups of theological educators, especially faculty interested in curricular development, planning, and assessment; junior faculty in the early years of formation as seminary teachers; doctoral students interested in theological education; and administrators of seminaries, Bible institutes, and other venues of ministry education who have leadership over the institution's mission and vision, planning processes, faculty development, and institutional assessment. As with the study *Educating Clergy*, we hope to foster an interfaith conversation with Jewish and Muslim administrators and faculty about integrating work in their contexts. We also hope to reach professional educators as well as undergraduate educators who are also seeking more integrative forms of teaching and learning.

Integrating Work in Theological Education has four main parts, though it need not be read from front to back. In part 1 we consider the school community. Edward Foley examines research on formal, semiformal, and informal education. Though rarely considered, a school's informal and semiformal spaces are crucial to integrating work. Each seminary embodies a particular tradition that shapes its communal life, rituals, symbols, behaviors, and physical spaces, from the dining room to the chapel. These activities and spaces constitute a seminary's foundational learning environment.

Three case studies examine how schools take up integrating work. Rebecca Slough, academic dean of Associated Mennonite Biblical School, scrutinizes a theology of theological education based on love of God, neighbor, and self and how this vision shapes her work in faculty development and renewal. In his case study of Calvin Theological Seminary, David Rylaarsdam, recounts the seminary's challenges regarding enrollment, finances, and the length of the MDiv program. This crisis spurred the administration and faculty to undertake an overhaul of the school's organizational structure, academic calendar, budgets, faculty hiring practices, and goals and strategies. Foley's case study examines Catholic Theological Union's formal, semiformal, and informal spaces of teaching and learning in which all community members participate.

Part 2 surveys curriculums as the primary building blocks of education. I examine leading philosophies of curriculums in the United States and their influence on theological education. Curricular revisions need to connect horizontal learning across time, within a semester or year, and vertical learning from the beginning to the end of a program, with its introduction and capstone components, with the diagonal, crosscutting pressures of personal and social life. Each case study in this section responds to four questions: What was the problem the school faced that prompted the revision? What was the solution or the plan and how was it designed? What was your role in the curriculum and in the change process? Since the implementation of the plan, what has been learned, including about its strengths and weaknesses?

David Rylaarsdam continues the story of Calvin's institutional overhaul in a case study on the redesigned curriculum, which began by first abolishing departments and divisions and creating new areas that represent its goals for competent ministry: person, message, context, and goal. Jeffery Jones's case examines a new approach to field education implemented in the fall of 2007 at Andover Newton Theological Seminary—the Professor-Practitioner Program (P3). It was designed to help students make connections between the courses they take and the learning they experience in the field. P3 courses are co-taught by full-time faculty and a resident ministry practitioner. David Jenkins assesses Candler School of Theology's innovative contextual education program, which launches students in a first-year experience of ministry in a social setting in which faculty members, local clergy, and students create a learning community while serving in prisons, food pantries, shelters, and service agencies.

Part 3 explores integrating work in courses through face-to-face, online, and immersion courses. Gordon Mikoski explores the classroom where faculty and students are making connections between ideas and concepts, skills and practices, and moral and spiritual formation. Course design is particularly important in connecting goals, activities, and assignments. Each case addresses four questions: What was the problem or issue that led to redesigning the course? What process or model of redesign was used? What are some salient features of implementing the design? What is your assessment of the course?

Emily Click, using L. Dee Fink's *Creating Significant Learning Experiences*, redesigned a course on leadership for Harvard Divinity School students. Of particular interest is that she discerns that her pedagogy is undermining the theory of leadership she advocates; using Fink, she discovers a way to teaching that embraces leading. David Jenkins's immersion course, "The Church on the Border," is taught in Arizona and Mexico and aims to engage students' capacities as public theologians. Jenkins discerns that the preparatory study and post-trip reflection are critical to integrative learning. Key to the course, however, is the disintegrating of participants' worldviews. In "Creating a New Course on Leadership in the Small Church," Jeffrey Jones designed a course in which students produced a case study of a small church, through interviews with members and leaders and participant observation. At Columbia Theological Seminary students were required to take three integrative courses, one each year of the MDiv program. The courses are designed to help students connect personal, ecclesial, biblical, theological, and ministerial perspectives. Jeffery Tribble explores the first of these courses, Intersections. The faculty teaching this team-taught class were surprised when students expressed concerns about course materials they perceived as racially offensive. Tribble explores what happens when faculty and students unpack the intentional and unintentional dimensions of course planning. Edward Foley explores the process, challenge, and delight of designing an online format for a course on the Eucharist that for decades he had taught in the classroom. His theology of the Eucharist shapes his pedagogy as well as students' learning; both students and instructor discover that embodied presence can be encountered in the virtual.

In part 4, the final section, the three editors step back to consider integrating work through the three lenses: as models, as practical wisdom, and as theology. In his essay, Gordon Mikoski analyzes five models of integrating (linked, fusion, mutual influence, networked, and complex open systems), the rhythms of integrating work, and Reformed theological themes. I argue that practical wisdom is the *telos* (goal) of theological education for ministry, which entails several kinds of knowing that become integrated over time: contextual awareness, embodied realizing, conceptual understanding, critical thinking, emotional attunement, creative insight, relational perception, and practical reasoning. I examine the ways these kinds of knowing emerge across professional education and practice, from being a novice to a competent practitioner, and challenge notions of an expert practitioner. The book concludes with a theological analysis of integrating by Edward Foley. In his essay, Foley compares and draws together some crucial elements that move toward a theology of integrating work.

We are deeply grateful to the Collegeville Institute for hosting the seminar, to the monks of Saint John's Abbey who welcomed us to their guest house and worship, to Corein Brown, our research assistant, and to Craig Dykstra and Chris Coble at Lilly Endowment, Inc., who have generously supported the work of theological education and in particular the Collegeville Institute Seminars.

We hope these essays and case studies spur theological educators to recognize the places they are already engaged in integrating work and to imagine further ways to interpret, understand, and expand its reach.

Bibliography

Brownell, Jayne E., and Lynn E. Swaner. "Integrated Approaches." In *Five High-Impact Practices: Research on Learning Outcomes, Completion, and Quality*. Washington, DC: Association of American Colleges and Universities, 2010.

Browning, Don S., ed. *Practical Theology: The Emerging Field in Theology, Church, and World*. San Francisco: Harper & Row, 1983.

Cahalan, Kathleen A. "Integration in Theological Education." In *The Wiley-Blackwell Companion to Practical Theology*, edited by Bonnie J. Miller-McLemore, 386–95. London: Wiley-Blackwell, 2011.

———. "Reframing Knowing, Being, and Doing in the Seminary Classroom." *Teaching Theology and Religion* 14 (2011) 343–53.

Collegeville Institute Seminars. "Research Seminars." http://collegevilleinstitute.org/the-seminars/.

DeShon, Richard P., and Abigail Quinn. "Job Analysis Generalizability Study for the Position of United Methodist Local Pastor: Focus Group Results." A Report to the Advisory Committee on Psychological Assessment for the United Methodist Church," December 15, 2007.

Farley, Edward. *Theologia: The Fragmentation and Unity of Theological Education.* 1983. Reprinted, Eugene, OR: Wipf & Stock, 2001.

Foley, Edward. *Theological Reflection across Religious Traditions: The Turn to Reflective Believing.* Lanham, MD: Rowman & Littlefield, 2015.

Foster, Charles R., et al. *Educating Clergy: Teaching Practices and Pastoral Imagination.* San Francisco: Jossey-Bass, 2006.

Kegan, Robert. *The Evolving Self: Problem and Process in Human Development.* Cambridge: Harvard, 1982.

Klimoski, Victor J., et al. *Educating Leaders for Ministry: Issues and Responses.* Collegeville, MN: Liturgical, 2005.

Nagel, Nancy G. *Learning through Real-World Problem Solving: The Power of Integrative Teaching.* Thousand Oaks, CA: Corwin, 1996.

Palmer, Parker J., and Arthur Zajonc. *The Heart of Higher Education: A Call to Renewal.* San Francisco: Jossey-Bass, 2010.

Scharen, Christian A. B., and Eileen R. Campbell-Reed. "Learning Pastoral Imagination: A Five-Year Report on How New Ministers Learn in Practice." *Auburn Studies* no. 21 (Winter 2016).

Sheppard, Sheri D., et al. *Educating Engineers: Designing for the Future of the Field.* San Francisco: Jossey-Bass, 2008.

Standards of Accreditation, A.1.3.2. Association of Theological Schools, 2012. http://www. ats.edu/accrediting/overview-accrediting.

Stevens-Long, Judith, and Greg Michaud. "Theory in Adult Development: The New Paradigm and the Problem of Direction." In *Handbook of Adult Development,* edited by Jack Demick and Carrie Andreoletti, 3–22. New York: Springer, 2003.

Wagoner, Walter D. "Theological Education: Integrated or Disintegrated?" The Association of Professional Education for Ministry. Unpublished report, 1972.

Wheeler, Barbara G., and Edward Farley, eds. *Shifting Boundaries: Contextual Approaches to the Structure of Theological Education.* Louisville: Westminster John Knox, 1991.

PART 1

Schools

Widening the Aperture

School as Agent of the Integrating Process

EDWARD FOLEY

While sometimes overworked, the oft-quoted African proverb "It takes a village to raise a child" is still rife with wisdom. In the context of this project, such a sociocentric view of child-rearing is an instructive, even powerful prod for expanding our imaginations about the integrating process, particularly when highlighting the key players in that process. In theological education circles, integration is too often understood narrowly, as some balance of knowledge and skills that a student must acquire to complete successfully their seminary training and be recommended for ministry, either as a layperson or as a member of the clergy. Contrary to a student-centered view of integrating—which not only seems unhelpful but even counterproductive—we the authors wish to widen the aperture for viewing the integrating project by beginning with the school as its own type of wisdom village.

The Proposal

It is true that a divinity school or seminary is not an independent entity, even if it defines itself as freestanding. Every institution committed to training people for ministry is embedded in a network of complex relationships that result in a labyrinth of responsibilities to sponsoring faith communities, to the judicatories that oversee a denomination or religious body, to alums and donors, to collaborating congregations and service organizations that mentor our students, to accrediting agencies, and to the local civic context. For example, my institution, Catholic Theological Union (CTU), describes itself as a free-standing school of theology and ministry. In a Roman Catholic context that means the institution is not an official part of any diocese and is not directly under the control of the local bishop. On the other hand, CTU is sponsored by twenty-four men's religious communities, and the leaders of each community together comprise the school's corporate board. There is also a board of trustees composed of representatives from each of the sponsoring religious communities as well as lay trustees. As member of the Association of Chicago Theological Schools (ACTS) CTU collaborates with ten other graduate institutions, especially with the four other ACTS schools and the University of Chicago Divinity School in the Hyde Park Cluster. It also has an official alliance with DePaul University in Chicago. Accredited through the Association of Theological Schools, CTU serves as a polling place for local, state, and national elections, opens its facility to the neighborhood for lectures or visits to our art gallery, and has been a worship site for small Protestant congregations. Thus, like other schools of ministry, CTU continuously navigates a mosaic of religious, academic, and civic relationships.

Without ignoring this web of interdependencies, it yet seems appropriate to consider an institution apart from these external partners. As demonstrated in the groundbreaking *Being There*,[1] a theological school such as CTU generates an influential environment that leaves its ministerial fingerprints all over its students. Similar to the impact a medical school has on the doctors it trains,[2] the ethos of an institution, style of leadership, morale of the staff, relationships among students, and multiple other often hidden factors influence students as much and sometimes more than classroom instruction or curriculum design. Our institutions also are places of enduring consequence for the faculty, staff, and administration who inhabit them often far longer than those who study with us. At this writing I am in my thirty-first year at CTU and share this long-standing engagement with other faculty and administrators as well as some in support services.

At its best, a seminary or divinity school endeavors to become what Etienne Wenger calls a "community of practice."[3] Such a community does

1. Carroll et al., *Being There*.

2. See, for example, Gofton and Regehr, "What We Don't Know We Are Teaching."

3. Wenger, *Communities of Practice*.

not arise through simple coexistence in some shared space, like workers at a plant or families in a neighborhood. Rather, this is a group of people bound together by mutual interest, common purpose, and even a shared passion for some work. Regular, often informal interaction enables such a community to strengthen its bonds and develop its ability to be even more effective in pursuing its common goal. I would contend that becoming a community of practice is a most appropriate goal for a school of theology and ministry.

Aspiring to be a community of practice in the service of ministry is a noble objective. Doing so, however, requires serious reflection on how the many people and programs, budgets and brochures, mission statements and marketing strategies contribute to or impair the integrating journey for the whole community of practice.[4] Yet, seminaries and divinity schools are seldom places of sustained self-examination regarding the integrating or disintegrating impact of these various factors. If such reflection is done at all, it is usually confined to an examination of the formal curriculum. If the integrating project is a lifelong sojourn, however, how do our institutions acknowledge and support this process for members of the maintenance staff, librarians, faculty, development officers, and the multiple others vital members of our communities of practice? We have unending assessment plans for what we expect of courses and programs and curriculum in service of our students, but do we assess how a school promotes and promises in accompanying staff, administrators, and faculty as well?

Seldom, for example, do boards of trustees or others responsible for institutional oversight examine the interrelatedness of the various groups, tasks, processes, and messages that reverberate through a school to discover how they converge or when they contradict each other. What is the degree of continuity, for example, between the vision of a school presented by recruiting and that experienced by a second year MDiv student? Or how does a school's mission statement stack up against its operating budget? Pondering how the web of policies, budgets, marketing strategies, hiring, and physical environment contribute to the integrating journey of students, staff, faculty, and administrators might at first seem overwhelming. At the same time, it is a necessary exploration if schools of ministry and theology are going to model what they hope is reflected in their graduates. Unfortunately, however, in the words of the Elizabethan bard, this is too often an

---

4. In addition to what is discussed here, other important places and processes contribute to a school's ethos, such as the dining hall, corporate worship, residential life, commuter patterns, and online communities.

"undiscovered country."[5] The closest some schools get to this process is the arduous work that faculty and administrators undertake in preparation for the decennial accrediting review. We are often so concerned with putting forth our best face in order to avoid notations that we seldom place a high priority on reflection on the integrating journey as a shared venture of all members of this potential wisdom village.

The goal of this overview article is admittedly more evocative than programmatic, more an exercise in advocacy than an outline of some detailed strategy. While programmatic and strategic suggestions will be forthcoming—especially in the articles that follow—the first and central hope here is to stir the imaginations of theological educators to begin thinking more systematically about how schools can be self-reflective agents of integrating. This means critically examining not only what schools say, but also what we do. Schools committed to training ministers are not just bastions of ideas but places of practice. While we spend untold hours crafting mission statements, curricula, and policies for faculty, staff, and students, it is not only or especially our written materials that need to be examined. Rather, viewing our schools as primary agents in this process requires examining the many practices that are meant to complement but sometimes obfuscate or even contravene those written canons intended to insure an honorable and mutual trek into integrating work.

To ground this advocacy in something more than my own personal experience or perspectives, I have chosen to consider how an entire institution has formative agency. If we can raise our awareness about how the various components of our educational ecosystems influence students in their ministerial maturation, then we might begin to perceive how these same ecosystems affect those of us who continue to inhabit them. At the end of this article, I will link these insights with three case studies on how seminary or divinity school is a key agent in the integrating process.

Formal, Semiformal, and Informal Learning

Many educational theorists and practitioners have something to say to theological educators regarding the nature of adult learning[6] and professional

---

5. Shakespeare, *Hamlet*, 3.1.

6. A fine overview of adult educational theories is Fenwick, *Learning through Experience*.

training that parallels ministerial training.[7] Our seminar has learned from visionaries such as Paulo Freire and his work on critical pedagogy;[8] Malcolm Knowles and his theories of adult centered education;[9] Donald Schön and his provocative work on the "reflective practitioner";[10] David Kolb's insights about experiential learning;[11] and Jack Mezirow's ideas about "transformative learning."[12] Many of these, however, focus on the individual—Freire is an exception here—and following their theories could lead us back to an unnecessarily narrow focus on students.

Intrigued by the work of Etienne Wenger and his collaboration with Jean Lave on the nature of "situated learning,"[13] I have chosen to consider the range of learnings that occur within a single institution through the rubrics of formal, semiformal (usually called nonformal in the literature), and informal education. I do so because this porous taxonomy allows me to envision in new ways not only how learning is nourished within an institution, but also how all members of a community of practice are potential and essential agents in the ongoing integrating process. It allows us to consider how the authority to teach—often centered in a professor or formal curriculum—can shift, and we can notice the more diffuse, decentralized dynamics throughout our institutions. It also allows one to consider not only learning opportunities that affect our students but also the extent to which our institutional environments enhance the integrating trajectory for other members of our communities of practice.

Formal Education

Distinctions between formal, semiformal, and informal education were first developed by economist and educator Philip Coombs (1915–2006). These were initially based upon organization categories. In 1973 Coombs and two colleagues defined formal education as "the hierarchically structured, chronologically graded education system," running from primary school through the university and including, in addition to general

7. See Benner et al., *Educating Nurses.*

8. Freire, *Pedagogy of the Oppressed.*

9. Knowles, *Modern Practice of Adult Education.*

10. Schön, *Reflective Practitioner*; also, Schön, *Educating the Reflective Practitioner.*

11. Kolb, *Experiential Learning.*

12. Mezirow, *Transformative Dimensions of Adult Learning.*

13. Lave and Wenger, *Situated Learning.*

academic studies, a variety of specialised programmes and institutions for full-time technical and professional training."[14] Tony Jeffs suggests that in the nineteenth century in the west, schools began to acquire elements that helped to define formal education; for example, the gap in status between adult teacher and child pupil, classrooms and desks, externally imposed curricula, and so on.[15] Semiformal education was also bureaucratically described as organized education outside any established formal system, and informal education was the more random lifelong learning process each of us encounters as an ordinary part of life.

While organization structures do help define these different learning genres, these descriptions can be more refined. David Hung and associates, for example, note that formal education operates through "extrinsic motivation and strict assessment."[16] They also conclude that learning in the formal curriculum is often decontextualized, typically "learning about" rather than "learning to be," framed by paradigms of "intellectual and individual excellence," and more focused on the individual than groups.[17] Formal learning ordinarily leads to some credential recognized across local and even national borders.

Informal Education

Informal education is virtually the polar opposite of formal education: a ubiquitous process and the aboriginal educational form for humans. John Dewey (1859–1952) apparently coined the term to contrast the subject treated in formal education with that which occurs in the matrix of social discourse.[18] Today it is often defined in contrast to formal education, for example, the "intellectual life beyond the classroom."[19] Thus, it is sometimes considered a "hidden"[20] or "third curriculum"[21] that shapes students

14. Coombs et al., *New Paths to Learning*, 149.

15. Jeffs, "First Lessons," 37.

16. Hung et al., "Authenticity in Learning," 1072.

17. Ibid., 1078.

18. Dewey, *Democracy and Education*, 10.

19. Sullivan, "Making the Graduate Curriculum Explicit."

20. Jackson seems to have coined the language of "hidden curriculum" in his *Life in Classrooms*.

21. Gofton and Regehr, "What We Don't Know We Are Teaching," 21.

engaged in formal education through unspoken academic, cultural, or social messages.

Rather than an invisible aspect of formal learning, however, informal education is better understood more broadly as the way we naturally learn. This seems closer to Dewey's understanding of informal education as the incidental by-product of social integration. Nat Colletta's definition captures this breadth: "'Informal education' is the incidental transmission of knowledge, skills and attitudes (with the stress on attitudes) with highly diverse and culturally relative patterns for the organization of time, space, and material, and also for personal roles and relationships, such as are implicit in varying configurations of the family, household and community."[22] Multiple characteristics of informal learning distinguish it from formal educational processes, for example, the primary mode of this type of learning is conversation,[23] including "gossip, rumour, story-telling and hearsay," and the accompanying "raised eyebrows, grins, shrugs, and body posture."[24] Because this is learning through unstructured dialogue, it is necessarily unpredictable,[25] unorganized, unsystematic, and regularly serendipitous,[26] whose outcomes are emergent and not explicitly foregrounded.[27]

Since this form of learning is both more contextualized[28] and completely voluntary, attention to place is critical.[29] While apt to transpire in virtually any environment, cultivating spaces (face-to-face or digital) in which people feel comfortable enough to engage may have more of an impact on outcomes in informal than in formal learning processes, where engagement is expected no matter what the environment. This geography of informal education requires a heedfulness—a distinctive assessment criterion—so that "spaces become places."[30] Preparing such an environment is complex, as it attempts to encourage interaction while at the same time imposing few controls on the learning activity.[31]

22. Colletta, "Formal, Nonformal and Informal Education," 22.

23. See, for example, Jeffs and Smith, *Informal Education*, 23, 78 *et passim*.

24. Gilchrist, "Working with Networks and Organizations in the Community," 109.

25. Jeffs and Smith, *Informal Education*, 33.

26. Selman et al., *Foundations of Adult Education in Canada*, 124.

27. Hung et al., 1072, 1089.

28. Ibid., 1076.

29. Jeffs and Smith, *Informal Education*, 24.

30. Smith, "Place, Space and Information Education," 144.

31. Schwier, "Comparison of Participation Patterns," 2.

Some characterize informal education as more affective than formal learning with its perceived emphasis on cognition.[32] This is linked to the voluntary nature of the former, whose effectiveness relies upon a level of group "effervescence" to sustain participation.[33] It also is tied to the role that emotions play in human development and in lifelong learning.[34] Connected to this affective flow is the parallel emphasis that some give to informal learning's power for influencing attitudes and ethics. Jeffs and Smith contend that informal education is a "moral craft" that not only requires but also communicates core values, for example, respect for persons and promotion of well-being, fairness, and equality.[35] Even when considered a "hidden curriculum" that shadows formal instruction, informal education is critical for shaping the attitudes and values of trainees and may be one of the most important elements in nurturing professional identity.[36]

Semiformal Education

The language of nonformal—though I prefer semiformal—education came into currency in the late 1960s. It was most often employed by economists, who believed that formal educational systems were too slow in responding to the socioeconomic demands of late modernity. Conversely, they emphasized the importance of investing in educational processes organized and administered outside the more conservative and relatively expensive venues of formal schooling.[37] Semiformal education should be relatively easy to define, as it sits between the previously discussed polarities of formal and informal education. However, so much distance spans the formal curriculum of a credentialing institution and the incidental learnings that happen throughout life that defining the learning that straddles that huge terrain is daunting. Even in early discussions, authors fretted about the difficulties in defining this educational genre with any clarity.[38]

---

32. Brebera and Hlouskova, "Searching for Bridges," 275. http://eric.ed.gov/?id=ED 542829.

33. Schwier, "Comparison of Participation Patterns," 10.

34. Tiffany, "Relationships and Learning," 98.

35. Jeffs and Smith, *Informal Education*, 94–95; also see Banks, "Professional Values."

36. Gofton and Regehr, "What We Don't Know We Are Teaching," especially 20.

37. See n. 13 above.

38. Ward et al., "Effective Learning," 38.

Semiformal learning is ordinarily defined in contrast to formal rather than to informal learning. Such definitions often explicitly critique formal educational, for example, the following: "[Semiformal] education theory questions the adequacy of learning that is rigidly organized within limited time periods and circumscribed space, the dogmatism of entrenched subject matter, the structural inequality inherent in social mobility patterns that neglect the needs of the poor, the illiterate, the unemployed and the alienation and wastage of youth reflected in high dropout rates."[39] Such a definition resonates with the crisis mentality that marked the 1967 conference so determinative for generating this term. This brittle caricature of formal education, however, diminishes the potential contribution of semiformal learning. Still a definition in contrast mode but more useful is the one proposed by Coombs and associates who define semiformal education as "any organised educational activity outside the established formal system—whether operating separately or as an important feature of some broader activity—that is intended to serve identifiable learning clienteles and learning objectives."[40]

Some have tried to bridge the definitional gap by contrasting characteristics of formal and semiformal education, as demonstrated in this chart adapted from the work of Tim Simkins:[41]

	Formal	**Nonformal**
Purposes	Long term and general	Short term and specific
	Credential based	Noncredential based
Timing	Long cycle, preparatory, full time	Short cycle, recurrent, part time
Content	Standardized, input centered	Individualized, output centered
	Academic	Practical
	Entry requirements determine clientele	Clientele determine entry requirements

39. Colletta, "Formal, Nonformal, and Informal Education," 1.
40. Smith, "Place, Space, and Information Education," 2.
41. Simkins, *Non-formal Education*, 4.

	Formal	Nonformal
Delivery System	Institution based	Environment based
	Isolated from environment	Community related
	Rigidly structured	Flexible
	Teacher centered and resource intensive	Learner centered and resource saving
Control	External, hierarchical	Self-governing, democratic

This binary approach has multiple difficulties, for example, the wide-spread movement to credential semiformal programs,[42] and the highly structured nature of some of these programs, especially in workplaces.[43] Claudio Zaki Dib would reduce the persistent features of semiformal education to (1) "centralization of the process on the student, as to his [*sic*] previously identified needs and possibilities; and (2) the immediate usefulness of the education for the student's personal and professional growth."[44] In general, there is agreement that semiformal learning is cued toward developing skills rather than abstract knowledge, and that to be effective, the learner must recognize its benefit for the present.

An undercurrent of liberation also flows through many understandings of semiformal learning. This could partially explain why some understand it as a challenge to formal educational settings, sometimes considered colonizing powers. Freire's *Pedagogy of the Oppressed* is sometimes understood as outlining a type of semiformal learning.[45] Among the wide range of initiatives that self-identify as semiformal are literacy and basic education programs, political and trade union education, catch-up programs for

---

42. See, for example, *European Guidelines*.

43. "Non-formal learning is also highly structured with specific aims and objectives. . . . In industry, non-formal learning . . . may be used to induct new employees into the culture of the company, develop the technical and inter-personal skills of experienced works, and hone the skills of managers and supervisors. For all workers, non-formal training . . . is the most common form of training after informal on-the-job training." Misko, *Combining Formal, Non-formal and Informal Learning*, 10.

44. Claudio Zaki Dib, "Formal, Non-Formal and Informal Education," 301.

45. Guldbrandsen, "Paulo Freire and the Problem of Consciousness."

school dropouts, and various educational endeavors linked with development initiatives, for example, agricultural training programs.[46]

More than the frameworks of formal and informal learning, that of semiformal demonstrates the limits of such frameworks if employed too strictly. Almost forty years ago Simkins noted: "Most [programs] are not either formal or non-formal in any meaningful sense, but exhibit various degrees of formality or non-formality depending on the particular characteristic which is being considered. Indeed, many programs become more or less formal over time as their objectives and characteristics evolve."[47]

Rather than a silo into which one can categorize certain forms of learning over against others, Alan Rogers suggests that the language of semiformal learning is a useful tool for analysis and planning.[48]

Staying Fresh

Having preached many years in the same parish, I find that a key challenge is trying to find something fresh to say in view of the prescribed texts and feasts that occur over and over again in my tradition. Thus, I scour old commentaries and new websites for that insightful exegesis, commentary, or story that not only enlivens my preaching but also renews my faith. In a similar way, thinking about the nature of the integrating project in theological education can become stale and repetitive for me. When that happens, I often launch into a similar quest for some constructive insight or optic that will stimulate my thinking and enhance my practice.

The linkage of formal, semiformal and informal has been such a framework for me. It has helped me to envision the entire landscape of my own institution—and not just the brick-and-mortar or digital classrooms—as a rich and fluid environment for untold forms of learning and formation. It helps me raise questions when we hire a new recruiter or development associate about how effective the person will be not only in bolstering enrollment or the bottom line but also as a formative guide for students and colleagues alike. It deepens my appreciation for the presence and pastoral care of receptionists and administrative assistants who in untold ways shepherd neophytes and some of us antediluvians on our journeys into ministry. It challenges me to reconfigure classrooms and curb my input in

46. Smith, "Place, Space, and Information Education," 3.

47. Simkins, *Non-formal Education and Development,* 19.

48. Rogers, *Non-Formal Education.*

seminars so that more voices are heard and informal exchange is honored in hopes of decentralizing power and decolonizing theological knowledge. It even gives me a frame for thinking about policies regarding academic probation or continuing registration, wondering sometimes aloud how they model ministry or care and not simply effective management.

This framework, of course, is not the only or even the best possible lens for seeing theological institutions with fresh eyes. In the case studies that follow, dialogue partners reflecting on the integrating task will cast a wide view of their own institutions in diverse ways. Rebecca Slough, for example, brings the optic of an experienced academic dean with wide involvement within her own denomination and with the Association of Theological Schools. With all her wisdom and bruises, Slough has a preferential option for love as the fundamental personal and theological spark for shaping faculties. More than engendering respect, love is a powerful integrating framework for reimagining how faculty members can be with each other. Envisioning the integrating task inside out from a faculty center generates neither competition nor siloization but *koinonia*. If a faculty can begin to figured out how and decide if this is their future, it will clearly resound to the well-being of the whole institution. This is integrating writ large in virtue and charity, authored by a faculty willing to temper guild expectations of individual achievement and consider faculty development as a shared venture and not personal accomplishment. This radically evangelical Anabaptist vision honors authentic love—not personal affect—as a faculty practice capable of engendering wider community commitment to mutual respect and regard.

While Slough digs deep into her evangelical roots through the New Testament to ponder how the integrating task might be reimagined through a faculty practicing gospel love, David Rylaarsdam takes an equally distinctive path to describe Calvin Theological Seminary, a school situated in the Reformed tradition. This case study centers on a recent school revision at Calvin. In this integrative revisioning, the steering committee intentionally avoided any frameworks that could enforce silos, fragmentation, and divisions. In addition to tackling the curriculum (described in a case study in part 2), the school had to reenvision its guiding values, organizational structure, assessment practices, academic calendar, finances, and language.

In a case study centered on CTU, I illustrate how formal, informal, and semiformal learning flow through the main academic building. This mapping exercise highlights the ways these three forms of learning flow freely to create multiple learning environments. More about attending than decision making, this consciousness-raising reflection is offered as an example of how faculties and administrations can begin to chart the integrating flows that are already operative in a space, as a first step toward capitalizing on them further.

Bibliography

Banks, Sarah. "Professional Values in Informal Education Work." In *Principles and Practice of Informal Education: Learning through Life*, edited by Linda Deer Richardson and Mary Wolfe, 62–73. London: Routledge, 2001.

Benner, Patricia, et al. *Educating Nurses: A Call for Radical Transformation.* San Francisco: Jossey-Bass, 2010.

Brebera, Pavel, and Jitka Hlouskova. "Searching for Bridges between Formal and Informal Language Education." In *IADIS International Conference on Cognition and Exploratory Learning in Digital Age*, edited by Demetrios Sampson et al., 274–77. Red Hook, NY: Curran Associates, 2012. http://eric.ed.gov/?id=ED542829.

Carroll, Jackson, et al. *Being There: Culture and Formation in Two Theological Schools.* New York: Oxford University Press, 1997.

Colletta, N. J. "Formal, Nonformal, and Informal Education." In *International Encyclopedia of Adult Education and Training*, edited by Albert Tuijnman, 22–27. Oxford: Pergamon, 1996.

Coombs, Philip, et al. *New Paths to Learning for Rural Children and Youth.* New York: International Council for Educational Development, 1973.

Dewey, John. *Democracy and Education: An Introduction to the Philosophy of Education.* New York: Macmillan, 1922.

European Guidelines for Validating Non-formal and Informal Learning. Luxembourg: Office for Official Publications of the European Communities, 2009. http://www.cedefop.europa.eu/EN/publications/5059.aspx.

Fenwick, Tara. *Learning through Experience: Troubling Orthodoxies and Intersecting Questions.* Malabar, FL: Krieger, 2003.

Freire, Paulo. *Pedagogy of the Oppressed.* Translated by Myra Bergman Ramos. New York: Seabury, 1970.

Gilchrist, Alison. "Working with Networks and Organizations in the Community." In *Principles and Practice of Informal Education: Learning through Life*, edited by Linda Deer Richardson and Mary Wolfe, 106–19. London: Routledge, 2001.

Gofton, Wade, and Glenn Regehr. "What We Don't Know We Are Teaching: Unveiling the Hidden Curriculum." *Clinical Orthopaedics and Related Research* 449 (2006) 20–27.

Guldbrandsen, Francis. "Paulo Freire and the Problem of Consciousness." In *Historical Perspectives on Non-Formal Education*, edited by Marvin Grandstaff, 70–75. East Lansing: Michigan State University, 1974.

Hung, David, et al. "Authenticity in Learning for the Twenty-First Century: Bridging the Formal and Informal." *Educational Technology Research Development* 60 (2012) 1071–91.

Jackson, Philip W. *Life in Classrooms.* New York: Holt, Rinehart, and Winston, 1968.

Jeffs, Tony. "First Lessons: Historical Perspectives on Information Education." In *Principles and Practice of Informal Education: Learning through Life*, edited by Linda Deer Richardson and Mary Wolfe, 35–49. London: Routledge, 2001.

Jeffs, Tony, and Mark K. Smith. *Informal Education: Conversation, Democracy and Learning*. 3rd ed. Bramcote, Nottingham: Educational Heretics, 2005.

Knowles, Malcolm. *The Modern Practice of Adult Education: Andragogy vs. Pedagogy*. New York: Cambridge, 1970.

Kolb, David. *Experiential Learning*. Englewood Cliffs, NJ: Prentice-Hall, 1984.

Lave, Jean, and Etienne Wenger. *Situated Learning: Legitimate Peripheral Participation*. Cambridge: Cambridge, 1991.

Mezirow, Jack. *Transformative Dimensions of Adult Learning*. San Francisco: Jossey-Bass, 1991.

Misko, Josie. *Combining Formal, Non-formal and Informal Learning for Workforce Skill Development*. Adelaide: National Centre for Vocational Educational Research, 2008. http://files.eric.ed.gov/fulltext/ED503360.pdf.

Rogers, Alan. *Non-Formal Education: Flexible Schooling or Participatory Education?* CERC Studies in Comparative Education 15, 239–42. Hong Kong: University of Hong Kong, 2004.

Schön, Donald. *Educating the Reflective Practitioner*. New York: Basic, 1987.

———. *The Reflective Practitioner*. New York: Basic, 1983.

Schwier, Richard A. "A Comparison of Participation Patterns in Selected Formal, Non-Formal and Informal Online Learning Environments." *Canadian Journal of Learning and Technology* 39.1 (2013) 1–15.

Selman, Gordon, et al. *The Foundations of Adult Education in Canada*. 2nd ed. Toronto: Thompson Educational, 1998.

Shakespeare, William. *Hamlet*.

Simkins, Tim. *Non-formal Education and Development: Some Critical Issues*. Manchester: University of Manchester, Department of Adult and Higher Education, 1977.

Smith, Mark. "Place, Space, and Information Education." In *Principles and Practice of Informal Education: Learning through Life*, edited by Linda Deer Richardson and Mary Wolfe, 138–47. London: Routledge, 2001.

Smith, M. K. "What Is Non-formal Education?" *The Encyclopedia of Informal Education*. http://infed.org/mobi/what-is-non-formal-education/.

Sullivan, Teresa A. "Making the Graduate Curriculum Explicit." *Teaching Sociology* 19 (1991) 408–13.

Tiffany, Graeme. "Relationships and Learning." In *Principles and Practice of Informal Education: Learning through Life*, edited by Linda Deer Richardson and Mary Wolfe, 93–105. London: Routledge, 2001.

Ward, Ted, et al. "Effective Learning." In *Effective Learning in Non-Formal Education*, edited by Ted Ward and William Herzog, 14–64. East Lansing: Michigan State University, 1974. http://eric.ed.gov/?id=ED100774.

Wenger, Etienne. *Communities of Practice: Learning, Meaning, and Identity*. Cambridge: Cambridge University Press, 1999.

Zaki Dib, Claudio. "Formal, Non-Formal, and Informal Education: Concepts/Applicability." In *Cooperative Networks in Physics Education: Oaxtepec, Mexico, 1987*, edited by Jorge Barojas, 300–315. AIP Conference Proceedings 173. New York: American Institute of Physics, 1988.

2

What's Love Got to Do with It?

Faculty Development in a Community of Practice

REBECCA SLOUGH

O ne achievement of my time as a theological school dean will be over-
seeing the generational shift of the faculty at Anabaptist Mennonite
Biblical Seminary. Sixty percent of our professors were hired in the last
four years, having recently completed doctoral work, and have limited
graduate-level teaching experience. The remaining 40 percent of the faculty
have taught for ten or more years with fluctuating degrees of contentment.
While we affirm basic Anabaptist values for expressing Christian life and
look to the theological traditions within the Bible for the church's guidance,
renewal, and inspiration, these commitments are not sufficient to orient
the faculty in its common work. One of my responsibilities is to help this
group of newer and seasoned professors become a community that uses the
strengths and vulnerabilities of each colleague to navigate the challenges
facing theological education and deepen Christian discipleship.

Faculties are critical guardians and nurturers of their learning community. If an educational goal of theological schools is helping students
embody dimensions of knowing, being, and doing, as the Collegeville Institute Seminars seek to explore, a starting place for determining how students
gain a vision for an integrative orientation to ministry lies in the character
and culture of the theological faculty.[1] Through teaching, scholarship,

---

1. I continue to be surprised that the Association of Theological School accreditation standard related to faculty (Standard 5) does not require an assessment of the health

curricular oversight, and commitments to service, faculty members are invited to demonstrate a deepening capacity for sustaining relationships of mutuality with colleagues and students, with God, and with themselves while stretching toward an integrating center, which in this essay I name as love.

The mystery of integrating work presents multiple quandaries. Two years ago, as I worked toward discernment, the synoptic Gospels' passages on the first and second commandments ambushed my imagination. I became intrigued by the potential of claiming love as an integrative center for promoting faculty development and deepening a theological faculty's maturity.

The First and Great Commandment

Each synoptic Gospel records a dialogue in which someone seeks to test Jesus's orthodoxy.[2] In all three cases, Jesus draws from Deuteronomy 6 and Leviticus 19: "You shall love the Lord your God with all your heart, and with all your soul, and with all your mind . . . And . . . your neighbor as yourself" (Matt 22:37–39; Mark and Luke add "strength" to this list of human characteristics). Within the biblical tradition, the human being is understood as a "biopsychospiritual" unity.[3] There is no heart without a body, no mind without a heart, no living body without a soul. The integration of these modes of human being is a blessing to be accepted, honored, and deepened.

In Jesus's exchanges with his questioners, he claims love as the integrative center. Love activates the unique capacities of mind, heart, soul, and body in relationships with God, neighbor, and self. The Gospel texts' trifocal approach to love illustrates brilliantly an essential balance of human social, psychological, and spiritual orientations. Loving God, neighbor, and self holds a self-correcting tension. Loving God but not neighbor or self can lead to excessive pietism or fanaticism. Loving neighbor but not God or self can lead to excesses of self-sacrifice and pride. Loving self but not God or neighbor gives rise to the excesses of narcissism, entitlement, and

---

of the relationships in the faculty, the collective well-being of the faculty, or the climate within the faculty that supports the growth of its individual members. Commission on Accrediting, *Bulletin 50, Part 1.*

2. See Matt 22:34–35; Mark 12:28–29; Luke 10:25–26.

3. Green, "Soul."

hubris. Jesus's teachings orient our full-bodied expressions of love beyond ourselves, beside ourselves, and inside ourselves.[4]

Commentators connect Matthew's and Luke's passages on loving enemies with the commandment to love the neighbor.[5] Loving our neighbors is easy enough when everyone follows the same rules and shows up for meetings on time. However, the costliness of Christian discipleship is best seen in Jesus's nearly impossible command for us to love our enemy. Christian love is not limited to those for whom we have positive feeling. It orients us to revere and act for the well-being of all people, especially those for whom we feel enmity.

The good news resounding in the two great commandments affirms the unity of human being and the complementary capacities of heart, mind, soul, and strength for the sake of love. Yet, the practices of many theological school faculties demonstrate an overwhelming preference for the capacities of the mind and sometimes disdain or resist knowledge arising from emotional or intuitional sources. How often are professors honored for brilliant scholarship while demonstrating staggering emotional immaturity?[6] Good teaching—that demands the integrated expressions of physical, emotional, and cognitive intelligences—may be considered of secondary importance to scholarly research in promotion processes. Most systems for evaluating faculty performance exclusively honor the production of intellectually sound writing and have no standards for discerning the scholarly merit of public performance, artistic production, or project design. Overemphasis on intellectual productivity belies our most basic nature.

The depth of these two great commandments dawns when we begin to grasp the truth that love is primarily an *action* of honoring and revering the irreducible worth of another being. Loving colleagues does not require deep affection but rather a sense of loyalty with attendant mutual respect and cooperation. It does not require unanimity in all matters and certainly

4. If asked today about the most important commandments, Jesus might extend the tradition by including love for God's creation. One can make a case for loving God by caring for God's creation; loving neighbor and enemy by caring for the natural environment we share; and loving ourselves by ensuring that our species be sustained with the company of every other species.

5. Perkins, *Love Commands*; also, Furnish, *Love Commandment*, 51–53, 54–56, 66.

6. During the years spanning this project, my school has addressed the history of a former professor's sexual misconduct—a person who was widely celebrated as intellectually brilliant while exhibiting significant social and emotional immaturity along with exceedingly poor judgment.

not preserving peace at all cost. Mature colleagues speak truth in loving-kindness that is free of rancor and inappropriate self-interest. The command to love God, neighbor, and self offers faculty members a perspective on human dignity that should bear on how they treat their most difficult colleagues. Even when a person challenges every strand of patience, it is possible for us to see another's gifts and quirks within this larger loving vision.

It is paradoxical to think that we can love ourselves well in the context of a theological school faculty, and it is equally counterintuitive to believe that this love is best expressed as a community of colleagues who hold us accountable and support us. Yet, in their presence and through our shared work, we have hope of rising to our best selves.

Theological School Faculties as Communities of Practice

Jean Lave and Etienne Wenger developed the "community of practice" concept to explain how people learn to function effectively in social environments. The researchers noted basic patterns that beginners or novices often follow as they gain competence for participating in practices of a community. Novices start with the most basic activities at the periphery of what they are seeking to learn by watching, listening, and talking with practitioners who are more adept. Beginners gain proficiency as performance expectations rise and move closer to the center of the community's action.[7] With their increasing competence comes knowledge as well as a sense of identity, belonging, and meaning.[8]

A community of practice nurtures the multidimensional relationships between individuals, shared activities, common purpose, and interactions with the larger world. From the interplay of these relationships a culture emerges that shapes both the community's character and its participants'

---

7. Lave and Wenger call this process of initiation and integration into a community of practice "legitimate peripheral participation." *Situated Learning*, 35–37.

8. Wenger, *Communities of Practice*, 4. Wenger's work is not rooted in a particular social, psychological, or philosophical framework. He borrows from a wide set of theoretical resources to analyze his ethnographic examples of situated learning (11). His is not a well-developed social learning theory. This is a strength insofar as it uses an interdisciplinary approach to the topic of social learning and a weakness in not providing sufficient analysis of the wide variety of sources from which he draws.

character while providing the means by which the community reproduces itself.[9]

I count theological school faculties as communities of practice who welcome new faculty colleagues into their circle. Practices of teaching, assessing, mentoring, implementing the curriculum, discerning, decision making, and governance characterize faculty work. New colleagues learn these practices from those who have been in the community longer. Faculties also welcome students into the school's unique learning ethos, introducing them to its academic, spiritual, and social practices. If Lave and Wenger are right, how a faculty sustains its practices as a community conditions how their students will learn important aspects of a ministerial vocation.[10]

The size of a faculty creates certain organizational necessities. Large faculties may be organized into disciplinary departments while smaller faculties may work as a total group or in committees. The location of office and meeting spaces plays a role in how a faculty may understand itself as a community. Not all members of a faculty gain a wide-angle perspective on their work as it relates to other colleagues, especially when competition for resources or a share of the credit hours in a degree program are at stake. New deans in theological schools, moving from their faculties into administration, are often shocked to discover the complexity of relational dynamics within faculties. They had no idea this was so, even after multiple years of teaching with colleagues they now oversee.[11]

Is it inappropriate to think that a commitment to continuing growth in love for God, neighbor, and oneself could provide faculty with an integrating center for a community of practice and the ongoing development of that community? Love requires a vision of work that draws colleagues into deeper respect and trust of one another and into an expanding love for God as well as themselves as individuals.

9. Lave and Wenger, *Situated Learning*, 98.

10. Brown and Reimer report on emerging evidence that shows virtue is learned by watching people around us acting virtuously. What virtues and integrative practices do students learn by observing their faculty at work together day after day? Brown and Reimer, "Embodied Cognition."

11. I have participated in three deans' colloquies (2010–2011, 2012–2013, 2013–2014) sponsored by the Wabash Center for Teaching and Learning in Theology and Religion, Crawfordsville, Indiana. I served as colloquy leader with another dean in two of these colloquies. In all three, the topic of faculty complexity (especially interpersonal complexity) was addressed. Nearly to a person, we confessed our shock and, at times, dismay that we had known so little about what we had stepped into with regard to our colleagues.

The dean plays a key role in realizing the vision for a mature faculty community. Without a biblical-theological perspective on how a theological faculty can function, a dean's vision can be distracted by administrative demands, causing one to lose the holistic vision of love for self and the faculties one leads.

As a beginning dean, I mistakenly thought that giving the faculty all the relevant factual information for a particular issue was enough to enable them to make a reasonable decision. When discussions revealed unexpected emotional currents, I learned the hard way that empirical data alone was not adequate. I valued efficient decision making more than the intellectual, emotional, spiritual, and sometimes physical knowledge these colleagues brought to the issue at hand. For quite a while, I did not know how to lead the faculty to its deepest wisdom or how to develop its growing capacities for discernment.

Dorothy Bass's and Craig Dykstra's work on specific theologically grounded practices provides a useful complement to Lave and Wenger's perspectives on social learning. Patterns of shared activity weave together and create a way of life.[12] Practices have particular shapes and orientations; they are a means to embody intention and meaning. Communities engage in holistic actions (requiring the engagement of mind, heart, soul, and body) over extended periods that form collective character and culture that orient them toward love for God, neighbors, and the world.[13]

Theological school faculties are enmeshed in myriad formal, informal, recognized, and misrecognized practices.[14] Here I want to explore the practice of time as it relates to faculty meetings and the qualities of presence, attentiveness, and emerging trust as expressions of love.[15]

At Anabaptist Mennonite Biblical Seminary, faculty meetings unofficially start with an informal lunch in the room where our formal meeting

12. Bass, *Practicing Our Faith*, 8.

13. Ibid., 200.

14. Examples of ever-present but rarely recognized practices that would influence how love might be developed within a faculty include managing anxiety and emotional reactivity, working with conflict, planning curricula, using power, promotion reviews, managing organizational or personal failure, processing disciplinary action, and negotiating resources.

15. I am very aware that what I describe here may not be an effective way for large faculties to organize their meetings. My hope, however, is that readers' imaginations might be sparked to consider how the smaller groupings within a faculty—for example, department or committee meetings—might also orient their practices toward love.

will be held; eating is accompanied by casual conversation, good humor, and usually a generosity of spirit. Some discussions capture the whole group's attention, but not always. For forty-five minutes, the largest block of unstructured faculty time in a week, no one is required to be productive. Lunch is a sabbath in the middle of the day, a space for being present with one another.

The official meeting starts with everyone responding briefly to a question that invites a personal response (for example, recent family events or travel, future plans, personal concerns, or a recent teaching discovery). Then we are led in worship by a colleague. The first twenty to twenty-five minutes of the meeting is utterly unproductive in the sense of what a meeting is to accomplish. But the Spirit of God and the presence of our collegial neighbors have our attention.

The day's agenda shifts the quality of our listening. Our intentions are refocused. Discussions can flow with ease, but may turn intense because they often stir emotions. At times we follow principles from the Circle Process to allow important intellectual, emotional, physical, and spiritual dimensions of an issue surface.[16] For example, we may use a simple discussion structure that slows down our talking and ensures that everyone has space to speak without interruption. We take time to breath and occasionally to stand and stretch. Treating conflict with respect and the graciousness of time has led to unexpected resolutions to issues that seemed intractable as they emerged. Meetings rarely close as gracefully as I would like, because I am still learning the grace-filled art of pacing and ending.

A number of small practices structure faculty meetings: eating together, breaking the day's work cycle, checking in, worship, and orderly discussion that can contain emotional and spiritual as well as intellectual information. These meetings attempt to attend to the relationships required for our community of practice to function with integrity. At times, we fail our best intentions, but the vision remains.

Practicing love for God, neighbor, and self takes qualities of time and activity: time that is already filled with God's presence before the gathering starts; time for laughter, tears, prayer, and the holy stories of our lives; time free from agenda and the demands to produce; time that allows for work that has turned difficult to unfold at a different pace that allows everyone

16. Christina Baldwin and Ann Linneas, cofounders of PeerSpirit, Inc., and the Circle Way Process, recently led the faculty retreat (see http://peerspirit.com/about/). Several colleagues have pursued Circle Way Process leadership training, which is building capacities for structured and careful listening and speaking from within the faculty.

to be heard and respected; and time to find and speak the heart's deepest wisdom. These practices require the vision and commitment of leadership from the dean and from the faculty.

I love the faculty. I am deeply invested in a vision for how this community of theological educators grows into vocational maturity. One of my leadership responsibilities is keeping our work practices oriented toward the love of God, neighbor, and self. This vision is not easy to keep in focus, and I often stumble toward it.

The mission of Anabaptist Mennonite Biblical Seminary is "to educate followers of Jesus Christ to be leaders for God's reconciling mission in the world." Through its shared work, the faculty shapes the character, culture, and climate of the community into which we invite and nurture students who are preparing for ministry. Capacities for spiritually grounded intercultural, interfaith, justice-attuned relational competencies are essential for ministry in the twenty-first century. How could our school possibly take Jesus's command to love enemies seriously if our faculty community does not stretch toward practices that deepen our love of God, our colleagues (who are neighbors and sometimes adversaries), and ourselves?

Bibliography

Bass, Dorothy C, ed. *Practicing Our Faith: A Way of Life for a Searching People*. Practices of Faith Series. San Francisco: Jossey-Bass, 1997.

Brown Warren S., and Kevin S. Reimer. "Embodied Cognition, Character Formation, and Virtue." *Zygon* 48 (2013) 841–43.

The Commission on Accrediting. *Bulletin 50, Part 1*. Pittsburgh: Association of Theological Schools, 2012. G-10–G-12.

Furnish, Victor Paul. *The Love Commandment in the New Testament*. Nashville: Abingdon, 1972.

Green, Joel. "Soul." In *New Interpreter's Bible Dictionary*, edited by Katherine Doob Sakenfeld, 5:359. Nashville: Abingdon, 2009.

Lave, Jean, and Etienne Wenger. *Situated Learning: Legitimate Peripheral Participation*. Learning in Doing. Cambridge: Cambridge University Press, 1991.

Perkins, Pheme. *Love Commands in the New Testament*. New York: Paulist, 1982.

Wenger, Etienne. *Communities of Practice: Learning, Meaning, and Identity*. Cambridge: Cambridge University Press, 1998.

3

Integrating Foci in a
School's Renewal Process

David Rylaarsdam

A crisis is a terrible thing to waste. In 2007 Calvin Theological Seminary (CTS) confronted a mounting crisis, and its leadership seized the opportunity. For over a century, CTS had enjoyed the advantages of being the denominational seminary of the Christian Reformed Church. By 2007 the financial support of the denomination was declining and alternative routes to denominational ministry were increasing. Furthermore, the economy was slumping, enrollment was slipping, a recent accreditation review resulted in a few nicks, and too many CTS graduates were expressing dissatisfaction with their seminary experience.

The seminary president formed a culture, pedagogy, and curriculum committee (CPC) whose mandate was the renewal of all things so that students could be better formed for ministry. The president asked me to help lead the renewal effort. Since I was untenured and the youngest full-time faculty member, the most highly respected senior faculty member was appointed chair of the committee. I would serve as a member of CPC and have course release time to facilitate the committee's work.

The culture, pedagogy, and curriculum committee assumed that improving theological education required more than curriculum revision and enhancing faculty pedagogy. The committee took a systems approach, attempting to reform the seminary's entire way of life: its culture, assessment process, organizational structure, hiring and faculty development practices, and relationships to colleges, churches, and the denomination. Integrating was identified as a central value in the process. In this essay, I will highlight ways in which CPC attempted to create a culture throughout the school in which integrating work could be fostered in an ongoing way.

Guiding Values for School-Wide Renewal

A few years before CPC, the seminary's board of trustees had declared that holistic, integrative formation for ministry was the new focus of a CTS education. The board insisted that this focus should not compromise rigorous academic training. It believed, however, that holistic formation rather than intellectual information alone must be the guiding principle when preparing people for ministry.

Building on the board's declaration, CPC began by analyzing recent data on alumni views of their CTS education. The committee also hosted small groups of faculty and staff listening sessions, wanting to give everyone an opportunity to voice what things to keep, reform, or eliminate at Calvin. Based on those listening sessions, CPC developed ten values to guide the renewal process and support the focus on formation for ministry. Six of the ten were concerned in some way with improving the integrating work of students and faculty.[1] For each value, the committee listed several examples. I have abbreviated them here.

1. Shape the whole person.
   - Form a pastoral identity that integrates being, knowing, and doing.
2. Strengthen the seminary community.
   - Attend to the ways CTS's culture is as formative as the curriculum.
   - Develop the faculty's character, pedagogy, and pastoral modeling to students.
3. Integrate
   - across subdisciplines;

---

1. The other four values were continue to confess Reformed theology and belief, adapt (to students' previous education and experiences, to learning styles, to a multicultural world), serve a wider range of students, and create buzz (proactively and creatively raise awareness of our school's renewal).

- between Mentored Ministries (formerly Field Education) and courses;

- between the church and CTS;

- between colleges and CTS;

- between head, hands, heart (that is, transcend the academic-practical-piety divides); and

- between CTS and the Grand Rapids community.

4. Collaborate, encourage, and hold each other accountable

   - across departments regarding the content of core courses and encouraging team-taught and interdisciplinary courses; and

   - between CTS and the church, seeking feedback from alums, congregations, and agencies.

5. Pursue lifelong learning.

   - Promote and model virtues and habits that set students on a path of continuous learning.

   - Set up workloads for students that encourage healthy, balanced living.

   - Develop a way of life at CTS that has more continuity with full-time ministry than discontinuity.

6. Sponsor regular faculty development.

   - Attend not only to what faculty teach but also to *how* faculty teach (tone, virtues modeled, integration with ministry, and so forth).

   - Engage in pedagogy that is appropriate to training people for ministry and encourages integration.

   - Develop not only students' critical thinking but also their practical wisdom.

While CPC was developing values for renewal, a newly formed assessment committee was creating an assessment plan for the school. In its 2007 accreditation review, the Association of Theological Schools (ATS) threatened to give the seminary a notation for a virtually nonexistent assessment process, but instead they scheduled a focused visit. Assessment suddenly became an institutional priority.

Assessment

Calvin Theological Seminary's small accreditation crisis was a gift. Just as it was embarking on institutional and curricular overhaul, CTS was forced to develop an assessment plan. Since integration is a criteria in the ATS standards, Calvin's assessment plan needed to measure how community life and curriculum encouraged integrating work. Assessment became an unexpected ally in promoting integrative living and learning at CTS.

In developing its plan, the seminary's assessment committee rewrote the goals of all degree programs; integration became integral to the structure and content of those goals. In a separate essay in this volume, I describe the curricular goals.[2] Integration also became an explicit theme in our newly developed assessment measures. For example, in our new case study rubric,[3] one criterion states:

> Integration: Was the student able to draw on all four areas (message, person, context, goal) of seminary education in approaching the case study scenario? Did the student articulate an approach to the issues and problems presented that drew together aspects of biblical, theological, and practical matters?

Calvin Theological Seminary made integrating a criterion in all student assessment rubrics: writing, preaching, theological reflections, service learning, and oral comprehensive exams. The course evaluation was rewritten, and various types of integration are now measured. The course form asks students not only to what degree the course was integrated with other courses in their program but also whether the teacher facilitated connections between the course and the practice of ministry and respectfully modeled what was taught.

Furthermore, CTS developed an exit interview for graduating students and a set of questions that could guide the faculty's assessment of degree programs. In all these measures, integration was an explicit criterion. Since faculty, students, mentors, and supervisors encounter these assessment measures frequently, the assessment committee assumed that attending to

2. See chapter 7, "Overhauling the Curriculum," in this volume.

3. The rubric is used to assess student work on ministry case studies. Students present or examine case studies at various points in their program, in courses as well as their mentoring groups (small groups which meet every week of their program). In the capstone course Integrative Seminar, each student receives a complex case study, prepares an approach to address the case, and discusses the approach with a panel consisting of two faculty members and a pastor.

the wording of these forms was a small but important way to encourage sustained self-examination of our integrating processes.

The Association of Theological Schools pushed CTS to build an assessment plan that paid special attention to how our community analyzed and acted upon its assessment data. The assessment committee concluded that constructive assessment discussions would be impossible within our current organizational structure.

Organizational Structure

The CPC committee was also troubled by the seminary's structure and doubted that it would sustain whatever forms of renewal the committee might accomplish. For years, curriculum discussions in our structure produced patches to fix problems. If most faculty acknowledged that there was a particular weakness in preparing people for ministry, an academic division would respond by adding a course. Such patches, without subtracting or integrating, produced a bloated curriculum that lacked pedagogical coherence and efficiency. More requirements meant that the MDiv degree took students five or six years to complete. Hence, prospective students were increasingly deciding to get their theological education elsewhere.

One of our organizational problems was the silo effect. Faculty members lived in one of three academic divisions (Bible, Theology, or Ministry) and lacked awareness of what was going on in other parts of the curriculum or institution. The director of field education was disconnected from two of the academic divisions. Collaboration, encouragement, and accountability across divisions—for example, development of interdisciplinary or team-taught courses, or improvement of faculty pedagogy—rarely occurred. Faculty did not interact with staff or discern together the ways to improve our communal life. Our "faculty-run institution," as some faculty adamantly considered CTS, was not discussing critical issues related to the needs of the church and the mission of the school, because these did not seem to fit the responsibility of any academic division. Although the assessment and CPC committees believed that structural changes are often a technical solution to adaptive challenges, as Ronald Heifetz describes,[4] they decided that our structure contributed to a depth of dysfunction that would make curriculum revision and other renewal efforts difficult. Some faculty wryly suggested that CTS should follow Paul's advice: "There should be no

4. See Heifetz, *Leadership without Easy Answers*.

divisions among you" (1 Cor 1:10) and a consensus developed around this exhortation. The seminary banished its academic divisions.

Divisions were replaced by three interdisciplinary committees: curriculum and pedagogy, community culture, and church relations.[5] Each of these is composed of faculty from each of the former academic divisions as well as staff members and one student. The committees are central to the school's organizational structure. They reflect our institutional identity as a school (Curriculum and Pedagogy) of the church (Church Relations) that is always seeking to reform itself (Community Culture). The new structure was intended to promote creative, interdisciplinary discussions on a host of important issues related to integrating work; for example, since community culture (the hidden curriculum) teaches as much as the curriculum itself, how can we improve our way of life together?

The faculty adopted its new organization in the spring of 2008, which facilitated intense curriculum discussions the following academic year. Consequently, the discussions became interdisciplinary, which kept them from stalling in internecine warfare and produced a new curriculum more likely to enhance the integrating task than divisional discussions would have accomplished in their silos.

Academic Calendar

The culture, pedagogy, and curriculum committee also persuaded the faculty in spring 2008 to adopt a new academic calendar. This replaced three quarters per academic year with two semesters, a January term, and a May term. The semesters are relatively brief (twelve weeks plus an exam week). This allows for a weeklong reading break one-third of the way into the semester and a weeklong Thanksgiving or spring break two-thirds of the way into the semester.

CPC's main arguments for the new semester system all related in some way to integrating living and learning.

1. The modern tendency toward fragmentation in theological education undermined a formation process in which practices and theology are integrated. Since our new semester system had 33 percent fewer

---

5. Although there are no longer divisions among us at CTS, academic departments still exist (Old Testament, New Testament, and so forth), but their role in institutional life is limited.

courses than our quarter system, the curriculum could potentially be taught more holistically.

2. Quarters tended to promote binge-and-purge learning, burnout instead of endurance, and short-term productivity rather than long-term fruitfulness. The rhythm of semesters, with two weeks of breaks each semester, could encourage a healthier rhythm that students could continue when they enter full-time ministry.

3. Discussion of the calendar changes pushed the faculty to consider more thoroughly how the entire curriculum and faculty pedagogy might contribute toward integrated formation for ministry. Rather than simply tweaking the number of credits allotted for various academic disciplines, the faculty was forced to begin curriculum revision by discussing the goals of an MDiv education and then develop a coherent curricular structure to meet those goals.

4. Reading breaks each semester as well as a January interim would allow opportunities in students' schedules for cross-cultural, international, or service-learning experiences.

5. Students could audit skill development courses during reading breaks. Integrative travel courses could be offered during the January and May terms.

Renewing Language and Budgets

As CPC engaged in this process of renewal, it became clear that some language in our community might encourage unhealthy dichotomies. Names for academic divisions such as "Theological" and "Ministry" might imply that so-called ministry courses are not theological and vice versa. Describing degree programs as "academic" or "ministry" might carry similar messages. In its renewal discussions and documents, CPC was attentive to language while recognizing that simply changing language was a technical solution with limited benefits if not accompanied by larger shifts in school culture and structures.

For example, field education was largely disconnected from the rest of a student's program and generally perceived as the opportunity for students to apply the theory they had learned in course work. To overcome this theory-praxis dichotomy, CTS needed not only to develop a curriculum that better integrated students' "course" and "field" learnings but also to change language, fee structures, and faculty involvement in "field" processes. The language of *field education* was replaced with *mentored ministries* and many faculty were appointed as mentoring group leaders. Furthermore, "credits" were redefined so that CTS no longer used different names or tuition rates for "field education" and "course" credits. Finally, in the new curriculum, mentored ministry requirements would be learning experiences structured more like courses (including a syllabus and rubrics) and more directly connected to the requirements of other courses.[6]

Besides greater attentiveness to language, CPC wrestled with the financial implications of valuing integration and changed the way in which faculty workloads were calculated. If faculty members co-taught a course across traditional disciplines, they were given more than half workload credit for that course. They were also given slightly greater workload credit for leading a mentoring group than for teaching a course. The seminary also increased its faculty development and assessment budgets. Administrators raised additional financial questions, but they were not resolved; for example, to increase the quality of students' internship experiences, was the seminary willing to invest in some excellent ministry contexts and supervisors?

Faculty Identity, Hiring, and Development

As part of its renewal process, Calvin Theological Seminary adopted a new statement regarding faculty identity and requirements. The decades-old former statement focused on faculty members' intelligence and capacity to be zealous defenders of Reformed dogma. But there was little or nothing about faculty character, pedagogical effectiveness, ongoing competence in ministry, or an ability to foster integrating work.

The new statement focuses on the character, wisdom, and skills of seminary teachers who are called upon to facilitate students' integrating journey into ministry.[7] The faculty who developed this statement assumed that CTS needed criteria for hiring new faculty who would embody some degree of personal, professional, and intellectual integration and a desire to accompany students. The new faculty identity statement was also intended to guide the orientation, encouragement, accountability, and promotion of

6. See chapter 7, "Overhauling the Curriculum," in this volume.

7. The new statement would have benefitted greatly from Rebecca Slough's essay "What's Love Got to Do with It?" in this volume.

faculty. It could also serve faculty as they wrote their development plans and annual reports to the board of trustees.

To facilitate students' integrating work, CTS also broadened its understanding of faculty. Categories of tenure track and adjunct can limit the number of gifted practitioners who regularly contribute to the community. Tenure-track faculty often have either limited ministry experience or experience several years in the past, and their current ministry is limited due to faculty responsibilities. Adjunct faculty parachute into a classroom to teach a course but are typically uninvolved in the seminary's discussions and decision making. Thus, CTS has broadened instructional categories to include vocational mentors, mentoring group leaders,[8] adjuncts, partner in ministry professors, pastors on capstone course panels, and tenure-track faculty.

A partner in ministry professor is a new category that enables CTS to develop a network of faculty who are engaged in various ministries around the world. Based on their gifts and interests, partner in ministry professors are involved in one or more parts of CTS life beyond teaching, such as committing to a period of residency on campus each year, participating in a learning forum with faculty members, and serving as a mentoring group leader.

The possibility of hiring teachers who promote integrating work has also increased due to the seminary's new organizational structure. Formerly composed of faculty in an academic division, search committees are now an interdisciplinary team of faculty who can attend seriously to a candidate's interest or ability to teach in an interdisciplinary or integrated way. Whether the new structure will help hire faculty who can promote the integrating task remains to be seen, but the door to that possibility has been opened wider.

Since too many faculty members have been trained in PhD programs that detract from integrating rather than promote it, CTS's new structure was intentional about assisting faculty development. For example, it called for two faculty meetings per month, no more than ninety minutes each. It also recommended that each faculty meeting should have only one or two agenda items rather than a laundry list of business items that other committees could address. The faculty agenda would consider substantive issues regarding the life and ministry of CTS and would arise out of the three new committees. At least four meetings per year would be related

---

8. See chapter 7, "Overhauling the Curriculum," in this volume.

to faculty development; for example, a pedagogical training event or an exercise related to assessment, such as review of a degree program.

Crises can be disintegrating moments in the life of a community. A crisis can also trigger much change in a short amount of time—a rare occurrence in academic institutions. Although CPC would have liked to accomplish more, there is a limit to the amount of change a system can digest. Moreover, the committee knew that renewal, like integrative teaching and learning, is a long-term project. Therefore, it attempted to create a context for moving a school away from only academic theological education and toward formational theological education with integration as an emphasis.[9] The committee initiated values, structures, and assessment processes that would continue its work. By the end of the 2007–2008 school year, after twelve months of labor, the culture, pedagogy, and curriculum committee dissolved. A newly formed committee, curriculum and pedagogy, continued to develop a new curriculum that would be implemented in fall 2009.

Through their efforts, the seminary's administrators and some faculty became increasingly persuaded that the institutional context of a curriculum significantly affects the quality of integrating in teaching and learning. Communal discussions across academic divisions, a good assessment process, revised understandings of faculty identity and hiring processes, and even attentiveness to the wording of course evaluation forms all matter because of their potential to improve the holistic formation of pastors.

As a result of promoting integration across the renewal process, some faculty have become more inclined to approve new initiatives to promote integrative teaching and learning. For example, since 2009 CTS has initiated a hybrid distance MDiv program and an education and ministry program in prisons, which provide new opportunities full of possibilities for integrating work. Distance education has pushed the faculty to rethink pedagogy, especially integrating theology with ministry practices. Distance students are typically embedded in ministry and connect their course work with issues from their personal and ministerial experiences. Online discussions often generate integrative questions and push learners to discern a practical, wise course of action. If their intensive face-to-face time is dominated by a transfer of information by the "sage on the stage," these students freely suggest a different pedagogy to the professor.

9. Aleshire in "2030" uses the terms *professional* and *formational* theological education to describe these two models of ministry training.

Distance students are pushing faculty and one another toward new forms and levels of integrating work.

Teaching in prison has also invited faculty on an integrating journey. For a few years, CTS has offered three courses per year in a local state prison and is now establishing an accredited BA degree in ministry training that plans to enroll students from thirty Michigan prisons. Sending faculty members to teach in prisons is a disintegrating experience for many of them. Far from the safety of a seminary classroom, professors are forced to consider how the content of their teaching fits a diverse audience in a challenging context. They face many pedagogical questions with multiple forms of integrating work embedded in them. For example, how does one teach a course on forgiveness and reconciliation to religiously diverse students, some of whom have not acknowledged the impact of their crimes and some of whom struggle with anger about their own experiences as victims?

Although the CTS renewal process assisted members of the community to become more reflective agents of integration, our theory is still better than our practice. Documents and structures can be renewed, but their functionality depends upon people, and people with tenure are not easily coaxed into changing practices. The faculty may, in theory, value collaboration, encouragement, and accountability, but we have not summoned the moral courage for much accountability. A committee, such as church relations, may have potential to assist integrative teaching and learning, but it may underfunction because our administration and faculty's imagination about how to relate to the church has not yet evolved. Faculty meetings have reverted to many hours, perhaps because listening to reports and tending to administrative details is less threatening and gives a sense of control compared to wrestling with core issues that will require integrating work and change.

Nonetheless, the renewal process certainly set a new direction for the future of Calvin Theological Seminary. Among all the noncurricular changes that CTS made, the most important was the faculty's decision about organizational structure. It was a critical moment in the life of the school. Although the vote was not close, there were more negative votes for changing than any proposal put forth by the renewal initiative. The debate was heated. The most outspoken, strongest personalities on the faculty were opposed to the change; they were satisfied with faculty discussions, relationships within divisions, the quality of the school's service to the church, and the clarity of distinct disciplines. They also correctly sensed that this vote meant a loss of power and the disappearance of well-known structures. It was a disintegrating moment. For a few, there was grief that an era of the school was ending and fear about what the future might hold. For most, the new processes of community relations and decision making opened the seminary to a future in which change and renewal would be common. Renewal is itself an integrating process and CPC hoped that it had begun to develop a context in which that process could be sustained.

Bibliography

Aleshire, Daniel. "2030: A Theological Odyssey of the Work of the Theological Educator." New Faculty Conference 2013, The Association of Theological Schools. http://www.ats.edu/uploads/resources/publications-presentations/colloquy-online/a-theological-odyssey.pdf.

Heifetz, Ronald. *Leadership without Easy Answers*. Cambridge: Harvard University Press, 1998.

————— 4 —————

The Ecosystem of
Theological Education

A Case Study

————— EDWARD FOLEY —————

An Ecological Introduction

The central preoccupation of this volume, and the five-year conversation that birthed it, has been the nature and process of integrating that should mark theological education. Earlier I proposed that it was both useful and necessary to think about an entire institution as having a critical role in the integrating process. To that end, I suggested that it could be helpful to view the educational enterprise through the lenses of formal, semiformal, and informal learning.

This case study is meant to concretize that claim by examining my own institution through these lenses. Pondering an institution as an integrating agent suggests considering it as an ecosystem. Educators have employed ecological frameworks for decades when pondering the dynamics of the educational process. Lawrence Cremin notably reimagined the role of schools in relationship to other educational endeavors and society at large with an approach he called the "ecology of education."[1] Some premier

1. Cremin, *Public Education*, 25.

educational institutions have programmatically formalized the linkage between ecology and education.[2]

Catholic Theological Union

For over thirty years I have been on the faculty of Catholic Theological Union (CTU), a freestanding graduate school of theology and ministry. Noted for the diversity of its student population, CTU is a relatively complex institution for its size, offering a range of academic and ministerial degrees, continuing education and sabbatical curricula, ministerial certificates, spiritual formation programs, daily worship, public lectures, Catholic-Jewish and Catholic-Muslim dialogues, travel programs, a peace initiative for high school students, and a vocational discovery program for young adults.

Similar to other graduate institutions, CTU faculty and academic administrators expend most energies on the formal curriculum. In the past dozen years, we have weathered two curriculum revision processes, initiated a new line of professional graduate degrees, and developed resources to enable students to complete one of CTU's standard degrees almost entirely online. Furthermore, an array of lectures, lunches, interest groups and other gatherings populate the weekly calendar. There have been small ventures to coordinate these learning events, but no attempts to map them or assess their impact on the wider learning and integrating processes.

As a small step in that direction, I will attempt to map student learnings that occur within the main academic facility of CTU.[3] To accomplish this task, I will first enumerate the various *types* of student educational processes that regularly occur, and then *categorize* them as formal, semiformal, or informal. Categorizations are admittedly arbitrary but I hope sufficient to allow for some useful analysis. Next I will employ the floor plans for the five stories of the Academic and Conference Center (ACC) to sketch the intertwining of these learning strands in order to illustrate how ecologies of learning coexist within the ACC.

2. An example is the Ohio State University's merger of its College of Human Ecology with the College of Education to form the College of Education and Human Ecology, http://ehe.osu.edu/about/history/.

3. There are learnings for faculty, staff, and administrators as well; for the sake of containment, however, the focus here is on students. Similarly, we did not map the various learnings that occur outside the ACC, such as field placements and online courses.

Styles of Learning	Specific Elements	Explanations, Illustrations
Formal learning processes	Credit granting courses	Online, face to face, independent studies
	Comprehensive exams	Academic MA requirement
	Thesis	Research MA and DMin requirement
	ESL classes	Required for select students
	Workshops	One MDiv track requires 11 workshops[A]
Semiformal learning processes	Lectures	Sponsored by departments, endowed chairs or one of the centers located at CTU[B]
	Organized interest group	For example, women in ministry
	Spiritual-ministerial formation	Required of all lay students in MDiv, MAPS, and MA programs[C]
	Spiritual direction	Required of virtually all nondoctoral degree-seeking students
	Student Representative Council	Organization for student input and action
	Required seminars for scholarship recipients	Bernardin, Romero, and Tolton scholars
	Orientations and academic advising	Required of all degree and certificate candidates
	Worship	Regularly scheduled and special seasonal worship
	Optional workshops	For example, research, library, writing skills

Styles of Learning	Specific Elements	Explanations, Illustrations
Informal learning processes	Random conversations	Between students, faculty, staff, and guests
	Personal electronic communications	E-mails, IMs, Skype
	General electronic communications	For example, weekly calendar, scriptural reflections, event announcements
	Electronic and low-tech bulletin boards	Often duplicating general electronic communications
	Open forums	For example, offered by major administrators
	Receptions	Following most public lectures or events
	Parties, athletic, or other recreational events	For example, soccer matches, Christmas and *Primavera* gatherings

A. For example, training to protect children from exploitation or abuse, issues in human sexuality, professional standards, and collaborative skills.

B. For example, the Bernardin Center for Theology and Ministry.

C. For example, the Augustus Tolton Scholars Program for Black Catholic scholarship students from Chicago, and the Oscar Romero Scholars Program for Hispanic Catholic scholarship students from Chicago.

An Eco-educational Mapping of the ACC

Our five-story, 101,000-square-foot Academic and Conference Center opened in 2006. This mapping is derived from my observations, subsequently reviewed by people in student services and facilities who schedule and manage these various spaces.[4] The material was also formally presented to faculty colleagues for comment and critique. Finally, five students in-

4. Thanks to Martin Fitzgerald, director of facilities; Christine Henderson, director of events planning and student affairs; Susan Hickman, administrative Assistant to the vice president for finance; and faculty colleagues, especially those who discussed a draft of this paper at the faculty seminar on December 6, 2014.

dividually mapped their use of the space over a two-week period. Their insights are particularly important for the analysis. The percentages employed are "guesstimations" based on the sometimes detailed input from the twenty-one students, staff, and faculty formally consulted in this process as well as my own observations. They are proposed as informed heuristics for considering what spaces students employ, for what type of learning, for what relative duration, and having what relative impact.

First Floor

The glass entrance of the ACC opens to an airy reception area. Over half of this first floor contains a large maintenance work room, loading dock, and mechanicals—not open to the public. Most people experience only the open hospitality space. With its long reception desk, chairs, banks of elevators, rest room, student locker room, and mail room, the first floor is environmentally cued to informal learning, which would characterize virtual 100 percent of the public space.

Learnings

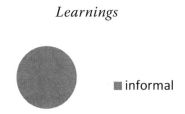

Second Floor

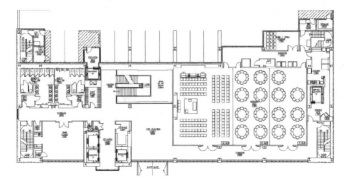

Ascending to the second floor by elevator or open staircase leads to the most public area of the building: the only floor without offices. The south side has large restrooms, a coat room, and a VIP lounge (right side of figure is North). North is a spacious area, often employed for receptions. Next are three large rooms: 210a, the semipermanent chapel with flexible seating for about 144; 210b and 210c, multipurpose rooms ordinarily used for lectures and large meetings. Behind are storage spaces and a kitchen. When walls are collapsed the space can seat up to 350 for worship or other gatherings. While some formal learning occurs on this level (for example, worship practica in the chapel), students largely experience the space for semiformal learning, for example, worship in 210a or lectures in 210b and 210c. While informal learning occurs in 210b and 210c, it is especially the open reception space that serves this purpose. The guesstimation for the learning distribution on this floor is 70 percent dedicated to semiformal,[5] 25 percent to informal, and only 5 percent to formal learning.

Learnings

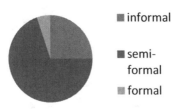

■ informal

■ semi-
formal

■ formal

5. As corroborated by the student informants in this study, students ordinarily do not go to the second floor except for worship or lectures.

Third Floor

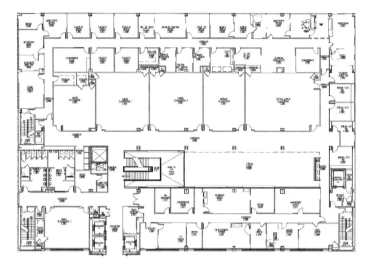

The third floor is the most complex and architecturally partitioned of the building, divided into four different zones.

The staircase leads into the first zone, the building's most open area: a 2175-square-foot atrium with a three-story ceiling crowned by a huge skylight. Dotted with tables and chairs, the atrium is an informal meeting place for students, staff, and faculty; the site of larger receptions; and a breakout space for the classrooms on this floor. Observation suggest that zone 1 is employed 80 percent of the time for informal learning and 20 percent of the time for formal learning.

Zone 2 comprises five classrooms with combined seating for 188 and four small study rooms. A seminar room on the southeast corner can accommodate twenty-four. Virtually all face-to-face classes occur in these spaces, sporadically employed for workshops and other gatherings. The four study rooms are sometimes employed for breakout sessions by formal classes, but most often for private study or informal learning. Observation suggests that zone 2 is employed 70 percent of the time for formal learning, 20 percent for semiformal learning, and 10 percent for informal learning.

Zone 3 includes multiple offices along an extended corridor, most for academic administration. There are also spaces for formation programs, the Bernardin Center, the Bible Study and Travel Program, IT, and student services. Conference rooms—occasionally used for thesis defenses—bookend this corridor. The spaces dedicated to formation work are the site of some semiformal learning. The vast majority of the space, however, is cued to informal learning. A rough estimation of this breakdown would be 3 percent formal learning, 12 percent semiformal learning, and 85 percent informal learning.

Zone 4 is a long corridor on the east side, populated by offices for business and finance, development, public relations, and the president. A small conference room occasionally employed for formal learning (such as a comprehensive exam). Observation suggestions that 98 percent of the student usage of this space is dedicated to informal learning with only 2 percent given over to formal learning.

Because students are most often present in classrooms on the third floor for extended periods (zone 2), frequently but for less time in the atrium (zone 1) as well as zone 3 (especially the registrar's office), and quite infrequently for sustained engagement in zone 4, my guesstimation of student usage of this floor is 65 percent formal learning, 10 percent semiformal learning, and 25 percent informal learning.

Learnings

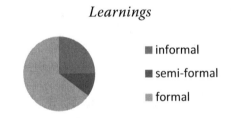

- informal
- semi-formal
- formal

Fourth Floor

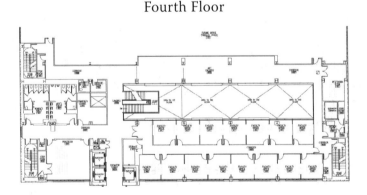

The fourth floor has the least amount of square footage than any public space, since the three-story atrium eliminates the center of this floor, and much of the west side is occupied by a storage area. East of that storage is an art gallery that runs the length of the building and is adjacent to a small interfaith meditation and prayer room. The east side of the floor has fifteen faculty offices, a seminar room seating eighteen, and restrooms. The gallery and meditation room are spaces of informal spaces learning with the occasional artist's lecture in the gallery. The seminar room is employed mostly for formal learning. The faculty offices, from the students' viewpoint, can be places for informal learning, semiformal learning (for example, academic advising) and even formal learning (such as independent studies). While students stop by for informal conversations, a student's presence in a faculty office is largely about semiformal and formal modes of learning. The art gallery is not widely visited by students, although some use this quiet space for personal study or informal gatherings. The meditation chapel seems less frequented. Student use of this floor appears to be for formal (40 percent) and semiformal (35 percent) learning; less with informal (25 percent) learning on staircases and spaces outside the practicum room (404).

Learnings

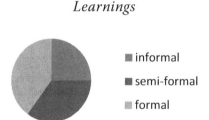

- informal
- semi-formal
- formal

Fifth Floor

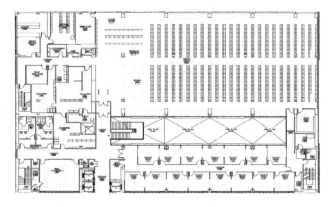

The fifth floor's design is similar to the fourth: faculty offices line the eastern corridor, a seminar room and rest rooms in the southeastern quadrant. The main difference is the library occupies the west side. Faculty offices and the seminar room have the same mix of learning identified for the fourth floor. Formal modes of learning occur in the library (such as comprehensive exams in the seminar room) and various modes of study and research. There are also semiformal ones (for example, a research librarian helping a student with a paper), as well as much informal interaction in the library. Consequently, a guesstimated distribution of learning on this floor would be 60 percent formal, 10 percent semiformal, and 30 percent informal.

Learnings

- informal
- semi-formal
- formal

Student Observations

The original draft of this essay did not have the benefit of student input: an obvious flaw. My challenge was to incorporate student insights that provided some overview of their engagement in these spaces in a coherent and intelligible manner. Since this is a more impressionistic than empirical contribution, I engaged five full-time Roman Catholic students willing to map their experience in these spaces. Their identities are masked at their request. The five were invited for multiple reasons: (1) each was in a different graduate program, (2) each claimed a different ecclesial status (layman, laywoman, religious sister, religious brother, ordination candidate), (3) they represented three countries of origin, (4) they lived in different proximities to the ACC, and (5) each had previously been experienced as smart, insightful, and responsible.

Informants agreed to map their usage of the ACC during the weeks of April 13 and April 27, 2015. Each person had copies of the ACC floor plans and was asked to document his or her presence in that space with this code:

A: Walked through that space

B: Had some brief encounters in that space

C: Had informative encounter in that space

D: Had an important encounter in that space

Informants were given the option to code the number of minutes in each space by employing a number, for example, "B:2 = spent a few minutes having a brief encounter." Their responses were impressive, thorough, and revelatory. Together they provided 361 incident reports of their presence in the ACC. Over 270 of those documented not only the space they traversed and the quality of the encounter but also how many minutes those encounters lasted.

Many of these mappings corroborated my guesstimations of the space usages noted above. On the other hand, two of the five had student work assignments on different floors of the ACC, and so their mappings were appropriately prejudiced toward their jobs. Most revelatory for me were the multiple ways in which these informants reported an "important encounter" in a space (D). Fifty (14 percent) of the 361 incidents were documented as important. They occurred at the front desk, in the chapel, in classrooms (14), in corridors, the atrium, the housing office, Bernardin Center, outside the registrar's office, and in the library (6). Some lasted three minutes, others forty-five minutes, and many (classes) almost three hours.

Also interesting is that the lowest number of reports (only 26) concerned "informative encounters" (C). This designation received one of the widest geographical mappings—documented next to the coffee bar off the atrium, in corridors, classrooms, the library—but also provided the only reporting about the prefunction space, the development office, the marketing office, and even the maintenance workshop on the first floor. This student input confirmed, in sometimes surprising ways, my hunch that learning occurs throughout the building. Furthermore, informative and significant encounters can occur not only in classrooms but also in the maintenance shop.

An Initial Analysis

My educational eco-mapping of the ACC is limited by my own social location, experiences, and prejudices. From a methodological perspective, it is more anecdotal than a systematic ethnographic study. At the same time, it is based on extensive and sustained observation of student movement throughout the ACC and conscious reflection on the same over the past eighteen months, critiqued and largely affirmed by faculty colleagues, staff members, and a select group of students.

Paul Ricoeur (1913–2005) proposed a hermeneutical method that begins with a hunch or the first naïveté.[6] My first hunch in this exercise concerned the ubiquity of informal learning throughout the ACC. In many respects, that hunch seems substantiated. There is not a floor of this five-story complex that does not allow for and support informal learning. While it is not the dominant form of learning in every space, it is a persistent, substantial, and even prevailing educational thread woven through all the spaces ordinarily open to students in the ACC.

A second hunch was about the imagined strength of semiformal learning throughout theses spaces, which would place formal learning in a somewhat diminished position. In some ways, this hunch appeared less well substantiated. There certainly was a clear thread of semiformal learning woven throughout this educational ecosystem, a thread that achieves a particular ascendancy on the second floor. However, many students seldom if ever take advantage of the many lecture series, worship, and other forms of semiformal learning programmed in those spaces. Similarly, while faculty offices on the fourth and fifth floors are potential locations for semiformal learning—for example, academic advising—such advising is increasingly accomplished through the multiple e-mail exchanges that have become an essential form of communication between students and advisors.

6. Ricoeur, *Rule of Metaphor*, 318 et passim.

Parallel to my surprise about the diminished amount of semiformal learning in the ACC was how much formal student learning took place throughout the space. My third hunch was almost to seal hermeneutically formal learning in the third floor classrooms. Upon reflection, however, it became clear how much such learning can be tracked throughout this ecosystem, excepting the first floor. Particularly striking was how often faculty offices were a place of not only informal and semiformal learning but also formal learning.

Conclusions

Various voices on these types of learning argue in favor of one or the other as the most important in institutions of higher education. While an early hunch in this research was the undervalued role of informal education in seminaries and divinity schools, and the implied corrective to bolster respect for this aboriginal form of learning, this integrating exploration suggested something more: each of these are critical pedagogical frameworks that together need to be more effectively integrated in the broad sweep of CTU's curriculum. While institutions like my own spend an inordinate amount of time on the formal curriculum, it is no little irony that most students who graduate from CTU will largely rely upon semiformal and informal types of education throughout the rest of their ministerial careers. Some might move into another formal educational program, but CTU alums are largely sustained in their ministry through reading, informal conversations or gatherings, and the occasional continuing education event. If the integrating trajectory that we cultivate at our institution is to help them beyond graduation, then we have to rehearse the effective integrating of the formal aspects of their education with the accompanying semiformal and informal aspects of that educational process.

As CTU faces one more curriculum revision in the coming years, a pointed way of addressing this integrating mix is bluntly to ask, how much control do students have over the ways they can fulfill requirements for their respective degree programs? Checklists have a certain efficiency about them, but most of them function in what could be considered a colonial, that is autocratic, mode. Does my institution have the chutzpah to allow students to propose informal and semiformal ways to fulfill degree requirements? My instinct is that until such an alternative is allowed—a portfolio approach to credentialing—the impact of semiformal and informal learning will be unacknowledged though not, however, diminished.

Bibliography

Cremin, Lawrence. *Public Education*. New York: Basic, 1976.

Ricoeur, Paul. *The Rule of Metaphor: Multi-disciplinary Studies of the Creation of Meaning in Language*. Translated by Robert Czerney, with K. McLaughlin and J. Costello. Toronto: University of Toronto Press, 1977 [1975].

5

Harvesting Insights

EDWARD FOLEY

Minding the Gaps

Anyone who has ever ridden on the London Underground is familiar with the phrase "mind the gap." Broadcast continuously over the sound system and emblazoned on tile floors and other surfaces throughout the Tube, the warning reminds travelers to practice caution when they cross the "gap" between the platform surface and the train door. An obvious safety alert, the phrase has also become something of a PR slogan for the Underground and can be found on T-shirts, mugs, and other souvenirs for sale across London and beyond.

Like many catchy phrases, this public safety announcement contains a kernel of wisdom. For those concerned about integrating work in theological education, the case studies in part 1 are examples of experienced educators who have recognized gaps—or even gaping fissures—in some aspect of their home institution. Furthermore, they are concerned with not only "minding" these gaps but also narrowing or even eliminating them altogether.

As an academic dean, for example, Slough monitors but often tries to resolve gaps, fissures, and divisions that are wont to occur among highly trained and sometimes competitive theological educators. Her gap-resolving solution is a virtue tactic: an approach seldom articulated or even attempted by most of theological school faculties. Let's face it, how many of us have a faculty contract, appointment, or job description that contains the word *love*? I admit, it sounds a bit outlandish, and many faculty might look askance at the suggestion that—aside from our scholarship, teaching responsibilities, and committee assignments—we are also called to exercise a deepening capacity for living in loving relationships with our colleagues, with God, and even with ourselves. Challenging times require inventive, resourceful, and equally challenging responses. Anyone with eyes wide open understands that these are challenging times for theological educators. Whether Slough's suggestion is the silver bullet that will put an end to our internecine squabbles and transform us into an *agapic* community is, to my way of thinking, not the point. Rather, she exemplifies a watchful administrator who has seen a gap and has chosen to do something about it. We need other gap prophets like her.

Similarly Rylaarsdam and colleagues experienced gaps, but this time in their institution. Prompted by the vision of the school's board of trustees that was pushing for more holistic and integrative formation for ministry, the faculty was sparked to action by concurrent challenges to its accreditation regarding the issue of assessment. Since integrating is a value in the accreditation process, the convergence of challenge and opportunity opened an important window for his school. As Rylaarsdam wryly notes, "A crisis is a terrible thing to waste." The gaps, as identified in the preliminary work to reimagining the school, were multiple. Some of these were collegial, with limited collaboration across disciplines and departments. Graduates perceived rifts between what they learned at Calvin and what they needed to equip them adequately for ministry. Then there were cracks in the support the school was receiving from its denomination. The wide-ranging proposals in calendar and faculty structures, budgets, and curricular design did not cure every ill. As noted, for example, the issue of faculty accountability as reflective agents of integrating work is yet to be seriously resolved. On the other hand, this comprehensive institutional response indicates that someone was paying attention with a wide-angle lens to the gaps and fissures that were diminishing the integrating capacity of the institution and its structures. Such quality of vision is to be applauded and emulated.

In my own reflections on the range of formal, semiformal, and informal learnings threading their way through the main academic facility at Catholic Theological Union, I was hoping to draw attention to a different kind of integrating gap. Like other institutions, the faculty has undertaken two major curriculum revisions in the last dozen years and is preparing for a third. Ordinarily these demanding exercises focus on the formal curriculum. In so doing, we have a tendency to overload that curriculum with discipline-specific requirements and up to eleven mandatory workshops for our MDiv students in the ordination track. While I proposed no specific plan or strategies in my case study—in the language of James and Evelyn Whitehead, I engaged in an exercise of pure "attending"[1]—such attending has influenced my thinking about the impending curriculum revision. Given all the informal learnings in which our students are engaged within our Academic and Conference Center, besides all the others in their ministry sites, faith communities, houses of formation, and various modes of socializing, would it not make sense to give them serious freedom in opting for those modes of formal and semiformal learning that actually might be more useful to them? Such attending makes me wonder whether my institution should be less concerned with a formal curriculum that minds every gap and more responsive to the semiformal and informal modes of gap minding often more beneficial to our students.

Disciplined Improvisation

Improvisation is not simply making something up on the spur of the moment but is a disciplined reinvention in the present, be that music making or comedy.[2] By definition, improvisation is virtually unrepeatable. As I learned from David Jenkins, one of the collaborators for this book, a basic rule of comedic improvisation—similar to playing in a jazz quartet—is the need to respect what others give you: to listen intently to the gift they offer and use it as a springboard to go where you have never been before.

Reading these case studies, and recalling the untold hours of conversations over four years that surrounded the authors' deliberations on integrating, I am struck how the work of integrating came out of a willingness to improvise. Calvin Seminary's broad-ranging curriculum-calendar-faculty plan was bold and imaginative. No proposal like that had ever before existed. In a true spirit of improvisation, they confronted the "crisis" that was handed to them, accepted it as a gift, paid serious attention to it, and used it as a springboard to envision a future not previously imagined. Improvisation requires working with what you have, be that crisis or grace, and wagering that it can be life giving. Sometimes musical, comedic, or

1. Whitehead and Whitehead, *Method in Ministry*, 67–75 et passim.
2. See my *Theological Reflection across Religious Traditions*, 34.

educational improvisations fall flat. That is the improvisational risk necessary if our institutions and theological education are to move forward. In this regard I am reminded of the folk wisdom of humorist Will Rogers (1879–1935), who once said that even if you are on the right track, you will still get run over if you just sit there!

Similarly, Slough's virtue strategy in the face of faculty estrangement or even division was not borrowed from some textbook on faculty development. While faculty cohesiveness is not a new issue, the specifics of her own institution, with new hires on a small faculty and some dark institutional moments that were addressed quite publicly, provided a unique conjunction for strategizing not only about faculty unity but also about faculty as *communitas*. The juxtaposition of scriptural and religious resources from their shared Mennonite tradition, galvanized by shifting faculty configurations of seasoned and junior colleagues, yields this fresh and even startling take on faculty development. It richly resonates with another integrating metaphor noted above: the combining of chemical compounds. Organic chemistry demonstrates that the chemical structure of certain elements promotes their reactivity and allows them to easily combine (for example, hydrogen and water into H_2O), whereas other elements only combine under extreme pressure or temperature. For example, methane gas combines with water to become carbon monoxide and hydrogen gas ($CH_4 + H_2O = Co + 3H_2$) only at high temperature (800–1000 degrees Celsius) with increased pressure (10–50 atmospheres) and requires a catalyst (such as nickel). Slough took the temperature of her own community of learning, brought together distinctive religious and personnel resources, and by invoking the biblical teaching of love as a particular catalyst in their institutional life, sparked a community-building chain reaction.

In my own case study of the various types of learning unfolding throughout CTU's Academic and Conference Center, I have begun to understand that the way students do and can opt for various modes of learning is a form of improvisation on their part. With discussions, alternative readings, and sometimes even subversive practices, they complement, counterpoint, and maybe even contradict what they learn in a formal setting. An unspoken aspect of theological education concerns the imbalance of power that ordinarily exists between students and professors or the institution at large. In some ways, affirming students' instincts for informal and semiformal styles of learning could be considered a mode of power improvisation. This becomes especially apparent when these various modes of learning converge in a shared learning environment. As noted in the overview essay for part 1, the frameworks of formal, semiformal, and informal learning are increasingly porous. All my lectures courses, for example, have morphed into hybrid learning experiences with small group work, online PowerPoint presentations, and even group exams and shared grading. My online teaching puts even more emphasis on student interaction, in the hopes of offsetting some of the power imbalance inherent in graduate education.

Conclusion

If we are going to take seriously the fundamental contention of this volume that integrating is a long-term process that is the proper work of entire institutions—and not just students—then many of us will be compelled to think differently about the entire theological education and formation process. Often institutions of higher learning and faithful adherents to academic guilds are reluctant to change. It is the world, however, that is changing: the world of higher education, religious adherence, and ecclesial credibility. Evolution is essential if we are to not only survive but also flourish. These case studies offer ideas about how some colleagues are thinking about and evening enacting such changes. These are challenging times, but these challenges are also gifts, and they would be a terrible thing to waste.

Bibliography

Foley, Edward. *Theological Reflection across Religious Traditions: The Turn to Reflective Believing*. Lanham, MD: Rowman & Littlefield, 2015.
Whitehead, James D., and Evelyn Eaton Whitehead. *Method in Ministry*. Rev. ed. Kansas City: Sheed & Ward, 1995.

PART 2

Curriculums

6

Integrating Dynamics in
the Seminary Curriculum

—— Kathleen A. Cahalan ——

At the heart of every curriculum is an argument. I do not mean a fight, though it has been known to happen. I mean an argument in the sense of tradition that is "extended through time in which certain fundamental agreements are defined and redefined."[1] Curriculums rest on philosophical, educational, theological, and pedagogical assumptions about what needs to be learned, in what ways, and toward what purposes. To undertake curricular review is to enter a school's tradition of arguments that constitute its identity and deepest commitments; the task is to negotiate and redefine its past claims and values in light of its present situation for a future that is all too rapidly approaching.

Many seminaries today strive to make their curriculums more integrative. To do so, they must make a case for what needs integrating, how it will happen, why it needs to be done, and how the school will know it happens. To do so requires that a faculty work toward some agreement about what gets defined, redefined, and negotiated. For many faculty members curriculum discussions can mean insuring that their interests or discipline are fairly represented. However, if faculty want education to be more integrative, they have to do more than rearrange the courses and credits and defend their turf. They have to make an argument for what a curriculum is and how it works.

1. MacIntyre, *Whose Justice?*, 12.

75

What Needs Integrating and Why

The three approaches to integrating work in theological education, discussed in the introduction to this book, each have a particular diagnoses for the curriculum's ills. First is the claim that the curriculum needs to be more interdisciplinary, connecting ideas from highly specialized bodies of knowledge that are too separate. Second is the claim that theology (usually meaning systematic theology) is not connected sufficiently with ministerial practice and requires closer alignment, and the third approach argues that professional competence must connect a body of knowledge with competent practice in a community of moral formation that aims toward the public good. Each of these approaches is a valid way of thinking about integrating in the curriculum.

Integrating Knowledge

A subject-centered curriculum is organized "according to how essential knowledge has developed in various subject areas."[2] In higher education, subject-centered curriculums are primarily discipline based and are designed to give students "a sweeping understanding of all content areas" and to "integrate content that fit together logically."[3]

North American theological education inherited the subject-centered curriculum from Friedrich Schleiermacher's threefold curricular pattern—philosophical theology, historical theology, and practical theology—that over time became four divisions: Bible, history, doctrine, and practical theology.[4] This organizational structure continues to frame most seminary curriculums. The arrangement rests on the claim that disciplines are specific bodies of knowledge that constitute a mode of inquiry, a conceptual structure, specialized language, a tradition of thought, and a community of theorists and instructors.[5] The school is understood to be a "microcosm of the world of intellect, reflected by such disciplines,"[6] and each discipline constitutes a particular method to study and make sense of that world. Such assumptions about knowledge and its organization is rooted in

2. Ornstein and Hunkins, *Curriculum*, 191.
3. Ibid., 194. Ornstein and Hunkins call this the "broad-fields design."
4. Farley, *Theologia*.
5. Ibid., 192.
6. Ibid.

perennialism, an educational philosophy that has long-shaped American education. It rests on the belief that there are a set of universal truths about human existence and morality that have stood the test of time, and the curriculum exists to organize that content into subject matter and disciplines.

Two concerns drive faculty to integrate ideas and disciplines across ever-expanding bodies of knowledge. First, disciplines are increasingly specialized, which leads to fragmentation both *within* a discipline and *between* the disciplines. The curriculum becomes a group of silos that have to connect or reconnect across subject matter. The second concern arises from the pressure faculty can feel to remain up-to-date. The curriculum, then, must continually be connecting and adding new content, but often at the cost of eliminating. The lack of connection and the responsibility to cover one's field can contribute to conflicts during curriculum revision.

The most common strategies to address these two concerns have been team teaching, which is cost prohibitive for many schools, or thematic courses that are interdisciplinary (for example, a course on forgiveness that draws upon biblical, theological, liturgical, and ministerial resources).

Integrating Theory and Practice

Theological educators became increasingly disgruntled with the perennial approach to knowledge and curriculum building as broad social changes affected churches and universities. For instance, mainline Protestants in the 1960s and '70s began to grapple with the decline of Christianity's influence on the culture. Seminaries realized that clergy ministry had become largely ineffective and they placed the blame, in part, at the feet of the curriculum in which students were expected to take the theology they learned in a classroom and apply it to congregational ministry. Churches would not be sustained or legitimate in a changing cultural context without ministers who were prepared to face its challenges.

The curriculum, its critics claimed, was based on a faulty notion of how theory and practice relate to each other. The perennial approach assumed that by knowing a body of knowledge, a practitioner would be able to apply these truths in his or her context. The emerging approaches claimed that praxis is an epistemological priority: theory derives from praxis and praxis is theory laden.[7] Various curricular strategies emerged in the 1980s that emphasized praxis at the heart of learning ministry: the shift from field to

---

7. Browning, *Fundamental Practical Theology*.

contextual education; greater emphasis on field supervisors' training and readiness to guide students; the movement of faculty out into contexts of ministry; clergy becoming teaching colleagues at seminaries; and the emergence of a new field—congregational studies.

A second shift arose from the postmodern critique of "universal truths" masked as power relationships. Critical pedagogy shifted the goal and practice of education toward the student's capacity to analyze, raise questions, and critique assumptions for the purpose of social reform and social justice. An institution's curricular responses could be seen in subject matter, critical pedagogies, and its growing awareness of the need to make the student body and faculty more racially and ethnically diverse.

The emphasis on praxis reflects the broader educational shift to learner-centered curricular designs. Critical of subject-centered learning in which the teacher is an expert and the student passively receives information, learner-centered curricula focus on students as active agents in learning environments. Students learn best when they focus on their lives, needs, and interests, allowing them to "actively construct their own understandings."[8] The curriculum places a strong emphasis on experience, constructing and revising knowledge, and active participation. The movement toward praxis is a direct outcome of both pragmatism and progressivism, initiated by John Dewey in the early twentieth century, in which learning focuses on active engagement in problem solving and students' growth and development. Critical theory is the philosophical foundation of critical pedagogy in which students learn the ability to analyze social, economic, and political activity toward the goal of equality, empowerment, and social change.

Nonetheless, the 1980s conversation about theory and praxis in theological education presumed the fourfold curriculum model: the goal was to make better connections between Bible, history, and theory (the "academic" areas) and pastoral practice. It did not question the categories of the fourfold pattern; that would take another step in thinking about curriculum.

Integrating the Professional Model

The third, and most recent, approach stems from professional educators who find the critical thinking paradigm in higher education deficient. According to William Sullivan and Matthew Rosen, higher education is based

8. Ornstein and Hunkins, *Curriculum*, 197.

upon an epistemological framework in which knowledge is conceptual, abstract, and disengaged; student learning focuses on understanding and critically assessing concepts, frameworks, and social practices.[9] They argue that practical reason is an "alternative educational agenda" in which the students learn to "think and act through a back-and-forth dialogue between analytical thought and the ongoing constitution of meaning."[10] This educational philosophy aims at "an engaged self" that links "self-conscious awareness to responsive engagement in projects in the world" and "values embodied responsiveness and responsibility over the detached critical expert."[11] Their focus on practical reason is a retrieval of Aristotle's *phronesis*, the capacity to make good judgments.

Several seminaries have experimented with curricular models that emphasize ministerial competencies, hinting at the professional ideal. The *telos* of theological education—thriving faith communities led by competent practitioners—becomes the horizon that informs their curricular model. These schools have abandoned the fourfold schema and organized the curriculum according to professional competencies they deem are foundational to effective ministry. In some cases, the school eliminated departments based on disciplines and created new groups and structures, composed of people from various disciplines, each contributing to defining and integrating their subjects and pedagogies in relation to a core competence. For example, Andover Newton's curriculum was structured according to four areas of ministerial competence: interpreting, communicating, leading, and embodying. Calvin Theological Seminary, discussed in a case study in part 2, revised the curriculum in 2007 based on a rhetorical paradigm—person, message, context, and goal of ministry—as well as an integrative stream that flows throughout courses, intentionally building competencies each year. Every course syllabus was required to reflect these four areas.[12] That these curricular experiments have met with varying

9. For a discussion of the four characteristics of critical thinking, see Sullivan and Rosin, *New Agenda*, 98–99.

10. Ibid., 104.

11. Ibid., 105.

12 It should be noted that each of these schools is a free-standing denominational seminary and a leader in theological education in its tradition. Another example is Catholic Theological Union. In 2003 the faculty created a curriculum with a "foundational core" of four courses in the first year: "Pastoral Practice: The Theology of Ministry," "The Art of Theology: Theological Method," "Religion in Context: Diversity in Dialogue," and "Tradition: Sources through History." In subsequent years students take courses in an

degrees of success is not surprising. One obstacle has been faculty loyalty to their guilds and reluctance to change from a discipline to a competency-framed curriculum.

Curriculums embody a tradition of theological beliefs, ecclesial identities, and educational philosophies and approaches. Each of these informs what faculty believe needs to be integrated. When integration is posed as a solution to the curricular problem, it is most often framed within this tradition. When fights break out over this set of arguments, it is most often the case that competing educational philosophies and approaches are at stake.

How Learning Is Integrated: Principles of Curricular Design

Curriculums constitute the intentional content and processes of an educational system. They are made up of various parts: objectives, content, instruction, and evaluation.[13] The curriculum design makes a case for how these parts are in relationship to one another. Curricular theorists point to two ways curriculums are designed: vertical and horizontal integration. Vertical integration refers to sequencing courses and requirements over time. Sequence is articulating the way learning should be organized: what comes first, second, and later. It describes what learning is foundational in order that subsequent learning can be built upon it. Sequencing can be designed in four ways: (1) simple-to-complex learning, (2) prerequisite learning, (3) whole-to-part learning, and (4) chronological learning. Horizontal integration refers to the way faculty and students integrate across courses, experiences, and disciplines.[14] Within these two movements, faculty must consider the scope of what is to be learned, which refers to the cognitive, affective, and behavior domains of learning.[15]

"integrating core" that specifically works to connect these four areas. Luther Seminary also designed a curriculum based on a rhetorical model in the early part of the 2000s: learning the story, interpreting and confessing, leading and mission, and living our callings.

13. Ornstein and Hunkins, *Curriculum*, 182.

14. Foster et al., *Educating Clergy*, 329–54.

15. Ornstein and Hunkins, *Curriculum*, 186.

Vertical Integration

Vertical integration refers to how students move through a curriculum over time, from beginning to end, from introductory courses to more advanced studies.[16] It is premised on sequencing events in the curriculum that build upon one another and move the learner toward the curriculum's outcome. An additional way to think about vertical integration is the continuous repetition of curricular parts, referred to as "continuity."[17]

Several seminaries have created interesting sequencing patterns.[18] Phillips Seminary has an intentional sequence of three courses in vocation and theology: an introduction to theological education for ministry (including faculties' stories of their vocational calls), the art and practices of ministry, and constructive theology for ministry. Calvin Theological Seminary follows a similar movement through four areas of competency: first year literacy courses that form the basic building blocks of knowledge, the second year that includes analytical and exploratory courses, and the third year that more intensely integrates knowledge and practice. Columbia Theological Seminary has three integration courses, one offered each year: the first, Intersections, focuses on vocation, call, and mission; the second, Explorations, is a cross-cultural immersion experience; and the third, Integrations, examines the boundary between seminary and the students' first call. The courses are team taught by professors across all areas; therefore, the course is a "course of the faculty, not the discipline," according to Jeffery Tribble.[19] The end point of curricula varies; many schools require capstone assignments, comprehensive exams, or ordination exams as the end point of the vertical axis. These approaches will be discussed below under assessment.

16. Foster et al., *Educating Clergy*, 330.

17. Ornstein and Hunkins, *Curriculum*, 188.

18. The examples here are primarily drawn from representatives of thirty theological schools that attended a Collegeville Institute consultation on integration in theological education in 2010. Cahalan and Fanucci, "Integration in Theological Education and Ministry."

19. Another example: Associated Mennonite Biblical Seminary sequenced their formation and curricular requirements over three years: the first semester is an orientation to theological and spiritual knowledge, followed by a ministry seminar on missional leadership and vocation; internships take place in the second year, and a final capstone course on growth in ministry includes a paper and a performance.

A number of seminaries use a bookend approach that presents integration in an introductory course and tests it in a capstone course.[20] Some schools have found this strategy to be challenging. For example, Columbia's first-year integrative course was dropped, because faculty felt it was not working well, and they replaced it with a course on worship. Harvard eliminated a first-year course that introduces students to ministry. Many faculty have struggled with teaching an integrative, introductory course that does not seem to work. Some schools are offering a first-year course on theological education or theological literacy, due to students' lack of understanding of both. In addition to theological vocabulary, students often require a "basic literacy of the self" at the outset of seminary education.[21]

Many schools have found that sequencing required courses is not feasible because of the large number of nonresidential students whose course selection is limited by their commuting schedule. Because of this constraint, faculty have argued that every course and teacher must enhance integrative connections, since sequencing is nearly impossible.

Horizontal Integration

Horizontal integration refers to how the various parts of the curriculum relate to, intersect, and affect each other. In one semester, a student may be enrolled in courses on patristic history, the doctrine of Jesus, the Hebrew prophets, and preaching or field education. The horizontal movement points to the connections made between subject matter and disciplines as well as practice.

Because most curriculums are discipline or subject based, integration is primarily horizontal. Faculties have designed several ways in which connections are made across courses, ideas, disciplines, and experiences. Iliff School of Theology intentionally incorporates the practice of "traveling knowledge" in which students are encouraged to share diverse experiences across classrooms; faculty also share with each other what they are teaching in order to facilitate the flow of knowledge between courses. Many schools facilitate this movement by having faculty intentionally share course syllabi with each other.

Much of horizontal integration happens within and between courses and tends to happen on an informal level, based on the connections

20. Cahalan, "Introducing Ministry," 65–74.
21. Reported by David O. Jenkins, Candler School of Theology.

individual students and teachers make between courses and disciplines. Horizontal integration may be less dependent on or determined by the curriculum, and instead relies on the distribution of courses according to semester offerings and students' schedules and on the particular pedagogies of faculty across the disciplines. When it happens well, it is due largely to how intentional faculty are in making connections to other subjects and experiences. It is usually under the radar and not witnessed by many outside the classroom.

In some cases, schools use small groups or cohorts to facilitate horizontal integration; some are sequenced over three years and contribute to vertical connections as well. For example, Wesley Theological Seminary requires a first-year course on pastoral identity, which is followed by reflection groups over two years that are led by a faculty person and practitioner. Candler School of Theology's contextual education program is a two-year experience, first in a social ministry setting and followed by an ecclesial setting. Faculty are partnered with a site supervisor in each context and team teach a seminar. In the beginning, every faculty member taught the seminar every three years in order to be exposed to students in their ministry sites. For a variety of reasons, which are discussed by David Jenkins in his case study, that requirement has changed, but the goal of faculty to increasingly integrate aspects of ministry practice into their courses has been successful.

The University of Chicago Divinity School, because of its small MDiv program, had a unique process of horizontal and vertical integration. Student learning is based on two fundamental principles: cohorts and conversation. A cohort of fifteen to eighteen students move through the program together, engaging in conversation in and outside class each semester. The learning is vertical as well: students write and share spiritual autobiographies in the first quarter, engage in a service-learning experience the second quarter, are in a yearlong congregation placement during the second year, and complete a capstone project during the third year.

Diagonal Integration

Students also experience what I have called "diagonal" integration.[22] While vertical and horizontal integration captures an intentional process working across time and content, *diagonal integration* refers to the unintentional events that cut across formal education but have a significant impact on

22. Cahalan, "Integration," 386–95.

students and faculty. School members experience life's joys (birth of children, marriage), challenges (failure, divorce, illness), ecclesial changes, and social and political events (elections, tragedies, injustices) as well as cultural opportunities (music performances, art exhibits). Each provides a context for learning and connecting what is happening in a course or the curriculum with events deemed outside the curriculum. Most often, spiritual formation programs are the curricular space that address issues arising across the diagonal spectrum, so while they may not be outside the curriculum, they are largely outside the classroom.[23] Diagonal movement is much less predictable than vertical or horizontal, which means it cannot be planned for, only responded to. Responding to the integrative possibilities of individual, communal, and social events requires that students and faculty have the time and space to make the necessary connections.

Assessing Integration

In most Association of Theological Schools the capstone experience is the key component of assessing integrating work. Capstone experiences can be a paper, a course, an exam, a thesis, a performance, a portfolio, a senior project, a public presentation, or a meeting with an advisor. In all cases, the purpose is for students to demonstrate their capacity to integrate what they have learned in relationship to the church's ministry.

Students' capacities for vertical and horizontal integration are assessed most often at the midpoint and the end of the degree program. For example, some denominations require mid-degree assessments of students' progress toward candidacy. Faculty of Lutheran seminaries complete a statement about each student's academic and intellectual competence, call and gifts to ministry, practical readiness, and professional and leadership skills. Columbia requires a similar midcourse assessment, but as a degree, not a denominational, requirement. The assessment board is composed of the academic advisor, two faculty members, and two students; the board reviews student reflection papers and assesses course work and reports from supervised ministry. The process provides an opportunity for vocational discernment by the student and allows the school to ask if this person should continue to pursue candidacy. These practices, as some have

23. For a discussion of the pedagogies of formation that focus on spiritual and professional identity in experiences outside the classroom, such as worship, prayer, spiritual practice, and service, see Foster et al., *Educating Clergy*, 100–126.

found, are quite formative for students but time and labor intensive for administrators and faculty.

Ordination exams are another point in a student's movement through ecclesial structures toward ministry. As in vertical integration, there is a movement toward the exams in which a student must accumulate a body of knowledge and insight, and, as in horizontal integration, the student must demonstrate his or her ability to pull together what he or she knows across various domains.

Capstone courses typically involve questions of vocational identity, the expression of one's theological beliefs, and critical reflection on both academic knowledge and pastoral experiences. The majority of capstone courses evaluate these integrative goals through one or more of the following student outcomes: preparing a paper or a public presentation or both, working through case studies, writing a personal statement of belief, articulating a vocational or ministerial identity, or engaging in reflection on the journey through seminary.

Seminaries take a variety of approaches to the capstone course. For example, the main requirement of McAfee School of Theology's capstone course is a synthesis of the entire seminary experience: students write a paper examining an experience of ministry through the four areas of the curriculum—biblically, historically, theologically, and pastorally—and relate how their experience at McAfee has affected their response to this experience. Other capstone courses focus more intentionally on processing the field education experience, as in Trinity Lutheran Seminary's two courses on "Pastor as Theologian" and "Pastor as Leader," both of which draw upon the third-year internship required of ELCA students. Calvin's capstone course prepares students for ordination exams and includes writing and analyzing case studies.

Many capstone courses require a significant writing component. In Western Theological Seminary's Credo course students write a forty-page statement expressing their theological and ministerial framework, which is to be written at a sixth-grade level in order to help them communicate clearly to a broad audience. Other schools have broadened the capstone project from a written assignment to a creative exploration of integration. Louisville Seminary's "Senior Integrating Seminar" is team taught by faculty from different disciplines and focuses on a broad theme, such as embodiment or attention, which invites integrative thinking and practice. Students are required to complete a large project, either a thesis paper or a project that engages the arts. Student projects have incorporated photography and dance.

Lutheran School of Theology at Chicago likewise uses a broad integrative theme to structure their senior interdisciplinary seminar; for example, "Fostering Narratives of Hope," which has been team taught by a systematic theology professor and pastoral care professor. Students examine narratives of hope and despair in parish life. The course aims to build collegiality among peers in order to reduce patterns of competition that can emerge among church staffs. Another example of promoting collegiality in capstone courses was Trinity's requirement to have four peers write responses to the student's final project. A more personal, vocational approach to the capstone is seen in Candler's course, designed in response to asking students what they wanted in a capstone experience. The class, "Becoming a Healthy Pastor," addresses spiritual growth, collegial relationships, financial health, and the pastor as theologian—issues of importance after students have witnessed some unhealthy habits in their site supervisors.

Capstone courses point in at least two directions: some are focused on students looking back over their seminary experience and pulling together knowledge, practice, and identity; others point forward, anticipating what students will be doing upon graduation as they enter ministry. An example of looking forward is Columbia's third-year integration course, which examines the boundary between seminary and the first call. The course has five objectives: to equip students to reflect on how the gospel and context shape Christians; to be theologically informed readers of their context; to engage in integrative imagining about ministerial leadership; to cultivate resiliency in the face of conflict; and to discern God's movement and opportunities for transformation.

Performative pedagogies are becoming increasingly viewed as a way to engage the whole self in learning. Much like jazz or juggling, as Foley notes above, integrating is an improvisational art that can be taught. This embodied, artistic sense of integration allows students to engage aesthetic intelligences and make interdisciplinary connections. Some schools are intentionally cultivating a culture of integration through the arts. Wesley Theological Seminary requires students to take a course in the arts in order to engage in artistic practice and to reflect theologically on their practice. The course is a "trans-cognitive work of integration," a recognition that words are not always adequate to fully integrate knowing, being, and doing.

Faculty were aided by Wesley's arts center to develop a rubric of questions for students and faculty to assess artistic practices.

Similarly, Anabaptist Mennonite Biblical Seminary faculty incorporated an "artful response" into their courses to give students the opportunity to explore a different kind of improvisation. Acknowledging that multiple intelligences mean written papers are not always the best way for students to demonstrate what they know, the artful response allows students to integrate their knowledge through a more embodied and sensory approach. Iliff recently created an end-of-the-year theological recital in which students will be asked to respond to an everyday theological question (as from a person on the street), to think theologically about a current event, to provide an interpretation of a biblical text for a given community, and to reflect on a case study related to their ministry context. The hope is that the theological recital will function like a capstone course in providing students an opportunity to synthesize their seminary experience, but will mimic the more public and performative reality of professional ministerial practice.

Integrating Work in the Implicit Curriculum

Much of the integration that happens for people is not programmed or set down by a curriculum. A community with wise mentors and elders is the primary context for integrating work, which is often taught and learned most deeply at an implicit level. Princeton Seminary students ranked key sources of integration in the following order: field education, conversations with peers in the dining hall, and the classroom.

As Foley notes in his essay "The Ecosystem of Theological Education," a school's culture, space, and time are integrating spaces, such as having a common mealtime that does not compete with a course. To guarantee some balance for students, Calvin Seminary instituted a workload policy of eighty hours of work a semester for a two-credit course to guard against faculty piling more and more work on students. Community building is central to McAfee, which was emphasized in the yearly retreat taken by faculty, staff, and students as part of first-year students' spiritual formation.

Three Approaches to Curricular Integrating

The three case studies that follow demonstrate three approaches to curricular change that shifted a seminary's curricular philosophy, structure and organization, and pedagogy. Much like a house that is being remodeled, each one had a different plan. Calvin Seminary's curricular redesign, reported by David Rylaarsdam, could be described as a teardown. The faculty and administrators rethought the school on nearly every level. In his curricular case study, he describes the redesign of the curriculum toward a competency-based model, which included disbanding the disciplines as its framework. Candler School of Theology, a long-time innovator in pedagogy and curriculum, created a two-year contextual education program that challenged the prevailing theory-to-practice model. As David Jenkins recounts, their redesign meant airing out the house by moving what was inside to the outside. Their faculty accompanied students and a field supervisor to sites of ministry, thereby enabling faculty to learn more about ministry and pulling that knowledge back into their classes. Andover Newton Theological Seminary, as Jeffrey Jones describes, had a similar approach, but in the opposite direction: they remodeled by bringing practitioners inside the house to be part of courses and experts on integrating theology and ministry practice.

Bibliography

Browning, Don S. *A Fundamental Practical Theology: Descriptive and Strategic Proposals.* Minneapolis: Fortress, 1991.

Cahalan, Kathleen A. "Integration in Theological Education." In *Wiley-Blackwell Companion to Practical Theology*, edited by Bonnie J. Miller-McLemore, 386–95. London: Wiley-Blackwell, 2011.

———. "Introducing Ministry and Fostering Integration: Teaching the Bookends of the Masters of Divinity Program." *Teaching Theology and Religion* 11.2 (2008) 65–74.

Cahalan, Kathleen A., and Laura Fanucci. "Integration in Theological Education and Ministry: Findings from Initial Meetings of the Collegeville Institute Seminars, Fall 2010." Unpublished report, April 20, 2011.

Farley, Edward. *Theologia: The Fragmentation and Unity of Theological Education.* Philadelphia: Fortress, 1983.

Foster, Charles R., et al. *Educating Clergy: Teaching Practices and Pastoral Imagination.* San Francisco: Jossey-Bass, 2006.

MacIntyre, Alasdair. *Whose Justice? Which Rationality?* Notre Dame, IN: University of Notre Dame Press, 1988.

Ornstein, Allan C., and Francis P. Hunkins. *Curriculum: Foundations, Principles, and Issues.* 6th ed. Upper Saddle River, NJ: Pearson, 2013.

Sullivan, William M., and Matthew S. Rosin. *A New Agenda for Higher Education: Shaping a Life of the Mind for Practice*. San Francisco: Jossey-Bass, 2008.

7

Overhauling the Curriculum

A Rhetorical Model of Integrating Work

DAVID RYLAARSDAM

I n 1989 I entered an MDiv program at Calvin Theological Seminary
(CTS), the denominational seminary of the Christian Reformed Church.
At orientation, the president showed new students the following pie chart
in order to illustrate that CTS took preparation for ministry very seriously.

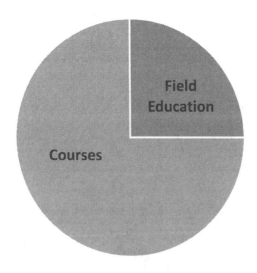

An entire year—one fourth of the MDiv program—was dedicated to internships. As a new student, I remember being impressed. When I entered full-time ministry four years later, I was not. In my seminary training, the two worlds in the pie chart intersected rarely and superficially. Although I learned a lot of good information and some skills, my fragmented education did not integrate the theory of courses and the practices of field education. My acquisition of theological knowledge prepared me for a doctoral program more than it equipped me for the complexity and ambiguity of sin and grace in the everyday life of a congregation. Moreover, as I began ministry, I had no idea how my preaching, administration, pastoral visits, and other ministry practices could work together in a coherent way.

When I became a faculty member at CTS, the pie chart process of formation was still operative for a few years. However, the school was increasingly facing challenges that persuaded a majority of the faculty that the curriculum needed to be overhauled. The general consensus was that CTS should form students effectively for ministry, but some faculty feared that intellectual rigor would be compromised if ministry skills and character formation were more thoroughly integrated into the curriculum and fewer courses in each traditional academic subdiscipline were offered. Other faculty argued that integrating work that developed students' practical wisdom was more intellectually rigorous than simply knowing lots of information. The following case study summarizes the ways in which the new MDiv curriculum seeks to value integrating work in the formation of students for ministry.

Integration in a Curricular Structure

Prior to curriculum revision, the structure of Calvin Seminary's MDiv program consisted of an equal number of courses in three academic divisions (Bible, Theology, and Ministry), plus two internships. Courses or assignments were rarely interdivisional and the internships were largely disconnected from coursework. The pedagogical assumption seemed to be that correct theory would lead to good practice. This assumption was so strong that for decades faculty were bewildered that intellectually gifted graduates adopted ministry practices remarkably inconsistent with the straight A exams that they wrote in seminary. Faculty lamented that these students had failed to apply the good theory they were taught; little did the faculty suspect that their own theory-application pedagogy might be problematic.

In 2008 CTS formed a curriculum revision committee, and the president adjusted my teaching load so that I could lead the revision process. After seeking the wisdom of alumni, church leaders, faculty, and other seminaries, the committee spent several months discussing the structure of the new curriculum. The committee considered many curricular frameworks, rejecting any that would unwittingly maintain dichotomies between theory and practice. Versions of knowledge, skills, and character or biblical, theological, ministerial paradigms were not accepted. The committee eventually persuaded the faculty to adopt a curriculum built around four areas of competency: person, message, context, and goal. This framework assumes that all ministry is interpersonal, that God chooses to minister to people through human beings (for example, John Calvin, *Institutes* 4.3). Drawing on an interpersonal or rhetorical model evident in patristic sources, the new CTS curriculum claims that every vocational situation for which students are preparing involves four elements: a biblical *message* communicated by a *person* in a particular *context* and for a specific *goal*. These competencies are intimately and necessarily related, whether one is visiting someone in the hospital, writing a theology book, leading a council meeting, having coffee with an agnostic, or preaching a sermon.

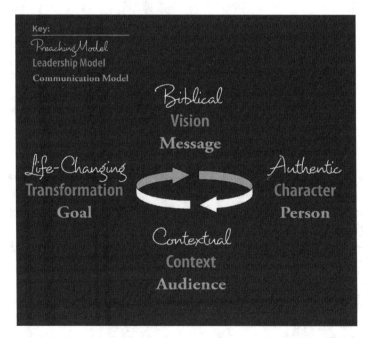

The curriculum committee favored this fourfold curricular framework for many reasons, including its integrative promise, its potential to push faculty to teach from a stance of practice, its focus on students' ability to use knowledge, its grounding in the Christian tradition (the ingredients of this rhetorical model can be found already in Augustine's *De Doctrina Christiana*), and its relevance for ministry in the twenty-first century.

We next developed new MDiv program goals for the four areas of the curriculum. The goals were stated as follows:

1. **Message**

1.1 Knowledgeable: students understand biblical languages and content, theological themes, the Reformed confessions, and the Christian tradition.

1.2 Theologically reflective: students integrate biblical, historical, theological, and pastoral reflection with all ministry practices.

1.3 Preaching and teaching: students explain and apply the biblical message clearly and engagingly.

2. **Person**

2.1 Spiritually mature: students exhibit the fruit of the Spirit, a commitment to the gospel of grace, and an eagerness to serve the mission of Christ's church.

2.2 Interpersonally intelligent: students demonstrate emotional health and relate to others with love and respect, even when expressing differences of belief, values, or practices.

3. **Context**

3.1 Discerning: students discern the ways in which theology and ministry practices are shaped by and respond to their historical and cultural contexts.

3.2 Engaging: students persuasively communicate the Gospel to people in a particular community, including religiously pluralistic, multicultural and cross-cultural settings.

4. **Goal**

4.1 Disciplining: students evangelize, respond to criticisms of Christianity, encourage moral formation, and provide pastoral care so that people at all stages of faith formation become more fully devoted followers of Jesus Christ.

4.2   Worshiping: students worship and help others worship in ways that are God-glorifying and spiritually renewing.

4.3   Serving: students promote service ministries that humbly seek justice, compassion, and reconciliation.

4.4   Leading: students help a group embody in its corporate life the Christian practices that shape vital Christian life, community and witness.[1]

Encouraging Integrating Work within Courses

Our next strategy was to connect each course to the fourfold curricular framework. All core course syllabi are required to list course objectives under the four curricular areas of person, message, context, and goal. Although many courses primarily develop one of the four areas, all core courses need to consider how other areas are represented in the course in some way. A course in history, for example, will focus primarily on context. Students will parachute into particular times and places in history and learn to think contextually by discerning the ways in which the ministry practices and theology of a particular community were shaped by and responded to their context. Students are pushed to investigate the degree of coherence in a particular community's interpretation of scripture, worship, ethical practices, and so on.

However, a history course must also strive to develop student competencies in other curricular areas. Faculty are expected to ask the following questions as they design a course: How can this course intentionally develop the character of a student? How can the knowledge and skills developed in this course help the student form a community of disciples? Simply asking, How can I cover the content of my subdiscipline most efficiently? is no longer adequate.

Although one goal of the new curriculum is that all courses should be integrative to some extent, some courses are more integrative than others. The third year of the MDiv program has integratively thick courses, because the curriculum has a vertical pedagogy. The predominant pedagogy in the first year is literacy; it moves to analysis and exploration in year two and to

1. *Calvin Theological Seminary Academic Catalog*, 2014-2015.

integration in third-year courses. During their first year, students receive the basic vocabulary and distinctions—the building blocks of their theological education—that they can further analyze, explore, and integrate in upper-level core, electives, and capstone courses.

A Central Integrative Stream in the Curriculum

Although the course sequencing in the new CTS curriculum has a generally developmental pedagogy, the three-year curriculum also has a central stream in which the tributaries of theological education are integrated and students are consistently encouraged to embody the faith as a way of life. As originally constructed, the central integrative stream of the new curriculum consisted of the following requirements:

1. "Gateway to Seminary" course, which new MDiv students take for two weeks prior to their first semester

2. "Theological Education as Formation for Ministry" course during the first semester

3. The following requirements that run simultaneously throughout the three-year program:

    mentoring groups

    vocational mentoring

    active involvement in a local congregation

    service learning

4. "Capstone course: Integrative Seminar" during the final semester

There are certainly other integratively thick courses in the new curriculum (for example, Introduction to Missional Ministry, Reading Ministry Contexts, various travel electives, and a capstone course in pastoral leadership), but the pieces of the central integrative stream are intentionally interrelated and draw together the rest of a student's education.

The Gateway to Seminary course is intended to whet students' appetite for their education by inductively examining ministry practices. For example, each day begins with worship, including a homily. The students then discuss with the preacher the development of the sermon—exegetical issues, consideration of audience and context, the person of the preacher, theological and ethical distinctions, and rhetorical and pastoral goals—so that students can begin to sense how the various parts of their education will form them for ministry.

The first-semester course Theological Education as Formation for Ministry provides students with a more detailed, holistic big picture of how the various parts of their program are intended to form them in an integrated way. The course seeks to persuade students that the habits developed during their education are integral to lifelong, discerning ministry practices. Topics include formation through spiritual disciplines, community, theological reflection, study, and ministry practices. One course assignment is to write a "rule of life," an intentional and adaptable plan by which each student hopes to be formed into the image of Christ for the sake of others. Based on their self-assessment (regarding spiritual gifts, academic and ministry practice strengths and weaknesses, emotional health, spiritual discipline preferences), students' rules describe how strategically chosen disciplines and practices will be integral to their way of life in seminary. This integrating work aims to cultivate habits that can sustain pastors over time.

Mentoring groups and vocational mentors keep the holistic concerns of the "Theological Education" course front and center during a student's three-year seminary program. Mentoring groups meet each week, and students receive one course credit each semester. Each group consists of seven students and a faculty leader. The purpose of mentoring groups is to form students for ministry by practicing mutual care and communal theological reflection. Mutual care takes many forms, such as encouragement and accountability for a rule of life, helping one another through the joys and concerns of life (family, finances, studies, discerning calls), and assessing and reflecting on one another's strengths and weaknesses as they become evident through various tools such as psychological tests and internship evaluations. Each semester, every student also presents a theological reflection (TR) based on a ministry experience and focused particularly on one of the four curricular coordinates. Although a TR focuses on one of the four coordinates, the interrelation of all the coordinates is also part of the communal reflection. The TR topics and internships are integrated according to the following schedule:

Semester	Theme	Projects
1–2	Person	Faith stories; rule of life; calling; assessments (psychological, ministry practices, and so forth)
Summer		Cross-cultural internship
3	Context	TR of a cross-cultural internship experience
4	Message	TR of a theological issue with which a student struggles
Summer		Congregation-based internship
5–6	Goal	TR of a congregation-based experience; TR of a service-learning experience

Students also reflect on ministry practices with their vocational mentors. By the end of the first semester, students select a ministry leader to serve as a mentor. Students meet with their mentors twice each month and are encouraged to bring to those meetings any topic that assists their formation for ministry: their faith story, assessment results, ministry experiences, theological issues, questions about specific ministry practices, or sense of call to ministry. The mentors share wisdom based on their life and ministry experiences. They ask questions, offer encouragement, practice theological reflection more informally than the mentoring groups, and model a maturing spiritual and pastoral identity for the student.

"Service Learning" is a three-credit course spread over three years. A student is required to complete a minimum of 120 hours of service through a ministry of justice or mercy. In consultation with their mentoring group leader, students choose a ministry that is strategic for their formation. The course has several purposes, one of which is integrating the other parts of seminary education with ongoing ministry practice. Through guided theological reflection on their service experiences, students learn about poverty, racism, incarceration, and countless other cultural realities in ways that books and traditional internships alone cannot teach them. The "Service Learning" course is integrated into other courses and into the theological reflections of mentoring groups. For example, based on some service experience, students must complete a major assignment (fifteen hours) related to another course in the curriculum. Each core course in the curriculum must provide ideas for completing this assignment, a strategy that pushes faculty (not simply students) to consider how their course relates to a wide variety of ministry practices. To fulfill this assignment, a student could write a sermon on the church's ministry to the poor for an ethics course or develop a curriculum for prisoners for an education course. Such integrating work intentionally seeks to transcend the divide between theory, praxis, and piety and to promote learning that simultaneously involves one's head, heart, and hands.

All MDiv students are also required to commit to a local congregation in which they will actively participate while they are enrolled in seminary. The pastor of the congregation may serve as the student's vocational mentor, and the student's service learning may be a ministry of that congregation. A student may present theological reflections based on his ministry experiences in this local congregation.

For three years, students are engaged in a local congregation and service learning at the same time as they are conversing with vocational mentors and mentoring groups. Running concurrently through the central integrative stream of their education, these requirements provide opportunities for students to reflect on the meaning of the knowledge and practice they are engaged in during seminary. Such guided reflection on current experiences and actions is critical for moving student practitioners to higher levels of expertise. In *Educating the Reflective Practitioner*, Donald Schön argues that the gap between the description of practice and the knowing-in-practice that corresponds to it must be filled by reflection-in-action. The central integrative stream in the MDiv curriculum seeks to fill the gap between description and practice with weekly reflective conversations on students' current practices.

A final section of the curriculum's central integrative stream is the capstone course, "Integrative Seminar." The course seeks to pull together the ways in which students have been formed during their seminary program. During the first half of the course, faculty members help students prepare for their oral comprehensive exam by demonstrating how to field integrative questions by drawing on various parts of their learning. Each student's exam panel includes a pastor and two faculty members. For the second half of the course, each student is given a ministry case study. Students prepare a nuanced response to the case in conversation with fellow students and the course professor. At the end of the semester, students present and discuss their response with the same panel that examined them earlier in the term.

Mentors and Integration

In developing a new curriculum, CTS decided to trade its curricular pie chart for a pinwheel.

Although all faculty and departments are responsible for integration in theological education, the mentored ministries office makes certain that each student and her mentors are attentive to how the breath of the Spirit is blowing the pinwheel and students are being formed for ministry. The director of mentored ministries (formerly known as the director of field education) oversees the mentoring that students receive from mentoring group leaders, vocational mentors, internship mentors and supervisors, and service learning supervisors.

Mentoring group leaders are important dialogue partners in the integrating work of students. Based on students' faith stories, psychological profiles, level of expertise in various ministry practices, and vocational aspirations, a mentoring group leader helps students choose a vocational mentor, a learning site, a local congregation, disciplines and habits for their rule of life, and the ways in which their ministry skills will be developed during their seminary education. Mentoring group leaders seek to guide a holistic formation process in which students' developing skills, knowledge, character, and sense of calling are integrated.

One goal of the new curriculum was to integrate course work with mentoring relationships and other so-called field education requirements much more than the old curriculum did. Rather than simply administering internships, the mentored ministries office was envisioned to be involved with several courses: Gateway to Seminary, Theological Education as Formation for Ministry, Introduction to Missional Ministry, Reading Ministry Contexts, Pastoral Leadership Capstone, and Integrative Seminar Capstone. Through such courses, the mentored ministries office teaches and helps students practice the art of theological reflection, including the habits of curiosity, inquisitiveness, and imaginative thinking about how the demands of ministry situations can be addressed in integrated ways.

Successes and Slippage in Integrating Work

Evidence shows that the new curriculum fosters integrating work more than the pie chart curriculum did. As demonstrated in the capstone course case studies, students develop habits of reflection on their ministry practices that integrate person, message, context, and goal. Moreover, students in other degree programs have envied some of the changes in the MDiv program and desire greater opportunities for integrating work in their programs. MTS students, for example, have requested mentoring groups, character formation plans, and greater integration of skill development in their course requirements.

Despite clear gains, the new curriculum, after five years of operation, has also suffered significant slippage between the original vision for encouraging integration and its actual implementation. Several integratively thick courses in the new curriculum have been cut, including "Reading Ministry Contexts," "Service Learning," and the integrative week of the "Gateway" course, primarily because CTS lacks sufficient faculty who are able to teach integrative courses well or who have the imagination to integrate and evaluate service learning in their courses. Compared to the original intentions of the new curriculum, the Mentored Ministries Office has not been integrated with course work. Moreover, half of the mentoring groups are not led by faculty members but by local pastors, because a number of faculty lack the appropriate skills. Thus, a number of faculty members remain disconnected from the central integrative stream of the curriculum and continue to function pedagogically out of the pie chart paradigm. As one faculty member commented when he was finding it difficult to teach a new integrative core course, "We have this wonderful new curriculum, but the wrong faculty to teach it."

Faculty members need to do their own integrating work in order to foster it in the curriculum and pedagogy of a school. Such work is a process, and progress is not straight and steady. Although the integration suggested by CTS's pinwheel diagram is still somewhat aspirational, the pedagogy of an increasing number of faculty reflects the belief that churches do not need leaders who are merely brains on a stick. The increasing desire is to facilitate the formation of leaders who have practical wisdom, an intelligence that is embodied, emotional, creative, spiritually mature, contextual, and theologically knowledgeable.

8

The Professor-Practitioner Program and Field Education

Jeffrey D. Jones

Andover Newton Theological School (ANTS) has a long and significant history in supervised education through field placements. In
the 1970s the school instituted a program that augmented student placement in ministry sites with theological reflection with trained supervisors
and on-campus peer groups. The stories that are told even now trace the
beginning of this approach to faculty overhearing student's talk as they
played basketball about the ways in which concepts from their classes applied to their experiences at their ministry sites. Whether fictional or not,
these stories point to the school's desire to utilize field education as a way
to help students integrate academic concepts with the practice of ministry.
During the two decades following the 1970s the school built an extensive
field education program that included formal training for supervisors in a
three-credit course and significant opportunities for student reflection on
their ministry experience.

As the realities of ministry changed in the late twentieth century it
became apparent that what had once been an excellent and thorough program was no longer achieving the results it once had in preparing students
for ministry. In addition, the school itself had changed significantly. An
all-male resident student body of recent college graduates was now significantly more diverse: students numbered almost evenly between males and
females; the majority of students were older and commuted to campus;

many were part-time students who had both family and job responsibilities. In additional, a much wider variety of denominations were represented among the students, including students from the United Church of Christ and American Baptist Churches USA (denominations with which the school was affiliated), but also significant numbers of students seeking ministry in the Unitarian Universalist Association. Because of these changes and their impact on field education, the faculty in 2005 charged the incoming director of field education with the responsibility for reenvisioning the program.

The desire to revise the field education program was also driven in some measure by Andover Newton's historical and theological orientation. The school has a long history of leadership in the practice of ministry, especially through its clinical pastoral education and field education programs. The theological traditions of both the United Church of Christ and the American Baptist Churches USA, emphasize the vital importance of active participation in ministry for all believers. Both have a long tradition that encourages believers to move beyond an intellectual understanding of faith into living a life of faith. In this context, it was especially important for the school to actively enable integrating theory and practice.

The Plan

In the fall of 2007 Andover Newton implemented a new approach to field education. Students would continue to do field education in approved sites with a trained supervisor for theological reflection. They would continue to work with an on-site teaching parish or site committee that would offer support and feedback. The new component was an on-campus experience of field education called the Professor-Practitioner Program (P3). This program was based in the belief that (1) all courses students pursue in seminary are relevant to ministry; (2) the best way for students to grasp the ministry implications of the subjects they study is through the immediate connection of theoretical concepts to the work of ministry; (3) this assists students both in their retention of theory and in their ministerial practice. The Professor-Practitioner Program was designed to help students make connections between the courses they were taking and their experiences in the field.

The plan included five courses each semester designated as P3 courses. These would be taught by full-time faculty members and also involve a resident ministry practitioner (RMP), men and women engaged in active ministry, mainly in parish settings, who had demonstrated a skill at reflective practice. The RMP role in the classroom would be to share ways in which the course material influenced their practice of ministry. In addition, RMPs would lead a ninety-minute breakout session for students in the course who were pursuing field education. These sessions would meet either shortly before or after the P3 course's meeting time. These breakout sessions, or P3 Sections, included no more than eight students. All field education students were required to take one P3 course concurrently with their required first two semesters of field education.

RMPs would play dual roles as course participant and section leader. The intent was that all students enrolled in the course would develop a better sense of the ways in which the course material informed the practice of ministry; the field education students would have the opportunity to connect course material in a specific way to in their field education setting and link insights from ministry back to the course. In most cases the RMP's input in the class took the form of a five- to ten-minute presentation about how a course concept appeared in or informed his or her ministry.

Recognizing that all students might not be able to arrange their schedules to participate in one of the designated P3 courses, the plan also called for one Integrative Seminar each semester that focused on a book the students read. This book was intended to substitute for the common content material the course provided.

In the early years of the P3 program I served a small church part time in addition to my part-time position on the ANTS faculty, which enabled me to function as an RMP. From 2012–2015 I was a full-time faculty member and served as director of ministry studies. One of my responsibilities in the role was to direct the field education program.

I served as an RMP in a variety of courses, including the introductory Hebrew Bible course, systematic theology, American religious history, and Christian education through the lifespan. In each case the responsibility of integrating course material with my current ministry proved to be an interesting challenge, but not an impossible one. Having to meet the challenge caused me to reflect more intentionally on my ministry, bringing a new perspective and often a deeper understanding of what I was about.

I also led the Integrative Seminar for several years. The absence of material from an entire course and reliance on the concepts from one book reduced the material students could draw on for their integrating work.

While this made the seminar experience somewhat less rich, it did enable the students to make significant connections between concepts and practice, which was the overall goal of the P3 program.

The student experience in both settings followed a similar pattern. In each seminar, students, with the leadership of the RMP, would create a covenant together that set guidelines for participation. These covenants typically covered issues such as confidentiality, respect, being on time, using "I statements," and nonjudgmental listening. Groups also tended to bring their own concerns, so some covenants included issues such as no fragrances, turning off cell phones, and praying for each other. These covenants provided the standards for participation in the seminar. On those relatively rare occasions when problems in the group's life developed, they also served as the reference point for addressing the situation.

P3 courses and the Integrative Seminar were graded satisfactory or unsatisfactory. The course syllabus stated that to receive a satisfactory grade students needed to (1) attend all sessions unless excused in advance by the seminar RMP; no more than two excused absences were permitted; (2) participate fully in the discussions; and, (3) present at least one integration exercise for the group.

For students in their first year of field education, P3 or the Integrative Seminar were part of the field education requirement. In the second year of field education, which some students took but was not required, they could participate in a seminar if there was room. In subsequent years the school offered an Advanced Field Education Seminar, not related to a specific course but still focused on integrating conceptual material and the practice of ministry. When that seminar was offered, second-year field education students were no longer permitted to participate in P3 sections or the first year Integrative Seminar.

Each P3 Section and the Integrative Seminar followed roughly the same format, although RMPs brought their own leadership style to the group. Similarly, groups varied in the way they worked together, so the format that was suggested and is described here often took on its own shape in the seminars. The suggested process for both P3 sections and the Integrative Seminar included time for checking in with each other and reporting on the integration exercise.

Checking In

The first portion of the P3 Section meeting time was devoted to checking in, facilitated by the RMPs. Each student was encouraged to take no more than three minutes to share with others what he or she was experiencing in field education without comment or discussion. After each shared, the group had an opportunity to share together for an additional ten to fifteen minutes. This time was typically devoted to common threads that appeared in the sharing and significant ministry issues that appeared. It was not intended to be a problem-solving exercise focusing on one person's concern, but rather a time in which students used a specific situation to look more deeply at a ministry issue they all shared.

Integration Exercise

After check-in (about forty-five minutes), the student who had previously been assigned responsibility for the integration exercise on that day shared his or her written document, which described intersections between the P3 course and ministry experiences in the field. During that discussion, the RMP functioned as coach and mentor, placing the student's presentation and the group's conversation into a wider ministry context. Students were encouraged to play a similar role for each other, helping one another see the wider implications of the integrative issue the presenting student was sharing with the group.

Both RMPs and students were encouraged to avoid providing answers to the problems students presented, especially when doing so focused the conversation upon the writer instead of upon the ministry issues presented. At the same time, students were encouraged to share their own experiences, as these could serve to normalize and broaden students' perspectives.

In preparing the integration exercise, students followed the three guidelines below. The exercise was meant to be brief—no more than one page—in order to provide a basis for conversation with the whole group and was intended to begin, not complete, the process of integrating theory and practice for ministry.

> *Description of Salient Concept from the P3 Course:* In this section, students wrote one or two paragraphs about a concept from the P3 course or seminar reading book that resonated with their ministry experience.

Description of the Ministry Event, Experience, or Dilemma: In this section, students briefly described (1) the backdrop of a certain happening in ministry, and (2) the basic characteristics of the event, experience, or dilemma under scrutiny.

Integration of Concept and Event: In this section, students reflected upon the intersecting points of the concept and the event.

The Ongoing Experience: Reflections in the Spring of 2015

In the eight years since the P3 program was established the faculty and partners have learned from their experience and encountered new realities. We have made several adaptations in order to respond to the needs of students and still maintain an emphasis on integrating theory and practice.

During the first year we offered one Integrative Seminar for students whose schedules and degree progress made it impossible for them to register for a designated P3 course. Students needed to petition the director of field education in order to be approved for participation in the seminar. During the first two weeks of the semester, students in the seminar read a book that served as the common reference point for integrating work. While we recognized this experience was not as comprehensive as a P3 course, it responded to a realistic scheduling need and still provided a setting for integrating work to be done.

In subsequent years the number of students requesting to participate in the Integrative Seminar has increased significantly. In the spring 2013 semester we had to make one of our planned P3 course groups an Integrative Seminar because of low registration in the course and the need to place students who were not registered for that course. We next conducted a comprehensive evaluation of P3 requirements, focusing on the ability of students to register for a designated P3 course and still meet the various demands of family, work, degree progress, and days on campus. We determined that given the large number of commuter and part-time students at the school and our inability to offer more than five P3 courses a semester, it was not realistic to expect that most students in field education would be able to register for a P3 course.

Our response to this situation was to reduce the number of P3 courses to two and offer three Integrative Seminars. One option would be available on each day of the week. The P3 courses have continued to function as they were originally designed and are still our preference if students can register for them. The Integrative Seminars in the new format have eliminated the book as the common reference point and allow students to use a concept from any of the courses they are currently taking when they write their integration exercise. Of course, students may not be familiar with a concept the presenter is using, which requires that person to be articulate in explaining it. The exercise still asks the student to explain the concept, describe a ministry experience, and provide his or her thoughts on the way in which the concept provides a perspective from which to view the experience. The written assignment becomes the basis for the discussion in the seminar led by the RMP.

In addition, there is ongoing discussion about the value of using a book rather than having students draw from any course they are taking. The book provides a common reference point, which makes the integrating discussion easier. At the present time we continue to opt for the alternative approach, believing it provides a more realistic experience for students, who will be integrating concepts from their studies and reading in settings in which no one else is familiar with them.

In a perfect world we would provide a full P3 experience for all students. It offers the richest integrating experience and places RMPs in the classroom, which benefits all students taking the course, not just field education students. We receive consistent feedback from nonfield education students that having an RMP in the course strengthens their learning and provides helpful insights for ministry. Given the realities we face, however, the use of the Integrative Seminar has proven a meaningful and effective way of enabling students to develop skill at integrative work.

Over the years the program has been operating we have seen a yearly pattern in which the students at first struggle with making the connections that make meaningful integrating work possible. This is clearly true in the fall semester. During the spring semester, however, they demonstrate a significantly greater ability to engage the integrating process. Their seminar evaluations indicate this, as does the anecdotal evidence we receive from RMPs.

9

Sanctifying Grace in the Integrating Work of Contextual Education

DAVID O. JENKINS

How does a seminary's formative practices of integrating work display its tradition's theological convictions? As one of thirteen US United Methodist seminaries, is there anything distinctively Wesleyan about Candler School of Theology's curriculum as an integrating context for students and faculty? I will argue not only that Candler's contextual education program is a fruitful model of a formative integrating process for students and faculty but that its theological inspiration finds its roots in John Wesley's doctrine of sanctification. I will examine Candler's first year curriculum, with an emphasis on the significance of the contextual education program.

For a number of years Candler's two-year contextual education program required nearly half of its full-time faculty to teach a year of either Contextual Education I or II almost every other year. Twelve or thirteen faculty members taught the first year Contextual Education seminars while serving as academic advisors for their contextual education students. Another twelve or more faculty members were paired with local pastors to co-teach the Contextual Education II ecclesial site seminars.

As the school experienced pressure to expand elective course offerings and cover required courses while half the faculty was teaching contextual education, it began to question the economic and curricular benefits of this deployment of faculty resources. Meanwhile, faculty expressed another concern: "How do we not try to become experts in the various context education sites (for example, refugee centers, homeless shelters, prisons), but rather find creative ways of designing courses that integrate our research interests with students preparing for congregational leadership?"

Seminaries simultaneously experienced additional pressures—both declining enrollment and declining revenue—so Candler sought to make creative changes within this new landscape of US theological education while maintaining its commitment to integrating field experience with classroom theological education and integrating faculty across disciplines into the contextual education program. A grant from the Lilly Endowment, Inc., provided the school that opportunity to respond to each of these problems, explore options, and reimagine the structure of our program.

In 2005 several years into the grant, Alice Rogers and I were hired to direct the two years of the contextual education program and related programs (CPE, Teaching Parish, summer ministry internships), complete the implementation of the grant, and bring a proposal before the faculty. After visiting other seminaries across the country, hosting conferences of field education directors who shared their best practices with one another, working closely with a Candler faculty committee on contextual education that included the academic dean, the current program that I describe below was developed and endorsed by the faculty. From 2005 through 2014 I directed Contextual Education I and CPE, after which I returned to full-time teaching.

Sanctification as Integrating Work

According to John Wesley, God nurtures Christians with sanctifying grace in their day-to-day transformation into holy people who—in heart, soul, mind, and strength—become filled with perfect love of God and neighbor. The *telos* of sanctification is Christian perfection.

United Methodist candidates for ordination are asked by their bishop several questions specified in *The Book of Discipline of the United Methodist Church*, one of which is "Are you going on to perfection?" Wesley claimed, "By perfection I mean the humble, gentle, patient love of God and man ruling all the tempers, words, and actions, the whole heart by the whole life."[1]

1. Wesley, "A Plain Account," 99.

This notion of perfection is the *telos* of the lifelong process of sanctification in which the individual believer, nurtured by the Holy Spirit, in the context and communion of the church, is transformed over time into a holy person bearing the likeness of Christ.

As Rex Matthews observes, Wesley conceived of perfection not as a static state of completion, but rather "understood 'perfection' in the sense of the Greek *teleiosis*—as 'perfecting,' as an ongoing process of growth and development in grace" that moves toward wholeness, maturity, and completion.[2] "For Wesley, then, Christian Perfection was that dynamic level of maturity within the process of sanctification characteristic of 'adult' Christian life."[3] In fact, one United Methodist bishop believes that the ordination question should be rephrased: "Are you earnestly trying to grow up?"[4]

One can see parallel meanings and dynamics between sanctification and integration: both are lifelong processes better characterized as sanctifying and integrating movements that lead to greater maturity and wholeness. Both require the intentional care and attention of the individual disciple, though the individual cannot become more integrated or sanctified on her or his own. Sanctification and integration require God's action through the Holy Spirit coupled with the communal, embodied attention of the church as the context for this movement toward wholeness.

In this regard, a grown-up is one who has matured in love over time, with the aid of the Holy Spirit and with help from fellow adults, all of whom continue to remain open to receiving God's perfect love that informs their loving care of one another and of the world and shapes their responsibility for the world. As Manfred Marquardt notes, "The aim of Wesley's preaching was therefore twofold: to lead individuals to renewal through God's grace in justification and sanctification and thus to meaningful life, and to guide them into activity suited to transform the whole of society from within."[5]

Candler School of Theology seeks to reflect its historic commitment to the Wesleyan tradition not only through a curricular design that calls on the collaborative work of faculty with contextual education sites and site supervisors, but also through its programmatic and curricular commitments to this Wesleyan notion of sanctification of people, the church,

2. Matthews, "'Words Get in the Way,'" 106.

3. Maddox, *Responsible Grace*, 187.

4. Jones, *United Methodist Doctrine*, 215.

5. Marquardt, *Wesley's Social Ethics*, 119.

and the world. The curricular design attempts to redress the traditional bifurcation of formal classroom theological education from the "practical" education of seminarians in the field. By constructing a more integrating curriculum, Candler hopes its faculty, as well as students and site supervisors, will become more integrated, whole adults equipped with skills and the desire to participate in God's sanctifying work in the world.

The School of Theology's curricular model is situated in a broader culture and context that offers daily worship, in addition to other opportunities for spiritual formation, social justice outreach, community life, and engagement with Emory University through dual degree programs and weekly guest lectures. Our curricular model—while flawed, susceptible to economic and institutional pressures, and facing regular resistance from the students and faculty who yet affirm its importance—attempts to display our convictions about integrating work in theological education and our commitment to participating in God's sanctifying work in the lives of students, faculty, staff, and partners.

In the first year of the MDiv program, most students enroll in five courses per semester: (1) Contextual Education I, (2) Contextualized Introduction to Pastoral Care, (3) Introduction to Old Testament, (4) History of Christian Thought, and (5) an elective, often a denominational requirement.

Contextual Education I:
Program Design and Goals for Integration

Contextual Education I is a yearlong integrating program in which students are placed in social service and clinical settings such as hospitals, prisons, refugee resettlement agencies, homeless shelters, or day programs for adults with mental illness and intellectual disabilities. Ten students are placed at the same site, forming a learning community. They are supervised by a site staff person, who is a practitioner and a graduate of a school of theology. In the fall semester the site supervisor teaches a weekly seminar and is joined in the spring semester by the faculty academic advisor for those ten students. Faculty advisors have met regularly with their advisees throughout the fall semester and have worked with the site supervisor to design the spring semester contextual education course. The goal is to integrate the faculty person's discipline and research interests with the experience of ministry at that particular site.

Both the site supervisor and the faculty person have the opportunity to expand their practical knowledge and areas of expertise as they collaborate with their teaching partner in the spring semester. For instance, a prison chaplain is partnered with an Old Testament professor but in the next year the chaplain might be paired with a pastoral care professor, and later an ethics professor. She is strengthened over time through her partnership with professors in different disciplines as well as a new cadre of students, who bring fresh questions, life experience, and their own maturation process to the course.

Interactions with a practitioner draw faculty out of their silos and allow them to learn from an expert in a particular area of ministry. Because faculty rotate through Contextual Education I once every three years, over time they will be asked to integrate their discipline with a variety of ministry contexts: refugees, homeless children and mothers, or patients on the oncology ward at Emory Hospital. As faculty have more exposure to metro-Atlanta neighborhoods, marginalized populations, social service ministries, and congregations in under-resourced communities, their course content and pedagogy can be reformed with an eye to identifying God's sanctifying activity in the world.

The faculty coleader is and remains the academic advisor for the ten students during their MDiv program. As a result of coleading the contextual education seminar, faculty have gained a richer insight into their advisees' capacities for ministry, heard students' deeply personal stories arising from challenges at the site, have been a member of a learning community during the first year of their advisees' studies, and are watching the process of sanctification occur in individual students, in the group, and in themselves. They become keenly aware of their students' intellectual and academic abilities while being responsible for assisting students to integrate learning across the first-year curriculum, with the students' vocational goals and with the students' previous experience of faith and Christian formation. They can observe their students' openness to receiving God's perfect love and their resistance to it. Students also observe their faculty advisor integrate her or his discipline with the ministry site, try to expand his or her role from professor to pastor and advisor, grapple with the same questions students bring to class, and collaborate—clumsily or effectively—with the site supervisor. Professors are often as uncomfortable and disoriented in this context as are students.

The Contextual Education Learning Community as a Place of Integration

The Contextual Education I seminar usually becomes more than a learning community focused on site work. Students often claim they met others in their group who became trusted friends throughout seminary. The contextual education class was the place of the profound formation, growth, and integration that resembles Wesley's notion of sanctification. "Con Ed is where it all came together," declared a first student last year. "I was loved by my colleagues and enabled to love [the refugees] at my Con Ed site." What students learned in Old Testament about justice and sin, about God's ongoing creative and redeeming action in the world, about the *imago Dei* (particularly their own embodiment of the *imago Dei*), found lasting meaning when brought into conversation with fellow students who were discussing a ten-year-old hospital patient they visited who had been shot by an Atlanta drug gang. The learning community is a safe place for students to do integrative work with those who can be quite different from them— theologically, socially, and politically. Trust, diversity, and the communal nature of the shared work are fundamental to the process of integration.

Candler's intent is to create diverse, intimate, integrative learning communities, facilitated by expert practitioners and faculty academic advisors, in order that students will (1) begin to practice the skills of integration in safe, communal contexts, (2) extend their integrative learning to other Candler courses, and (3) be inspired to participate in these sorts of integrative, reflective, communal learning communities throughout their professional careers. Being made aware of their sinfulness, their skills, and their maturing capacities for love of the other, the contextual education experience mirrors Wesleyan small discipleship groups that nurture the process of sanctification.

Contextual Education Pedagogy for Integrative Learning

Although the contextual education faculty committee regularly reviews syllabi, no template is imposed on individual contextual education seminars. Requirements such as site work hours, evaluation forms, attendance policies, and the amount of required reading remain the same throughout the program, while the individual class dynamic and pedagogy will vary.

Students lead the seminars through discussion of verbatims, case studies, or ministry experiences. Praxis reflection is the pedagogical norm.

Verbatims—the literal account of a pastoral encounter and conversation—emerged in the clinical pastoral education and counseling fields in the 1930s. The traditional format has been expanded to include social analysis and the expectation that the student identify his or her social location, analyze the overarching context as well as the immediate situation, and illustrate how the student is not only integrating her or his theological education and ministry experience but also becoming a reflective practitioner.

Case studies require a critical level of integrative capacities, drawing on pastoral-care theory and practices, theological reflection, social analysis, self-awareness, institutional analysis, and moral reasoning. Case studies can help students anticipate certain dilemmas and complex situations and are a safe way to tease out diverse perspectives.

Because contextual education is often the first experience students have of social analysis, Joe Holland and Peter Henriot's pastoral circle is sometimes a fruitful pedagogical resource.

The Pastoral Circle[6]

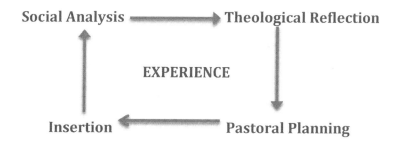

As noted in the diagram of the pastoral circle, the first action is insertion, in which the student steps into the ministry site or the seminar. Both social analysis and self-awareness are occurring. Questions to be considered during this first stage are these: "Where and with whom are we locating ourselves as we begin the process? Whose experience is being considered? Are there any groups that are 'left out' when experience is discussed? Does the experience of the poor and oppressed have a privileged role in the

6. Holland and Henriot, *Social Analysis*, 8.

process?"[7] Students work collaboratively through the four pastoral circle steps and have found this pedagogy useful in congregational leadership and community development for years to come.

The praxis-reflection pedagogy is an integrative communal learning process; it values experience, practices and skills, social analysis, theological reflection, and maturing self-awareness. Differing views are respected, valued, and needed in order for honest and transparent reflection and action to occur.

Assessing Integration in Contextual Education I

Regarding assessment, what are the most constructive ways to (1) assess a student's growth during the first year, (2) communicate promising growth and need for change when the evaluations will be available to ordaining bodies and future employers, and (3) examine the site, class, and culture of Contextual Education I?

If we theological educators believe that integrating work and sanctification are lifelong transformative activities requiring integrative communities and mentors, then we ought to be assessing students' growth, resistance to growth, and future areas of growth, rather than their capacity for ministry at any one point in time. While the first year offers nine months of observations, we can make some informed observations. We observe, for example, that people can change habits in briefer periods, can seek help making changes or resist help, can exemplify defensive or open postures toward peers, and can engage in integrative practices over the first year of seminary. Or they can refuse to do so or lack the capacity to do so, both of which are warning signs for the church. Assessing integration is an assessment of movement, growth, and transformation over time.

As students participate in assessing one another, they become more astute observers of growth, resistance to transformation and specific areas needing maturation, enhanced skill level, and additional knowledge and insight. We hope this assessment experience models possibilities for them as they assume congregational leadership positions with multiple staff members. Assessment ought to nurture students' desire for integrating over a lifetime.

7. Ibid., 9.

To examine transformation of individuals and communities over time, seminaries can evaluate students over a three-year period, but we also need to develop tools for long-term assessment of ministry practice. How could schools of theology collaborate with judicatories to measure the slow, steady transformation and integration of our alumni?

Who is equipped to assess our students' integrating trajectories, let alone measure our students' journey toward sanctification and holiness? How do we evaluate a student's love of God, neighbor, self, and enemy or the capacity of the school to nurture that love? If we can identify our elders who have matured in their faith and love of God and who are leading more integrative lives, if those elders have acquired the practical wisdom and skills for authentic ministry, then they should be engaged in our assessment process, perhaps complementing the site supervisor, faculty academic advisor, fellow students, and the student being evaluated. Yet we also know from experience that some of our youngest students possess wisdom and keen judgment. They bring a remarkable self-awareness to bear on the task of self-assessments and can teach faculty and site supervisors new ways of interpreting situations.

The entire community can also participate in the regular evaluation of the seminary as an integrative context for formation. How could staff, faculty, students, and site supervisors regularly and safely reflect on their experience of integrating work within the culture of the school? How could we elicit creative, constructive wisdom from all our members that would lead to greater integrative activities, personal and institutional relationships, scheduling, curricular designs, worship life, and spiritual formation?

As expressed earlier in this case, Candler set about to design a contextual education program that reduced the number of faculty members teaching contextual education courses each year, while continuing to integrate faculty into the program in substantive ways. It did so by reducing the faculty's involvement in Contextual Education I from a full year to one semester, and then replacing faculty teaching responsibilities for a full year of Contextual Education II seminars with teaching one-semester Contextual Education II electives for students in ecclesial settings.

Do faculty members continue to be fully engaged in the program that resides at the heart of Candler's curriculum? Undoubtedly, yes. Have more faculty been made available to teach other electives and required courses? Yes. Have faculty celebrated the opportunity to design contextualized electives from their disciplines for ecclesial sites instead of teaching a standard curriculum for students in congregational settings? Absolutely. Do students evaluate the program, the faculty, their site supervisors, and their field education experience with the highest marks across both years? With surprisingly few exceptions, detailed evaluations of the program offer compelling endorsement of the effectiveness of the program.

Does this new program succeed in attaining the fundamental goals that Candler has for its students, that they become integrating, sanctified human beings and disciples of Christ as a result of being participants in this particular experience of theological education? Perhaps we have yet to develop assessment tools that can carefully and honestly note our students' and faculty's growth in love, justice, faith, and movement toward holiness. These are the tools most needed by our boards of ordained ministry.

Bibliography

Holland, Joe, and Peter Henriot. *Social Analysis: Linking Faith and Justice*. Rev. ed. Maryknoll, NY: Orbis, 1983.

Jones, Scott J. *United Methodist Doctrine: The Extreme Center*. Nashville: Abingdon, 2002.

Maddox, Randy L. *Responsible Grace: John Wesley's Practical Theology*. Nashville: Kingswood/Abingdon, 1994.

Marquardt, Manfred. *John Wesley's Social Ethics: Praxis and Principles*. Translated by John E. Steely and W. Stephen Gunter. Nashville: Abingdon, 1992.

Matthews, Rex. "'The Words Get in the Way': Rethinking John Wesley's Idea of Christian Perfection." *Revista Caminhando* 18.2 (2013) 97–114.

Wesley, John. "A Plain Account of Christian Perfection." *The Works of John Wesley*. Edited by Paul W. Chilcote and Kenneth Collins. Nashville: Abingdon, 2013.

10

Harvesting Insights

── KATHLEEN A. CAHALAN ──

Designing a curricula to be more integrative requires significant change regarding several key issues. Curriculum work raises questions about a school's tradition and educational philosophies, especially those that compete with each other. It means identifying and articulating what content, experiences, and processes are included, which also means that faculty have to wrestle with what will not be included or emphasized. Creating an integrating trajectory in the curriculum means distinguishing the vertical and horizontal movements about which faculty and students can be intentional; of course other movement, learning, and dynamics will happen that are unintentional, such as the crisscrossing of events, experiences, opportunities, and tragedies that invite spontaneous and creative responses. Finally, faculties have to wrestle with how best to construct a curriculum to respond to the current challenges of ministry as well as internal pressures of finances, enrollment, and changing ecclesial contexts.

Calvin Theological Seminary provides an excellent case study of the move away from the applied theory-to-practice model toward a competency-based curriculum. The faculty determined that the pie-chart curriculum was no longer tenable, but not without significant resistance from those that believed good information can be easily translated into right practice. In many ways, Calvin jumped from the fourfold model (Bible, history, theology, and pastoral practice) to a competency-based curriculum in one leap. In terms of reconstructing their house, this was a teardown. Yet the reconstruction was based on the faculty wrestling with what the church needed to be and to do in order to thrive. The outside pressures from alumni and the denomination brought the question of integrating work to the fore.

Several important aspects of this new house are noteworthy. First, the Christian tradition remains an important source for them—they replaced the fourfold pattern with a model they discerned in Augustinian and patristic thought. Because the four competencies are grounded in the tradition, most faculty could understand and embrace the framework. Calvin's Reformed theology had been shaped by the epistemology of perennial educational philosophy; in order to shift to a new model some stability in the tradition was necessary.

Second, in addition to creating an integrating framework built around the four competencies, the faculty also looked at integrating work from the bottom up. Because each course focuses on one competency and takes account of the other three, faculty have to both consider how a course is related to curricular goals and how the competencies are addressed in their course. They have to do some integrating work before they ask students to do it.

Third, the faculty is intentional about vertical and horizontal integration. The four competencies are addressed in integrative courses each year, which creates movement and scaffolding for student learning. Horizontal learning is emphasized through small groups and ministry in local contexts over the four years—these provide a variety of learning communities for students where they continue the integrating work of the four goals of the curriculum.

The repetition of the four competencies in every part of the curriculum provides a solid foundation upon which this house is built. But even the best architects build a structure that not everyone can live in. As Rylaarsdam points out, many faculty may like the curricular plan but find that they cannot change their pedagogy to match the aspirations of integrating the four competencies. Their own competencies are limited or insufficient.

Andover's Professor-Practitioner Program focused its integrating work on drawing ministry into the classroom by including an expert from the outside. Many seminaries have recognized that pastors are theological educators who can be invited to the academic table as partners, and that they bring knowledge and insight about ministry that most faculty do not have, at least as readily. In this case, Andover welcomed to the table an expertise they did not have.

Their model shows the multifaceted dimensions of integrating work in the way that it fosters conversation among a faculty person, a practitioner, and the students. Together they grapple with texts, ideas, and practices in relationship to communities of faith. Students are able to see how both professors and practitioners approach the meaning of faith and the challenge of leadership. In this model, no one gets off the hook—the struggle, challenge, and delight of integrating work belongs to the whole classroom.

Despite that Andover can show that student learning is significantly better in P3 courses, based on student feedback, they cannot retain as many of these courses as originally planned. In this case, the ways student are engaging theological education poses a greater challenge than faculty resistance.

Candler School of Theology, like Andover, has been on the leading edge of contextual education. But unlike Andover, which brought experts into the house, Candler decided to take their faculty experts out into the field. In addition, rather than one student attending a field education site, they placed students in groups and created a learning community at one site. This cohort model provides a unique context for integrating work by shifting the traditional classroom to the ministry site and inviting faculty to be both expert and student.

Candler has both vertical and horizontal integrative dynamics happening, but the power of their model is the repetition of learning. Because faculty are exposed to different sites, and site supervisors are working with different courses, they have a greater opportunity to learn the nuances of integrating work—between ideas, practice, and theory and in relationship to competency.

Candler, like Calvin, turned to its own tradition to find a theological way of thinking about the integrating work of the curriculum. Through Wesley's theology of sanctification, they have a theology of learning that values both the process and the end goal. It places learning within a broader dynamic of sin and grace, failure and success, loss and opportunity. It identifies God's grace as *the* integrating power and movement through persons and communities, and it points to the way in which teachers and students participate in that movement and are changed by it.

The story of Candler's program also reveals the need for adapting innovative programs like Contextual Education I and II when other curricular demands emerge. In Jenkins's account, the shift from twelve faculty working in the first year and twelve in the second year, over both semesters, to faculty rotating into the program every three years, and for one rather than two semesters, is not a tragedy or a failure. It is a realistic adjustment, given the challenges facing seminaries regarding time, resources, and student enrollment. It also requires imagination. In Candler's case, they retained the unique pedagogical aim with a similar, albeit shorter, process. But the impact is still quite significant.

The three case studies point to a number of challenges in curricular redesigns that aim toward greater integrating, and they raise significant questions.

First, each of the three models required most faculty to do something they were not explicitly trained to do, including designing a curriculum and making it an integrative learning experience. How can doctoral training and faculty development better prepare faculty to be curricular thinkers?

Second, most faculty outside the practical areas are not ordinarily prepared to work with or think along with ministry site supervisors, either in their classroom or out in the field. How can faculty in all areas integrate aspects of pastoral practice into their work?

Third, most faculty have little experience in assessing integrating work. Many rely on the vertical movement toward a capstone or exam, but this is not the only strategy for capturing student learning. How can faculty build assessment into courses that are linked to curricular goals? What are the best ways to capture integrating work among faculty and students?

Fourth, each model added significantly to the workload of faculty as well as the time and work of clergy and supervisors who are part of these programs. What is realistic faculty involvement in contextual education, service learning, and immersion experiences?

Fifth, integrating work requires more time, resources, and intentionality on the part of a faculty. What competencies do faculty need to be able to do integrating work? Clearly, a plan can be too ambitious and outpace a faculty's competencies. What is too much, and at what point is a plan too ambitious for the skills and abilities of a faculty?

Sixth, in schools with multiple degree programs, ministry students are not the only students for which faculty are responsible. How does integrating work happen across degree programs, especially when students are in the same courses?

PART 3

Courses

11

Integrating Work at the Course Level

Gordon S. Mikoski

Faculty members engage in course design or redesign that emphasizes integrating work for several reasons. Outside pressures—usually from changing standards of accrediting bodies—can stimulate instructors to increase their efforts to make meaningful connections in the classroom. Sometimes student interest or demand inspires faculty members to overhaul courses in a more integrating direction. Changing landscapes of professional practice and context can also stimulate increased attention to integrating work at the course level. In some cases, developments in an academic's field of expertise can lead to course development or revision that gives higher profile to integrating trajectories. Whatever the motivation, much of the freight of integrating work in theological education takes place in the way courses are designed and carried out.

The degree to which such integrating concerns function in courses varies considerably. While many courses have at least one explicit integrating dimension (for example, courses that require learners to make meaningful connections between subject matter and the practice of ministry), some courses—often due to the nature of the subject matter—have only limited integrating emphasis. Upper-level departmental capstone courses or "issues and problems" courses usually contain significant integrating dimensions. While not all courses need to have the same degree of commitment to this issue, many, if not most, courses could be significantly strengthened by greater attentiveness and intentionality to this set of pedagogical concerns.[1]

Courses that help learners develop facility in integrating activities vary in the way the task is defined. Integrating work at the course level can emphasize making connections between various areas within one body of knowledge or discipline, as in the case of a course in early church history that helps learners make meaningful links between material culture, liturgical practice, theological beliefs, and political context in a particular region and period in history. Courses can also help learners make connections across disciplinary lines, as in the case of an Old Testament course that introduces various methods of interpretation that could contribute to preaching practices or approaches to religious education. Some courses use ministerial leadership as an organizing principle for drawing diverse knowledge to bear on one or more ministry settings. Still other offerings call upon learners to correlate key theological themes and issues with important aspects of their lives, self-definition, or spiritual practices. Although the way integrating is conceived can vary considerably across a curriculum, helping learners make meaningful connections between different kinds of knowledge and experience that previously might have been treated separately tends to promote breadth of vision, flexibility of judgment, and maturity of character.

The highly rewarding work of course design or redesign in service of this larger integrating vision generally has more satisfying results when instructors exercise educational imagination in relation to five interlocking elements that need to be considered both individually and in an integrated way in course design:

---

1. The sequencing of courses in a curriculum for a particular degree program that address the integrating process also varies. Some existing courses that give pervasive attention to this issue have a capstone function and, therefore, fall in the latter part of the sequence of courses in a degree program. However, some theological schools that hope to foster habits of mind and to develop skills relevant to integrating work throughout the curriculum take a different approach. They foreground integrating tasks at the beginning of the program and emphasize the development of relevant concepts and skills throughout a degree's sequence of courses. In such cases, an integrating thread can spiral through several courses in the beginning, middle, and end of degree program. In principle, there is no reason why each course in a degree program could not give significant attention to the integrating task. For further discussion of the way the integrating task can function in the curriculum as a whole, see Kathleen Cahalan's chapter "Integrating Dynamics in the Seminary Curriculum" in this volume.

1. Aims, goals, and objectives

2. Context

3. Roles of the teacher and learner

4. Curricular content

5. Methods of instruction

Each of these elements conditions and influences every other in course design or redesign. The integrating project at the course level cannot focus on only one element (for example, curricular content) in order to work effectively. The aims and the context exert shaping influence on the dynamic interaction of subject matter and instructional methods, which in turn also shape commitments about the roles of the teacher and the learner in the educational process. In principle, one can begin with any one of these elements and work one's way toward the others. In practice, it is usually best to begin with a careful consideration of aims and context ("from above" and "from below") as the larger frame within which the other elements receive appropriate treatment.

The case studies offered in part 3 provide some generative possibilities for promoting effective integrating work at the course level. Before turning to the cases, some brief consideration of each of the five interlocking elements in relation to the larger integrating concern can help both with the analysis of the cases and with stimulating educational imaginations when theological educators design or redevelop courses.

Aims, Goals, and Objectives

Theological education is teleologically oriented. Theological schools work toward an eschatological vision of reconciliation and harmony between God, human beings, and all creation through the education and formation of competent, caring, and capable leaders for Christian communities. Effective theological education serves God's redeeming work in the world and, we hope, contributes something to the final integration of all things in God's reign. Whether at the level of the institution, the curriculum, or courses, all integrating work in theological education needs to keep in view this ultimate horizon in which God will ultimately bring all things into dynamic and life-sustaining wholeness.

At the level of course design and implementation, larger teleological concerns provide the background for working toward the realization of immediate and intermediate educational ends. Most courses have four to six learning outcomes for learners. Those outcomes focus on what learners should be able to understand, do, or perceive in relation to a focal concern of the course. Many courses will have learning outcomes that include one or more aspects of the integrating task. In other courses, all the outcomes will have to do with central aspects of integrating work. On the most immediate scale, individual learning sessions that make up a particular course can include specific learning objectives explicitly focused on an integrating aspect. In Emily Click's chapter, for example, we find a cluster of learning goals that address several dimensions of the integrating project.

In theological education today, it never suffices to operate solely on the basis of educational intentions about aims and goals. Theological educators must also pay serious and sustained attention to the assessment of learning that has actually occurred in relation to stated goals and objectives. This also applies to integrating work at the course level. Ways of gauging the degree to which learners have attained learning goals and objectives pertinent to those aspects of the integrating task, which is specified in the course design and incarnated in the execution of the course, must play a prominent role in the educational cycle, particularly with respect to course (re)design. Assessment data relevant to the degree of the integrating project's effectiveness can arise from metalevel analysis of final papers and projects, especially when using grading rubrics that include criteria related to assessment work. Portfolio assessment works particularly well for this purpose. Random sampling of several course artifacts while using a rubric designed specifically for integrating work can also yield important results. Depending upon how well they are designed, student course evaluations can also provide important insights about the ways in which the integrating aspects of the course were effective. Several cases of course redesign offered in part 3 grew out of an instructor's grappling with the significance of assessment data that arose from versions of a course in which integrating work was either largely absent or not sufficiently developed.

Context

Theological education never occurs in the abstract. It always takes place in particular sociocultural settings and institutions populated by complex and multidimensional people. Each theological school has a unique history and ethos. The zip code, the predominant instructional language or languages, the ecclesial heritage, the location and layout of the spaces, as well as the cast of characters in faculty, student body, and administration of a theological school all shape the conditions under which integrating takes place at the course level.

Theologically speaking, context matters a great deal in education for ministry inasmuch as human life unfolds only in specific situations and never in rarified abstraction. Moreover, the decisive salvific action of God in Jesus Christ by the power of the Holy Spirit occurred in scandalous particularity with regard to time, place, and social context. In short, context matters for theological education.

Not all integrating at the course level will occur in the physical space of the theological school classroom. Some of this work can take place off-site through field trips, retreats, cross-cultural immersion experiences, or travel seminars. Sometimes this work occurs best in the intentional juxtaposition of the theological school's context and some other context of life and learning. The interplay between the liminal space of a classroom and a textured life situation arising from exposure to a context outside the school can set the stage for generative connections between the somewhat abstracted conceptual model and the thickly interwove textures of daily life.

Integrating at the course level can also take place in a digital learning environment. Either as courses offered completely online or as hybrids (a combination of digitally mediated distance learning and face-to-face contact), integrating themes and learning activities can work effectively. Edward Foley's case in part 3 offers a credible and proven example of how such work can take place in a digital learning environment. Much work in the future regarding issues of integrating will involve combinations of real and virtual contexts. The key to success with the integrating project in these kinds of courses lies in intentional course design and vigilant execution of the course. Conversely, lack of intention in planning for the integrating aspect of digital learning courses will result in even more fragmentation and disconnection than might be the case in pervasively face-to-face courses.

Roles of Teacher and Learners

Within the dynamics of a particular course, the contexts experienced in the learning environment by the instructor and the students also exert significant impact on the way in which integrating is realized. Each person's life experience, personality, and current location on one's own integrating journey affects how integrating work is realized in a course. The same course design will play out differently from one year to the next because of the different dynamics learners and instructors bring into performing the course. One can truly never teach the same course twice. The experience always has an improvisational character, even with consistent structure from one offering of the course to the next. As faculty execute a course they have taught before, they must spend time reflecting on assessment data provided by previous learners as well as their own appraisal. They must also gather information—through activities such as personal sharing, pretests, or a brief in-class writing assignment—about individual learners at the beginning of a course that will help establish a baseline of existing knowledge, learning interests, and vocational trajectory, which provide clues for adapting the subject matter and instructional methods of the course in order to maximize meaningful connections.

Establishing a healthy learning community that emphasizes the integrating project involves appropriate personal disclosure and modeling by the instructor. By sharing appropriately from the instructor's own life experience and intellectual journey, the learners have such work modeled for them, and the instructor begins to establish a learning climate characterized by reflection, personal engagement, and dialogue. Because integrating depends heavily on the initiative and work of the learner, the instructor functions best as coach or catalyst rather than dispenser of all wisdom, emphasizing more the "guide on the side" than the "sage on the stage." The instructor also promotes this work on the part of learners when she poses generative questions for reflection or suggests possible connections that students do not see or might see only dimly. It cannot be stressed enough that integrating takes place most effectively in a constructivist orientation in which the learner does the heavy lifting of making connections with the support and guidance of the teacher.[2]

---

2. Constructivism refers to an orientation to learning in which the learner actively makes meaning out of the interplay of her or his prior knowledge and new information or experiences. Instructors cannot do the work of learning for the learner, nor can the instructor simply transfer knowledge into the framework of the learner. The roots of this approach to the active construction of knowledge by the learner lie in the epistemologies of Immanuel Kant and G. W. F. Hegel, run through the educational vision of John Dewey, and come to fruition in contemporary neuroscience and educational psychology as well as several liberationist pedagogies.

The role of the learner, then, has determinative significance in ii___ grating work in courses. Instructors cannot make learners undertake this task; only learners can effectively make the necessary connections that promote greater, deeper, and more lasting connections between subject matter, self-concept, spirituality, and vocation. Making such connections at the course level works most effectively if students see themselves as in charge of their own learning as emerging ministerial leaders. For effective integrating to take place, learners have to possess a sense of agency and voice to establish significant and relevant connections between things that may have been previously separated or never connected in their experience of theological education.

It should be noted that not all learners want to take charge of their own learning. Even among those who do, one can often find resistance to learning that has an integrative character—particularly if the learner has not had much experience or occasion to engage in such work. In such cases, the instructor has to play the role of encourager or even prodder. Providing a safe space in which to take risks—perhaps small at first—in the direction of making meaningful connections can help aversive or resistant learners to try their hand at this work. Rewarding the smallest of steps in the desired direction with affirmation can open up creative possibilities for even the most recalcitrant integrators.

As with aims and context, the roles of the teacher and the learner in theological education matter a great deal at the level of particular courses. What people experience in their interactions with one another in relation to power and agency profoundly influences the kind of integrating that takes place in courses and the degree to which it develops.

Curricular Content

The content of a course has a key role to play in promoting the integrating process. Curriculum theorist Elliot Eisner argues that all schools—and, by extension, all courses—actually teach three things simultaneously: the explicit, the implicit, and the null curriculum.[3] The explicit curricular content pertains to the subject matter mapped out in a course syllabus. Often focused on topics like leadership, such courses provide students with opportunities to learn frameworks and to develop skills that will enable them to make meaningful connections among the various other courses

3. Eisner, *Educational Imagination*, 87–107.

they have taken over the trajectory of a degree program. Experiences in field education or internships sometimes play a role in the integrating work of capstone courses. These courses tend to emphasize reflective engagement with the sum total of what learners have experienced in the school to that point. Sometimes, they also provide experiences or case studies that help learners build intentional bridges of understanding and practice with actual situations of ministry. Some capstone courses also function as the pinnacle of a disciplinary arch that coordinates the various courses taken in a particular discipline or department. Theological schools that emphasize the importance of integrating across the curriculum will sometimes offer courses in which concepts and skills relevant for integrating work occur at the beginning and in the middle of the student's journey through a degree program, not just at the end of the journey.

Explicit curriculum, with respect to the integrating task in theological education, has a much broader scope than simply capstone courses. Course topics and outcomes of various kinds can and should lift up the central importance for learners of making meaningful connections between elements such as subject matter, intellectual disciplines, persons, ministry, society, spirituality, and the wider cosmos. Nothing in creation or redemption stands in utter and complete isolation. Less like independent atoms and more like extended and overlapping networks, all things exist in connection with other things. Full and deep consideration of any particular topic requires learners to make meaningful connections with other topics or realities at the course level.

Implicit curricular content has to do with subject matter communicated by the manner in which the course is taught, including the emotional climate fostered by the teacher and the use of space in the learning environment. A teacher who models integrative thinking or demonstrates integrating skills can teach relevant curricular content as much as the explicit content of a course. Of course, the reverse can also take place: the teacher's lack of understanding or skill relating to integrating work can convey more content about integrating than a lecture or assigned readings the teacher might give to the learner. The chapter by Jeffrey Jones in part 3 illustrates how the teacher models integrative thinking by the way in which he both redesigns a course and positions himself within the execution of the course. When the emotional and physical climate as well as the processes and power dynamics of a course function in congruence with the explicit subject matter of the course, deep and even transformative learning of an integrating nature will likely take place.

Somewhat counterintuitively, the null curriculum also teaches powerfully in any given course. The null curriculum teaches by virtue of what content is omitted from focal consideration or by what processes are excluded in a course.[4] For example, a course on ministerial leadership that never addresses matters relevant to the integrating process actually teaches something about the integrating dimension of the subject matter. Unfortunately, making integrating work part of the null curriculum is all too prevalent in theological education founded upon Enlightenment or modernist principles. This book came into being, in part, to shift the integrating task from the null to the explicit curriculum in theological schools.

Theologically, curricular content matters a great deal in education for ministry. Taking cues from Augustine, the explicit curriculum of God's love for humanity in Jesus Christ and one's response of love for God, self, and neighbor has to correspond to loving methods of instruction administered by a loving teacher in order for the transformative character of grace to have full sway.[5] In the end, love is the inner meaning and the highest significance of integrating work in theological education. It might not be a great stretch to say that to relegate integrating processes to the null curriculum runs the risk of omitting the transforming power of divine love from a course.

Methods of Instruction

The ways by which learners encounter and interact with course content matters as much as the curricular content itself when considering the integrating role of courses in a theological school. Considerations of instructional method have important links with the implicit and null curriculums discussed above, because the ways in which learners encounter subject matter teach as much about integrating as does the explicit curricular content of a course.

---

4. This should not be confused with poor pedagogy or the unfortunate effects of an uncongenial learning environment. "Null curriculum" pertains to what is omitted or excluded for consideration. For more on this concept, see Eisner, *Educational Imagination*, 97–100.

5. Augustine, *First Catechetical Instruction*, 36.

Instructional theorists Hellmut R. Lang and David N. Evans have identified five major families of instructional methods: direct, indirect, independent, collaborative, and experiential.[6] Instructional methods exist within each of these clusters that can promote effective learning in relation to the integrating task.

In the *direct* instructional family—often featuring lecture or video presentation—learners encounter subject matter related to integrating work in concepts or demonstrations that highlight key frameworks or skills pertinent to this dimension of theological education. Learners hear or see something that helps them grasp something of the importance, dynamics, or challenges involved in making meaningful connections within a discipline, between disciplines, and between disciplinary knowledge and vocational or spiritual life. To enhance the effectiveness of learning in this family of instructional methods, teachers need to provide ample opportunities for learners to ask questions and to try out the new information conveyed to them by lecture or demonstration. Of the five families of instructional methods identified by Lang and Evans, the methods in this family run the greatest risks of having a disjunction between explicit and implicit curricular content primarily because the instructor does most of the work and the connections made between areas of knowledge or experience are only received—not established by—the learner.

The *indirect* family of instructional methods emphasizes the importance of learner-initiated and conducted inquiry into questions relevant to integrating work. Methods in this family often allow learners to pursue questions or interests in a minimally or semistructured manner through case studies, concept mapping, or guided inquiry.[7] In addition to shifting much of the locus of instructional authority to the learner, these methods work best when the teacher legitimates divergent learning outcomes.[8] For example, using cases that have no single right answer can help teams of learners establish meaningful connections as part of a proposed solution and give reasoned accounts of those connections to other students in the class who may have developed alternate solutions.[9]

---

6. Lang and Evans, *Models, Strategies, and Methods*, 335–473.

7. Ibid., 368–83.

8. Divergent learning outcomes allow many possible answers or outcomes. By contrast, convergent learning outcomes stress the importance of coming to the "right" answer or outcome.

9. For further treatment of teaching through cases, see Ellet, *Case Study Handbook*.

The *independent* family of instructional methods similarly puts the emphasis on learner initiative and motivation. Here, the learner works to develop a project or a paper that provides an opportunity to consolidate and express integrative learning regarding a particular issue. For example, a course on leadership in ministry may require learners to write a paper or develop some form of creative expression that demonstrates the learner's integrative understanding and skill in relation to a key aspect of leadership.

Collaborative instructional methods call for two or more students to learn, teach, or express something relevant to the understanding and skills relevant to integrating work. In this family of instructional methods, groups of learners encounter, produce, or present content themselves. In these approaches, the learning takes place through some form of peer interaction with each other and with the subject matter. This family of instructional methods—featuring techniques like panels, role plays, round table discussion, jigsaw teaching, reciprocal peer instruction, and problem-solving groups—works particularly well in promoting integrating work.

Experiential instructional methods like case studies, field trips, role plays, and simulations also work exceptionally well for fostering integrating work in theological education. Merely having an intense or rich raw experience, however, will not usually promote integrative insight. Raw experiences must include some element of effective preparation as well as structured reflection subsequent to or even in the midst of the experience. David Kolb, the most well-known educational theorist of experiential learning, argues that following a raw experience, learners must work through several indispensible phases of processing the experience: reflective description of what was experienced; analysis of key insights and principles; identification of transferable learning; and implementation of new learning.[10] When learners work through all phases involved in the experiential learning cycle, the educational payoff for integrating work can be quite high.

The ways by which learners encounter subject matter in a course has theological significance related to the integrating task because learners acquire as much from the processes of instruction as they do from the nature of the subject matter itself. As with the Incarnation, the means of communication and encounter matter as much as the core content to be conveyed. To push this one step farther, subject matter has to be incarnated through particular means and processes of interaction.

10. Kolb, *Experiential Learning.*

Resources

Attending to the five interlocking elements of education—aims, goals, and objectives; context; roles of teacher and learner; curricular content; and instructional methods—when seeking to design integrating work at the course level requires both educational imagination and not a little trial and error. Several resources can aid the course (re)design in relation to the integrating project. Many theological educators have found two resources particularly helpful. Grant Wiggins and Jay McTighe's work *Understanding by Design* calls for a educational imagination at the course level in which the instructor engages in reverse engineering.[11] Instead of beginning by carving up curricular content (thereby running the risk of "content tyranny"), Wiggins and McTighe urge instructors to begin with the learning outcomes that they want students to take away from the course. After the instructor establishes a clear sense of the educational outcomes for the learners, Wiggins and McTighe then call for the instructor to identify ways by which the learners will demonstrate what they have actually learned about course content or the skills they have developed. Only after getting clear on these two aspects of the course can instructors turn their attention to the selection of curricular content and instructional methods. This "backward design" approach to course (re)design works very effectively, and it often has appeal only after failures in course design that begin with "covering content" and leaving instructional methods, assessment of learning, and outcomes as an afterthought. The backward design approach offered by Wiggins and McTighe can prove exceptionally valuable for course (re)design in relation to integrating work. In fact, this approach virtually ensures that learner outcomes, assessment procedures, curricular content, and instructional methods will themselves form a well-integrated and balanced whole. It cuts down on extraneous content and mismatched content and methods.

L. Dee Fink's course design framework is the second resource used by participants in the authors' seminar.[12] Fink's model—used in Click's and Jones's cases in part 3—provides a particularly compelling approach to course (re)design, integrating courses in two senses. Like Wiggins and McTighe (and sometimes interfacing directly with their work), Fink provides a step-by-step approach to educational imagination such that all the pieces for a course can be made to fit together in a holistic manner. It functions

11. Wiggins and McTighe, *Understanding by Design*.
12. Fink, *Creating Significant Learning Experiences*.

as "a model of integrated course design."[13] Fink's model emphasizes "significant learning experiences" in which each learning component has an intentional purpose and relates appropriately to other parts of the course.

Fink's model also promotes integrating work *in a second way*. He includes integration as one of six core elements for handling subject matter. Fink holds that an integrating vision must become one of the six dimensions for the content of any given course: "When students are able to see and understand the connections between different things, an important kind of learning has occurred. Sometimes they make connections between specific ideas, between whole realms of ideas, between people, or between different realms of life (say, between school and work or between school and leisure life)."[14] Fink argues that promoting such integrating work as part of the warp and woof of the explicit curriculum helps learners develop a sense of power or agency. He holds that learners develop intellectual and personal strength when integrating is made part of the learning outcomes for every course.

Overview of the Chapters

Part 3 features five cases of integrating work at the course level. Each of the instructors undertook course redesign in order to incorporate what they learned from trial and error and with the explicit purpose of making the instructional content and methods more integrative. Emily Click's chapter uses the course (re)design framework provided by Fink to improve a course on ministerial leadership. David Jenkins's chapter demonstrates the role of *dis*integrating work as a prerequisite process in relation to a travel seminar to the borderlands of Arizona and Sonora, Mexico. Also demonstrating how Fink's framework can function as a valuable resource for course (re) design, Jeffrey Jones's chapter focuses on the dynamics of ministerial leadership for small churches. Jeffery Tribble's chapter chronicles the challenges of integrating work in relation to an introductory course dealing with the complex dynamics of race and gender. Edward Foley's chapter explores integrating in an online learning environment. While not exhaustive of the range of possibilities for promoting integrating work at the course level, these five cases provide helpful models of ways this work can be carried out in individual courses.

13. Ibid., xiii.
14. Ibid., 31.

Bibliography

Augustine. *The First Catechetical Instruction [De Catechizandis Rudibus]*. Translated by Joseph P. Christopher. Ancient Christian Writers 2. New York: Newman, 1978.

Eisner, Elliot W. *The Educational Imagination: On the Design and Evaluation of School Programs*. 3rd ed. Upper Saddle River, NJ: Pearson, 2002.

Ellet, William. *The Case Study Handbook: How to Read, Discuss, and Write Persuasively about Cases*. Boston: Harvard Business School, 2007.

Fink, L. Dee. *Creating Significant Learning Experiences: An Integrated Approach to Designing College Courses*. Jossey-Bass Higher and Adult Education Series. San Francisco: Jossey-Bass, 2003.

Joyce, Bruce, Marsha Weil, and Emily Calhoun. *Models of Teaching*. 9th ed. Boston: Pearson, 2014.

Kolb, David A. *Experiential Learning: Experience as the Source of Learning and Development*. 2nd ed. Upper Saddle River, NJ: Prentice Hall, 2015.

Lang, Hellmut R., and David N. Evans. *Models, Strategies, and Methods for Effective Teaching*. Boston: Pearson 2006.

Ornstein, Allan C., and Francis P. Hunkins. *Curriculum: Foundations, Principles, and Issues*. 5th ed. Boston: Pearson, 2009.

Wiggins, Grant, and Jay McTighe. *Understanding by Design*. 2nd ed. Alexandria, VA: Association for Supervision and Curriculum Development, 2005.

Woolfolk, Anita. *Educational Psychology*. 12th ed. Boston: Pearson, 2012.

12

Using Adaptive Leadership in Redesigning a Leadership Course

EMILY CLICK

At Harvard Divinity School, I taught a Leadership and Administration course in essentially the identical format for seven years. Based on student feedback and my own dissatisfaction, I decided to redesign the course to make it more dynamic and integrating by using L. Dee Fink's twelve-step plan of course design.[1] Vibrant experiential learning, innovative community projects, and significantly improved student evaluations evidenced the effects of the redesigned learning process. The pedagogy became the message. New ways of engaging students enabled them to absorb material central to the course's intended focus.

A new paradigm of leadership now drives the course. Drawing from Ronald Heifetz and his colleagues, leaders engage communities in "mobilizing for adaptive change."[2] Rather than leaders providing answers, being charismatic, or acting as domineering figureheads leaders structure dynamic community-wide engagement in making meaning. In adaptive change, leaders pace the rate of engagement with complex problems. The leader's responsibility is to maintain vision and perspective on problems while steering a group's carefully paced engagement with the issues at hand. Courses teaching this version of leadership must enable those leaders to build communities. An ideal leadership course would enable students to be-

---

1. Fink, *Creating Significant Learning Experiences.*
2. Heifetz et al., *Practice of Adaptive Leadership.*

gin understanding the multiple layers involved when leading a community to work on complex challenges.

During the previous years of teaching the course, I followed an established pedagogical paradigm. Roughly sketched, the course structure called for me to master the subject area of leadership and administration, to select appropriate texts, and then to present key ideas to students. I sequenced the order of key ideas through PowerPoint presentations, lectures, and in-class discussions. Students demonstrated their mastery of important ideas by speaking in class or by writing excellent papers.

In spite of presenting materials that compellingly captured new models of leadership, the course consistently fell short of its goals. Students demonstrated continued allegiance to old paradigms of leadership when they were asked to lead class discussions or make in-class presentations. The pedagogy was undermining the intended central message of the course. When as the resident leader I perpetuated the model of a leader as providing all answers and dominating the generation of ideas, the intended purpose was subverted. By using pedagogies characterized as a "banking model" by Paulo Freire, I created an environment in which learners experienced the implicit value of maintaining passivity relative to an individual leader who holds the answers to all problems.[3] The old lecture-based pedagogy (dressed in the new clothes of PowerPoint) actually conveyed an underlying, undermining message: the new ideas about leadership would not work in practice. The teaching strategies employed trumped the new ideas conveyed in lectures. Pedagogy based in expert professors transferring content-based knowledge to passive learners powerfully communicates implicitly that the role of leader is to provide expertise and answers.

Shifting the Course Design

The former paradigm for course design could be captured by a metaphor: the professor built courses the way a train engineer couples train cars together. Designing a course meant artfully stringing along discreet elements of the subject matter. The major question in developing a syllabus was, how do I order various elements required to master the subject of a course? The usual tools were to assign readings thoughtfully on relevant texts and test student knowledge. In-class activities were usually brief question-and-answer sessions about the central issues presented by texts within each

3. Freire, *Pedagogy of the Oppressed*, 53.

individual element of the overall course. However, this contrasting, new model for how to create significant learning experiences radically decoupled every aspect of the former approach to course design.

Fink begins the new model with three integrated steps: "One very important feature of this model of course design is the proposition that . . . three initial decisions need to be integrated: the learning goals, the teaching and learning activities, and the feedback and assessment must all reflect and support each other." The professor begins with goals, imagines how to assess those goals, and moves right into activities that will enflesh such goals. The texts, while important, are still on the sidelines. The professor's expertise relative to influential texts is assumed. The course design demands that such mastery first moves into selecting learning goals prior to winnowing the field of textual materials.

The new goals for the leadership course resulted from an extended "dreaming session" at the beginning of the redesign process. Fink advises teachers to start by paying attention to relevant situational factors, to particular attributes of the students, and to where the course fits into the larger ecology of the curriculum. I began the redesign by spending hours imagining what graduates of this course might experience as significant to ministerial leadership. The new course goals conveyed these ideas:

1. Leaders know their own moral compass, which guides their actions.

2. Leaders understand the connections between their own values, strengths, and immunities to change.

3. Leadership begins with humble listening (to self and to others as well as to new information).

4. Leaders pay attention to the complex layers of problems. This means they distinguish between technical and adaptive challenges. They attend to what matters most in each situation.

5. Leaders build groups motivated to sustain their work on adaptive problems. The leadership art of understanding human interactions, motivations, and fears plays a crucial role in developing groups' capacities for courageous action.

6. Leaders develop strategic approaches. Two crucial aspects of strategic leadership include developing a holding environment and pacing the engagement of the group with their problems.

7. Leaders shape meaning through shared processes.

Fink's next segment of course design focuses on developing a thematic structure. Note that unlike traditional course designs, the professor still has not compiled a traditional syllabus that lists texts in order of study. Instead, the professor works to build a teaching strategy that supports a thematic structure for the overall course. After the teaching strategies have been sketched, the learning activities are imagined. This radical upturning of the process embeds the wisdom that pedagogy teaches message. Each subject matter demands attendant teaching strategies and overall themes. For the leadership course, that theme was leaders build webs of communities that enable the stakeholders to mobilize problem-solving strategies. The pedagogy, therefore, needed to energize students to experience the power of community processes that surface and address implicit challenges in the learning community itself.

Only during the final segment of course planning does the professor address traditional issues such as grading, building a syllabus, and course evaluation. Delaying the production of a list of texts, tasks, and outcomes enables the professor to sit with the material and imagine what kinds of significant learning will generate desired outcomes for the course. Professors must frontload tremendous effort in course planning, which virtually quadruples the time expended at the early stage. However, intense initial planning frees up energies for highly productive class sessions throughout the semester and actually frees up flexibility in teaching. The well-developed awareness of what is at the core of the entire course enables greater agility for the professor to respond to student learning needs.

My new paradigm for the leadership course is to weave a web of collective learning, a stark contrast to the prior paradigm that resembled train construction. My new pedagogical process surfaces ways leaders can respect and utilize community members' capacities instead of dominating the process in the interests of arriving at a predetermined solution. The teacher's orientation to the class shifts radically, yet the teacher's role in no way diminishes in significance. Instead, the teacher nurtures a learning community in which key concepts are experienced as well as discussed. Teaching demonstrates ways a new model for leadership engages the power of mobilizing people for adaptive work. The train metaphor illustrates that flexibility can be experienced as going off the rails. The new, web-based image mirrors a central concept of adaptive leadership. By building a holding environment leaders enable groups to do the hard work of addressing challenges without easy answers.

Teaching the Redesigned Course

The overall themes of the course showed a flow between four major aspects of leadership: (1) leadership begins with listening, (2) leaders know their own moral compass, (3) leaders diagnose complex problems, and (4) leaders mobilize groups to build meaning. For each module there were assigned readings. These modules showed a high level schema within which students could organize their radically evolving models for ministerial leadership.

Each individual class session included an initial reflective exercise, followed by a collaborative learning experience done in small groups, after which the entire class usually engaged in discussion with free-flowing questions. Every student received an empty journal in which to write during the reflective exercises at the beginning of each class. The flow of the class session modeled the desired shift in understanding leadership: each week students moved from individualized ideation to partnered learning. Full participation during in-class exercises required that students master subject matter in advance of attending class. Therefore, those exercises needed to be engaging enough to motivate students to arrive prepared. The energy level during class consistently was so high that students reported they felt responsible not just for their own learning but also for supporting the learning of others in the collective learning environment.

The class itself became the focus for collaborative learning. Often students discussed case studies they had prepared in advance of class. Some weeks students debated a key concept, with teams representing various sides of an issue. Students identified their long-cultivated bias for individualized learning as they experienced the challenges of discussing crucial concepts in various small groups and in the larger classroom as a whole.

Homework assignments included writing prompts for the journals for each week. These assignments, which were additional to the start-of-class exercises, built in the reflective component Fink identifies as a crucial component of active learning. A web-based course site facilitated the students posting their reflections, upon which I commented each week. Another reflective component came from the assignment for each student to select a spiritual practice to focus on during the semester. The spiritual practice could be the required journaling or something else of their choosing. These exercises served purposes including three of Fink's course goals: learning how to learn, learning to care, and applying key concepts (through engaging a spiritual practice).[4]

While the class focused on experiential learning, it still included some exercises that enabled assessment of mastery of key subject content. For example, students wrote three short papers that demonstrated understanding of assigned texts. The format for these papers was traditional for academia: requiring an argument of a controversial thesis, footnotes, and excellent writing to receive a top grade. These assignments assured the course incorporated the old maxim that "good writing makes for good thinking." All combined, the writing exercises reinforced the principle that excellence in leadership includes good thinking, which often arises from reflection.

Students also worked in pairs to interview a community leader of their choice. The pairs gave an in-class, jointly prepared presentation about what they learned from their leader. Pairs then wrote a five-page paper integrating assigned readings with whatever lessons they learned through the interview. They were required to quote at least one other group's presentation in this paper. The assignment assured that students would experience a way of conveying material that incorporated respectful partnership with another leader (the other student) as well as the discipline of listening not just to leaders but also to their student colleagues.

Pairs experienced all the real challenges of addressing problems that arise while working with others, which was quite different from the usual student experience of producing their individual best. One team of learners integrated course goals by humorously creating a fine and reward system through which they could nondefensively name their points of friction. One member, chronically late, fined herself upon being tardy. The other member, chronically uptight and judgmental, fined herself for losing her cool. Once the project was completed, they treated themselves by going out, which was financed through the system they created.

The final project called for creating an integrative portfolio. Students reviewed all their journal entries, their papers, their leader interview, and in-class exercises. They wrote a paper about what they learned in the course. They applied what they had learned to a new case study. Then they wrote a one-page letter to next year's class participants. Students often said that only through the iterative process of reflection did they finally realize how defensive they were at the outset of the course. They realized that by

4. Fink, *Creating Significant Learning Experiences*, 83–84.

discussing frictions and difficulties they relaxed and unleashed their imaginative selves. Students were amazed to discover the creative power hidden behind conflicts. Instead of emerging from the course with reinforced allergies to addressing problems, they felt equipped to dive into the realm of real-life complexity by orchestrating the conflict and making crucial issues discussable.

Giving the Problem to the People to Whom It Belongs: Creating a Learning Environment

Students spent an early class period creating a class agreement about norms for classroom behavior. Students prepared in advance how to express their own learning preferences. The class then discussed their answers to questions such as these: Is it okay to check e-mail or to text during class? What if a class member shares something confidential and someone else shares that publicly? Is it okay to come and participate in class when you have done none of the required preparation? This was the first time most students had been offered the opportunity to take responsibility for their own learning environment.

This exercise of creating a language of public agreement served several purposes.[5] It embodied the learning in Heifetz's seminal leadership text about giving the work over to the people. Heifetz recommends that leaders decide to whom the problem belongs, and then lead in a way that enables effective engagement by those to whom the problem belongs. He contrasts this with leaders owning the problem and trying to solve it on behalf of others.

Feedback and Assessment

The redesigned course incorporated multiple layers of feedback and assessment. Often an exercise incorporated assessment in ways students might not otherwise notice. For example, students received feedback on the quality of their own presentations when they learned that others had quoted their in-class presentation when writing their papers. Late in the course, students wrote about leadership strengths they observed in other students.

---

5. I have loosely based this exercise on a chapter in Kegan and Laskow Lahey's *How the Way We Talk*.

This provided assessment: learners developed a sense of how they are perceived, a matter of great impact for every leader. During the final session, when students read the comments made by others, faces shined with delight in discovering the ways in which they had been seen. Students who usually sat passively experienced themselves as actors who make a difference. The purpose for this was tied to the content for the course: leaders must learn how to harvest relevant aspects of what can be an overwhelming array of opinions about how they approach problem solving. These assessments upended the usual assumption that the professor is the superior judge of how students have engaged in learning with other students.

Conclusion: Nondefensive Teaching Can Be the Most Rewarding

In conclusion, this form of teaching is much more risky than simply presenting material in lectures or through structured discussions proceeding from carefully crafted PowerPoint presentations. The professor must be intently observant throughout every class period. Such intense participation enables highlighting spontaneous moments when course goals surface through learning activities. As a result, this course also became a highly rewarding one to teach.

In general, students rise to the occasion when they are treated respectfully and are trusted with higher levels of responsibility. In the end, the course evaluations for this redesigned course were dramatically improved. Students recognized that the risks taken in the classroom were undertaken on behalf of learning relevant to this course.

The Fink course design process helps teachers identify their dreams for how taking the class will make a difference to students one year later. This sharpens the identification of which are the most crucial concepts. Working through which concepts are foundational to others allows a conceptualization of how to build a learning theme rather than randomly stringing parts together. Furthermore, learning exercises that reinforce learning experienced in prior modules is made possible with sufficient advance planning. When learning builds upon prior learning, students report a far higher level of significance from taking the course.

Finally, this experiential type of course requires interpretation. Just as leaders must learn how to disappoint people at a rate they can stand, so must professors. Students expect to hear lectures and sit as passive learners.

Professors must create an inviting atmosphere that includes interpreting why students are being asked to take more responsibility for their own learning. Such expectations better prepare students to become effective beyond the college or graduate school experience. However, the need for them to invest fully in every class for experiential exchanges may be unfamiliar and therefore demands orientation. Students who are engaged learners are, on the whole, happy learners. They are also more likely to long recall such significant learning experiences.

Bibliography

Fink, L. Dee. *Creating Significant Learning Experiences: An Integrated Approach to Designing College Courses.* Jossey-Bass Higher and Adult Education Series. San Francisco: Jossey-Bass, 2003.

Freire, Paulo. *Pedagogy of the Oppressed.* New York: Continuum, 1994.

Heifetz, Ronald, et al. *The Practice of Adaptive Leadership: Tools and Tactics for Changing Your Organization and the World.* Boston: Harvard Business Press, 2009.

Kegan, Robert, and Lisa Laskow Lahey. *How the Way We Talk Can Change the Way We Work: Seven Languages for Transformation.* San Francisco: Jossey-Bass, 2001.

13

A Travel Seminar and the Unfamiliar Self

DAVID O. JENKINS

The practical theology course that inspired this reflection is a travel seminar, The Church on the Border, which I teach at Candler School of Theology, Emory University. In this chapter I will examine integrating work common to travel seminars as well as the experiences of disintegration that students often experience when they are intensely immersed in unfamiliar contexts, cultures, and landscapes. Similar dislocation, disintegration, and integration can happen when students do field education in prisons or homeless shelters, with refugees or those with profound disabilities, or in cross-racial settings. It could be argued that some level of disintegration is critical for authentic integrating, for the transformation of convictions and self-knowledge.

The course is taught in the spring semester so that a trip to southern Arizona and northern Sonora, Mexico, can occur during spring break, roughly midway through the term. Students study economic, agriculture, and immigration policies and the effects of those policies on Mexican and US communities and congregations, and they observe realities facing communities, congregations, and immigrants on both sides of the US–Mexico border. Students also explore their church's teaching and practices about immigration. The course is intended to enhance students' skills of moral and social analysis and strengthen their capacities as public theologians who are creative and strategic leaders in an increasingly diverse culture.

Our host on the border is BorderLinks, a nonprofit agency with offices in Tucson, Arizona, and Nogales, Sonora, whose mission is to "connect divided communities, raise awareness about the impact of border and immigration policies, and inspire action for social transformation."[1] Border-Links arranges homestays with Mexican host families, conversations with migrants preparing to cross the Sonoran Desert or those who have been captured and deported back to Mexico, US and Mexican federal agents, social justice agencies and movements, community organizers, and congregational leaders on both sides of the border. The agency organizes visits to federal detention centers, to the "fast track" federal trials of undocumented immigrants, and to South Side Presbyterian Church in Tucson, the founding church of the Sanctuary Movement and *No Mas Muertes* (No More Deaths). Following the trip to the border, Candler students meet in metro Atlanta with Hispanic residents, pastors, state legislators, and community leaders and have the opportunity to visit a detention center in South Georgia.

The course is designed to respond to Candler's mission "to educate faithful and creative leaders for the church's ministries throughout the world" and to address a number of the school's historic commitments to "teaching and learning to transform Christian congregations and public life; scholarship to inspire the production of knowledge in critical and collegial conversation with the traditions of both church and academy; and service to the world to form leaders dedicated to ministries of justice, righteousness, peace, and the flourishing of all creation."[2]

Congregational short-term mission teams, spiritual pilgrimages, and academic travel seminars are characterized by intense experiential learning. Research of short-term mission teams suggests that of the three components of that experience—the study and preparation, the trip itself, and the post-trip reflection and integration process—the first and third components are most critical. Not only will the site experiences be interpreted and enhanced through the learning prior to the trip, but the long-term transformative effects of the trip are often determined by the depth and duration of the post-trip reflection and integrating process.[3] Locating the travel experience in the middle of a semester-long course affords the opportunity

---

1. BorderLinks, http://www.borderlinks.org/.

2. Candler website and 2014–15 Candler catalog, 8–9.

3. Ver Beek, "The Impact of Short-Term Missions."

to prepare students for a new and complex social location and allows for a dialectic, integrative learning process on return.

As is the case with mission teams and pilgrimages, a typical travel seminar is marked by disintegration, a prerequisite for transformational growth. Traditional, institutional, and familiar integrating processes are interrupted—perhaps shocked—by the change of landscape; intense communal living and learning experience; and unfamiliar language, smells, climate, food, and daily routines. Our bodies are the first to disintegrate. Students experience the vulnerability that comes with a loss of familiar forms of control and power, loss of unconscious forms of knowing, and a loss of habituated patterns of navigating public, shared spaces, even the space of worship, when worship occurs in a different language, in a sanctuary lit by kerosene lamps, with unfamiliar music and unfamiliar bodily practices. Our capacity for salience is called into question. We no longer are certain what to do in most situations or how to learn what it is we ought to do, especially if we do not speak the language.

For many students, disintegration happens as a result of the loss of privacy and the physical demands of travel to the border: eating new food, perhaps sharing a latrine, sleeping in uncomfortable beds in strangers' homes, experiencing the heat or cold of the high desert, not knowing how to receive the hospitality that is offered, being escorted into a high-security detention center by armed guards, and all at five thousand feet. Body language is easily misinterpreted, as is humor. If technology is their primary way to gain access to resources and support systems, students become disoriented when they don't have access to their cell phone, the Internet, and social media.

They are often dislocated precisely as students. Traditional classrooms are replaced by living rooms, clinics, the central plaza, hotel lobbies, the swept ground under a shade tree, a sandy trail winding through cacti in the Sonoran Desert. Course instructors step aside as local residents—sometimes children, *campesinos*, undocumented migrants, or factory workers—become the teachers. Traditional texts are replaced by barrios, a border wall, a courtroom, a Pentecostal healing service, or a soccer game. Skills acquired over decades in academic and institutional settings are valued less than new skills and virtues such as collaboration, flexibility, patience, careful observation, and quiet listening, kindness, and humility. Students are often unclear what is expected of them, how they will be assessed, how they can succeed.

It is also not uncommon on international travel seminars for students to experience hostility directed to Americans, particularly if history suggests that the United States is responsible for the injustices local residents suffer. Students' assumptions, worldviews, and deeply held convictions about themselves, their country, and their religious tradition are often challenged.[4] At a point of disorientation and disintegration, students who are open to reforming these assumptions and convictions wonder who they are, what they actually believe, what they can do in response to this experience. They are more aware of how they have been shaped by their class and class values, by their social location within complex US cultures, and they begin to imagine new narratives for their lives. Their visceral reactions—their emotional and physical discomfort—can display a dissonance between what they have publically claimed and what they actually believe, whether those claims are about "the poor," themselves, their church, their country, or their God.[5]

Disintegration is often easy to observe. Some students begin to retreat from the group, both physically and emotionally. Often students revert to conversations common at home as they talk about their courses, basketball teams, favorite music, and favorite food. They resist being fully present to a reality that's difficult to interpret and integrate into their life experience and future plans. Familiar prayers, texts, and modes of interpretation, not to mention modes of behavior, are failing them. It's not unusual to watch tears flow as frustration, insecurity, and anger mount.

Students encounter an unfamiliar self and begin to search for the tools to integrate this emerging person with their history, self-image, and the perceptions others have of them. As one student declared, "I thought I knew how to hold it all together, but this new 'I' is unsure how to do that and even more uncertain how to hold it together in this place."

The travel seminar gives a mature faculty leader multiple opportunities to respond to students in pastoral ways, not rescuing them from vulnerable experiences but responding with kindness, patience, and wisdom.

---

4. Brelsford and Senior discuss this experience of "catching theology in action" and the process of making assumptions public in communal theological reflection in "Theological Thinking as Contextual Practice," in Brelsford and Rogers, *Contextualizing Theological Education*, 42–55.

5. Fulkerson, *Places of Redemption*. Fulkerson highlights the significance of visceral responses and embodied practices as means of examining deeply held claims and convictions that are tested when our bodies encounter the bodies of the other and the centrality of the body in redeeming habituated beliefs and practices.

Faculty can model ways of accompanying others in times of crisis, loss, disorientation, and loss of faith.

It is also an occasion in which a more integrated faculty person can model astute pedagogy of small group leadership. The experience of disorientation and disintegration affects the relationship students have with local residents and hosts, and affects the group dynamic. A more holistic response will engage the entire class in a communal response as students hold one another accountable to agreed-upon ways of relating, behaving, and processing their experiences. The hope is that the community of learners has been prepared for this group dynamic and given tools to assist them as a small group to respond. Many activities of congregational leadership involve small group leadership (teaching Sunday school and Bible studies, leading youth groups and spiritual direction groups, chairing committees, and so forth), so once again an integrated faculty person will model constructive small group leadership skills useful in these other contexts as well.

As noted earlier, the preparation for the trip and the post-trip integrating process are as significant to the learning experience as the trip itself. The formation of the class into an integrated learning community before leaving home—as much as is possible in six weeks—coupled with the ongoing reflection of the trip experience on return, are essential to transformation. Designing assignments that involve the entire class in analysis and implementation is one way of forging a communal learning environment. Inviting students on return to engage their learning with contexts and situations that require an integrating process that has coherency and familiarity is also productive. As students share their integrating projects with one another in class (not simply submit them to the instructor for evaluation), students once again experience a broader community of teachers like they had during the trip. Their youth group members, congregations, and fellow clergy respond to their projects in ways that contribute to an integrating process.

Disintegration and integration occur in bodies, individual physical bodies and communal, ecclesial, and political bodies. When individual students begin to decompensate in response to their disorientation, a well-integrated community of learners and leaders will provide individual support and a healthy process and space for integrating work to occur. Developing a community of learners begins before the class meets for the first time in January, with communication to students who enrolled in the course. The syllabus details expectations, anticipates struggles, and calls on

students to prepare themselves for an intense week of communal livi
learning. Once the class begins, time is set aside each week for comr
building that draws on students' gifts, strengths, and previous experiences
of collaboration, respect, inclusion, reconciliation, and care. The pedagogy
creates the opportunities for collective learning, for careful listening, for
critical disagreement and respectful resolution to conflict, while the professor steps back from the traditional role of expert. Films, documentaries,
food, music, guest speakers, literature, and weekly devotions are critical
elements for introducing students to a new culture and new modes of
thinking, worshiping, experiencing, and relating.

Engaging the body is central to the first movement of the pastoral
circle, a "circle of praxis" outlined by Joe Holland and Peter Henriot in their
introduction to social analysis as a theological practice.[6] Because the requirements of the border class include an action plan developed in response
to the integration of classroom learning and site learning, the pastoral circle
helps shape the communal, integrative process of designing an action as it
anticipates the communal response to new and disorienting experiences,
knowledge, and landscapes on the border. Holland and Henriot note that
this ongoing, four-movement process of social analysis is "related to what
has been called the 'hermeneutical circle,' or the method of interpretation
that sees new questions continually raised to challenge older theories by the
force of new situations."[7]

The first movement of the pastoral circle is insertion, in which one
engages the "lived experiences of individuals and communities."[8] To taste
food, hear and sing hymns in Spanish, watch documentaries of migrants,
interact with local residents who are undocumented, read journals and
other literature from *campesino* and migrant communities is a gentle form
of insertion that prepares students for the trip, the more intense experience
of insertion that is the trip.

Social analysis, theological reflection, and pastoral planning are the
movements that follow insertion. Social analysis not only calls students to
examine root causes of systemic injustice, it also calls students to greater
self-awareness of their own agency, access, and uses of power and privilege.
This second step of the pastoral circle is one that embodies hope and a

---

6. Holland and Henriot, *Social Analysis*, 8–10. See also Jenkins, chapter 9, in this
volume.

7. Ibid., 8.

8. Ibid.

theology of life, as the authors claim, while it raises students' consciousness about the world's suffering and oppression.

The third movement of the pastoral circle, theological reflection, is a dynamic opportunity for integrative work as students are asked to draw on church teaching, biblical texts and exegetical work, and their faithful understanding of situations in a communal, ecclesial process to better interpret the situation and their own lives.

Finally, students engage in the fourth stage, pastoral planning. The final class projects offer students the opportunity to engage their church communities as they integrate learning and experience, theology, particular ecclesial contexts, and their own evolving self-awareness in the design of an action plan.

Each step of the pastoral circle is a communal practice that continues to integrate learning from the previous movements into a rich understanding for action. Lived experiences inform a breadth of theological reflections from a variety of traditions; these inform the communal design of an action plan that subsequently draws the actors back into engagement and relationships with local residents, communities, and congregations. The process begins again. It is circular without a point of completion. The pastoral circle mirrors the circular, ongoing communal process of integration.

Another pedagogical resource that helps prepare students for the trip is a reflection on the border itself, or as Gary Gunderson describes the space, a boundary zone in which particular leadership skills, practical wisdom, and presence are required. According to Gunderson,

> boundary leadership is the practice of leadership in the boundary zone, the space in between settled zones of authority, where relationships are more fluid, dynamic, and itinerant . . . Boundary leaders are attracted to the broken, and broken-open, spaces in between formal structure and "legible" functioning. More than just being in between boundaries, and more than seeing the complex and turbulent reality of boundary zones, they consciously, intentionally seek to engage and influence the social networks alive in them. Boundary leadership . . . is thus critical for how leaders work with religious health assets in seeking the health of the public.[9]

When the border can be framed as a dynamic space of hopeful possibilities, students encounter the place with less anxiety and with eyes searching for opportunities. Integrating is, after all, a hope-filled, creative

9. Gunderson and Cochrane, *Religion and the Health of the Public*, 119–20.

experience, as all three steps of the pastoral circle exemplify. Prior to the trip when we discuss the skills and practical wisdom required of boundary leaders, and when we identify the multiple boundary zones students have already learned to navigate, students approach the border with greater confidence, then return to their familiar contexts having located a proposed action within a boundary zone with which they have experience. The relationship and integration of new and old experiences of boundary zones (some of which exist at Candler), of new and familiar spaces, and of new and familiar skills nurture an organic process that becomes a useful practice for the future.[10] After returning from a travel seminar, it is not uncommon to hear students declare, "My role at the women's prison each week for my contextual education work is clearer to me now that I've been to the border," or "I know better how to relate to my peers and professor in the New Testament class than before the trip."

When students return to Candler following the border trip, they are asked to collaborate with fellow students on an action plan that integrates learning across the semester with a particular audience and context, to engage the four movements of the pastoral circle, and to respond to a generative theme they experienced. It so happened that the most recent Church on the Border class was offered while Candler was completing construction of a new library building, which is attached to the primary classroom and office building. Between the two buildings, where the passageways would be located, were temporary plywood walls. Three first-year students chose the Candler community as their primary context and began to examine how Candler was itself a boundary zone. The temporary plywood walls became for them an opportunity to recreate the border wall between Mexico and the United States. After getting permission from the dean to paint the plywood walls, they set out to document how and why many Protestant seminaries in the United States have so few Hispanic students enrolled, and consequently why most mainline Protestant churches have ordained so few Hispanic women and men.

The wall became a place for educating the larger Candler community about this issue and the number of migrants who have died in the Sonoran Desert as a result of US policies. The stories or photos of some of those migrants who died were posted on a map of the desert trails. The Candler border wall became a sacred space as students were encouraged to stop

10. Throughout, I have relied on MacIntyre's understanding of a practice from *After Virtue*, 187, 191.

and pray at the wall for those making the crossing, to recite Psalm 23 from the perspective of a migrant making the desert crossing, and to seek God's wisdom as they pastored congregations and communities where undocumented sisters and brothers lived and worshiped. Resources and additional information were available to anyone who requested it.

Another team of students, each of whom was working part time in rural Appalachian congregations, developed curriculums to teach youth and adults about the complex immigration situation using biblical narratives of migration, diaspora, alienation, and pilgrimage. Another team designed strategies to engage congregations in lobbying the Georgia state legislature in response to proposed state legislation. Whatever the action plan, students had to do the communal work as they followed the pastoral circle movements, highlighting the theological reflection for their class presentation. As students articulated theological claims—about the Incarnation, about the nature and mission of the church, about justice—they did so from a place in the desert and in an Atlanta classroom where the profound work of disintegration and integration had helped form them as public theologians, moral agents, and more integrated neighbors. They did so with a greater appreciation for a communal process of theological reflection and action planning, with greater awareness and confidence of their skills to navigate boundary zones of many kinds, and with memories of a landscape and people who had become their teachers and companions.

In all these regards, travel seminars can be microcosms of the larger, longer process of disintegrating and integrating that occurs when students encounter unfamiliar landscapes. They experience profound dissonance between their public convictions and embodied practices when they experience people who do not share their theology but share in communion, or when they proclaim God's preferential option for the poor while they experience bodily discomfort being around people with disabilities, undocumented persons held in detention centers, transgendered persons, or homeless men who are addicts.

As students struggle with their faith, vocation, self-worth, and skills for ministry as critiqued by faculty, peers, and site supervisors, the normal processes of disintegrating and reintegrating are occurring every week. The challenges to the familiar and predictable ways of interpreting the world, sacred texts and traditions, and the self, result in disorientation that is vital for growth and integration. Travel seminars are extraordinary opportunities for students to experience a community of learners who are intentional about identifying the disintegration and opportunities for integration that lead to transformation.

Bibliography

Brelsford, Theodore, and P. Alice Rogers, eds. *Contextualizing Theological Education.* Cleveland: Pilgrim, 2008.

Fulkerson, Mary McClintock. *Places of Redemption: Theology for a Worldly Church.* Oxford: Oxford University, 2007.

Gunderson, Gary R., and James R. Cochrane. *Religion and the Health of the Public: Shifting the Paradigm.* New York: St. Martin, 2012.

Holland, Joe, and Peter Henriot. *Social Analysis: Linking Faith to Justice.* Maryknoll, NY: Orbis, 1983.

MacIntyre, Alasdair. *After Virtue: A Study in Moral Theology.* Notre Dame, IN: Notre Dame University, 1984.

Ver Beek, Kurt Alan. "The Impact of Short-Term Missions: A Case Study of House Construction in Honduras after Hurricane Mitch." *Missiology: An International Review* 34.4 (2006).

14

Creating a New Course on Leadership in the Small Church

Jeffrey D. Jones

A ndover Newton Theological Seminary is a progressive seminary historically aligned with the United Church of Christ and the American
Baptist Churches USA. The student body also includes a significant number of students seeking ministry in the Unitarian Universalist Association.
A majority of its students entered seminary later in life, usually following
a career in business. Many will serve small churches. On the theological
spectrum, the students range from charismatic conservatives to nonde-
ists. The school would characterize itself is being progressively Christian.
As is true with most free-standing seminaries, financial realities have led
the school to explore new ways of teaching and learning and new degree
programs. Deep in the ethos of the school is a commitment to training for
ministry.

I began serving the school in 2002 in a part-time position as coordina-
tor of e-learning. In 2005 that role expanded to a half-time position that
included developing nondegree initiatives and serving as a member of the
faculty teaching in the area of ministerial leadership. During that time I
also served as the half-time pastor of a small church. In 2012 I became
a full-time faculty member and director of ministerial studies, a position
from which I retired in June 2015.

Course Design

In 2013, attempting to fill what I perceived to be a gap in course offerings, I developed a new course on ministerial leadership in the small church to be offered during the spring 2014 semester. I knew that many students taking the course would either already or very soon be pastors of small churches, so I wanted to emphasize the practical dimension of the course without sacrificing the conceptual knowledge that is essential to effective ministry. The aim in all the school's ministerial leadership courses is to integrate conceptual knowledge related to leadership and change theories with the practical realities of leading in a congregation. Although most of my courses had attempted this, I sensed a need to do more, and so I took on the discipline of using the course design process outlined in L. Dee Fink's *Creating Significant Learning Experiences*.[1] I soon discovered that the process was comprehensive and sometimes bordered on being tedious; at times I wanted to abandon it. Ultimately, however, I learned that it provided a vehicle for thinking creatively about the way in which I could integrate theory and practice more effectively in my teaching.

Situational Factors

The process begins with extensive attention to "situational factors," many of which seem obvious but in typical course planning often remain unstated, perhaps even unconscious. These include factors such as the time and setting for the course and its place in the curriculum. Also included among situation factors are broader concerns of the academy or judicatory that might affect the course. These were some situational factors I noted:

1. The course will meet once a week for three hours in a classroom setting. Online resources and sharing capability will be available. Students will also visit small churches.

2. The course will fulfill a ministerial leadership curriculum requirement.

3. Congregations expect caring, competent pastors. Judicatories expect knowledgeable, skilled pastors. Both are concerned that small churches cannot pay a living salary but still desire full-time pastors.

---

1. Fink, *Creating Significant Learning Experiences*.

4. Both cognitive knowledge and skills are needed to function as a small church pastor. The context for ministry is rapidly changing, which creates competing paradigms. A recent history of denigrating small churches has led to a reactive stance that celebrates the virtues of small churches while tending to ignore, or at least significantly downplay, their struggles, foibles, and challenges.

Situational factors also include characteristics of the learners and the teacher. Attention to these led me to be clear about the diversity of learners that would be present in the classroom: age, full or part-time, commuter or residential, currently involved in a congregation or not, interested in the topic or fulfilling a requirement. While the diversity would be significant, I also stated a number of likely common factors. For example, they would be seeking answers about what to do as a small church pastor, and most of them would have had experience working in small groups in other classes.

It proved to be a bit more challenging to address honestly what I was bringing to the course and the ways in which that would shape my teaching. I probably would not have been conscious of many of the perspectives I brought to teaching the course without needing to state them as part of the design process. That lack of awareness might well have affected the course in ways I did not anticipate and for which I was not prepared. Here's what I had to recognize about myself:

1. I have recent experience as a small church pastor and have studied and taught leadership for over thirty years.

2. I am skeptical about the ability of most small churches to change, but I am not without hope.

3. I am not seeking growth but more faithful and missional ministry.

4. I expect to use insights from this course to inform a book project on effective and faithful leadership in churches that are getting smaller.

Full disclosure always helps—even if it's only to yourself!

Describing the array of situational factors Fink includes was tedious to the point that I kept saying to myself, "I know all this stuff. Why bother writing it down?" Doing so, however, led me to see the big picture in a way I had not seen it before; it made me aware of some contextual issues, such as my personal experience with the topic, that I probably would have ignored, or at least not recognized as my experience.

Learning Goals

The next step in the process involved defining learning goals for the course. The approach advocated by Fink varied from what I had previously done in two significant ways. First, he suggests that all goals be formulated based on what students will know and be able to do one year after the course is over. Second, rather than setting a limited number of goals, Fink's process requires setting goals in a variety of areas: foundational knowledge (what students will know), application (what students will be able to do), integration (connections they will be able to make), human dimension (learning about themselves and others), caring (changes in their feelings, interests, and values), and learning how to learn (interest in and skills for continued learning).[2]

Here's a sampling of the goals I developed:

1. *Foundational Knowledge*: A year after this course is over students will

    a. know several elements involved in creating a description of an organization that includes both personal and system dynamics and

    b. recognize the unique qualities of small churches.

2. *Application*: A year after this course is over students will

    a. be able to construct questions that enable deeper insight into a congregation and

    b. assess appropriate leadership stances in a particular small church setting.

3. *Integration*: A year after this course is over students will

    a. be able to compare the reality of a small congregation to the generally accepted characteristics of congregations in general and small churches in particular and

    b. be able to integrate concepts of leadership into their own leadership style.

4. *Human Dimension*: A year after this course is over students will

    a. be able to assess themselves and their role as pastors of small congregations, while still growing in their practice of leadership and

---

2. Fink, *Creating Significant Learning Experiences*, 3–81.

b. understand members of the congregation in terms of their own personal and corporate history.

5. *Caring:* A year after this course is over students will

    a. be open to both the realities and the possibilities that small churches offer and

    b. be more patient with those who need their leadership but still resist if not challenge it.

6. *Learning How to Learn:* A year after this course is over students will

    a. be aware of resources that will enable them to continue to study and learn about small churches and leadership in them and

    b. be eager to construct a "thick description" of the specific small church in which they are located.

After reviewing all the goals I had written, I determined that these were the significant ones that I would include in the syllabus: Students who participate in this course will be able to (1) describe and analyze the characteristics of a small church, (2) determine the challenges and potential of a small church, and (3) assess their own ability to provide leadership in a small church setting.

Setting goals related to what students would know and be able to do one year after the course was finished significantly changed how I approached the course so that I focused primarily on skills and concepts related to ministry rather than specific information about small churches.

The design process requires setting more goals than a single course can achieve. Doing so broadened my perspective, however, and got me thinking beyond the content. Having the goals clearly stated proved to be a helpful reference point for me, not only in the initial course design but also as I made adjustments in the course as it unfolded.

Feedback and Assessment Procedures

Fink offers several areas that need to be considered in the development of feedback and assessment. I have included a brief summary of my plans in each of them below:

Forward-looking Assessment

Along with setting goals for a year after the course is over, forward-looking assessment was another significantly different approach to course design. Assessment that is forward-looking focuses on the way in which students will use concepts from the course in the future. Assessment vehicles need to provide an approximation of the setting in which students will find themselves and the concerns they will be facing. I planned to use a case study and a report on a visit to a small church and interviews with its pastor and laity as the basis for assessment. The plan stated, "The case study, which they will be asked to analyze and determine appropriate actions, will present concerns and issues that students will likely encounter in their ministry. The interviews of clergy and laity will place students in situations similar to those they will encounter as pastors. The final exam will be constructed so that they will need to analyze a setting and determine how they would respond."

Criteria and Standards

The syllabus presented clear standards for written work. Several class sessions would be devoted to developing the questions and criteria for the visits to churches. Based on the assumption that the class is a learning community, we would determine qualities that are important for our work together and regularly ask, How are we doing?

Self-assessment

Students would have regular opportunities to assess their learning and their sense of themselves as pastors of small churches through the written assignments, their responses to the case study, their interviews in small churches, and the final exam.

Teaching and Learning Activities

Fink encourages the use of learning activities that also provide the opportunity for assessment. In my planning for the course I discovered that this was an effective approach and not difficult to implement. I planned a few brief lectures on key concepts of leadership in the small church and some direct discussion of the reading. However, most of the learning took place during work on the two significant assessment vehicles: the case study and the visits.

Case Study

I planned to use the same case study of a small church twice in the class. At the first session the case study would be distributed along with a set of questions. Students would have time for individual work and then share in groups and the entire class. I also planned to use the same case study in the middle of the course, after the class had spent time exploring issues related to the small church. I intended to use the same process as in the first week, with the hope that students would see more going on in the case than they had the first week.

Interviews

Students would work in teams of two or three to visit a small church and interview the pastor and lay leaders separately. In small groups and as an entire class they would work to shape the interview questions, based on their understanding of key issues for small churches. Prior to this work I planned to share basic information on qualitative research.

Reading and Discussion

Students would select a book that focused on a specific area of ministry in the small church (for example, worship, Christian education, pastoral care, or administration). They would write a reflection paper on the book to share with a group composed of those who read books about the same area of ministry. The group then had the responsibility to develop a presentation on its area of ministry to share with the class.

What Could Go Wrong?

Another of Fink's helpful suggestions is to think before the class begins about what might go wrong, making the initial design unworkable or at least in need of adaptation. Here are a few of the possibilities I considered for this course:

1. Diversity in the class could be greater than I anticipated.

2. The interviews might be seen as overwhelming.

3. There may be too much material to integrate.

4. It might be difficult to find enough small churches and pastors willing to be interviewed.

5. Snow may force cancellation of class, requiring a readjustment of the schedule in order do the interviews on the established days.

Evaluating the Course

Regular assessment would take place by asking, How are we doing? in both the class and the groups. Further evaluation markers would consider (1) the quality of the case study reflections and final exam, (2) standardized course evaluations from the school, and (3) a specific course evaluation that I developed.

Teaching the Course

The course unfolded much as I expected in relation to the integrating course design process. Students were engaged. They were excited about the interview opportunities. Recruiting enough churches for the interviews was not difficult. Then the snow came! Since the interview date had already been set, I needed to adjust the course schedule in order to cover the material that was essential before the interviews. Some of this was done through online discussion.

The most significant change in the course involved the use of the case study.[3] My original intention was to use the same case study at two points in the course, hoping that students would see more dynamics at work in the case after we had covered most of the course content. Students did a fairly good job of working with the case study the first time, however, so I sensed a need to provide different content. Also, as the course progressed, it became apparent that many students could see surface problems present in

---

3. For helpful guidance on the use of case studies see Mahan et al., *Shared Wisdom*.

a congregation, but they were struggling to grasp the underlying dynamics that would allow them to develop "thick descriptions." This would mean, for example, going beyond looking at a conflict between two people to seeing the deeper systems issues present. Similarly, it would mean addressing issues from the perspective of the adaptive challenge that was present rather than just the technical problems to be solved. (Students had both read about and discussed this insight from the writing of Ronald Heifetz.[4]) As often as we talked about this in class, most students did not demonstrate an ability to engage in this type of analysis. This led me to create a different case study for use as the midterm exam. The first case was about a pastor after his first year in the church; the second was about this same pastor following his third year in the church. I also decided to develop a third case study about the same pastor at the end of five years, at the time he was considering whether he should stay in the church or seek placement elsewhere.

I designed the second case study to include a variety of issues and problems, but also with content that pointed to the deeper issues that would be part of a "thick description." My plan was to grade their work primarily on whether they discussed and dealt with the underlying issues in a significant way. Many did not, and grades were low. However, I had the students' attention on this issue in ways I had not before. In the following classes we spent significant time developing a process that could be used to move from the surface problem to the deeper issue. All this proved to be a significant learning opportunity, which became evident in the student reports on their interviews and in their work on the third case study, which served as the final exam.

The design process presented by Fink is a comprehensive one. In this chapter I have focused on the elements of the process that enhance integrating work. Two elements were particularly significant for me. First, the goal-setting process encouraged me to think more holistically about the students I would be teaching, recognizing that learning would be taking place at a number of levels. This moved my thinking beyond the conceptual and cerebral. It provided significant information about the way in which the concepts of the course could affect the experience of the students as they applied them, integrated them into their experience as leaders, deepened their understanding of themselves, and enhanced their care for others and their role as leaders. Also, setting goals about what students would know

4. See Heifetz and Linsky, *Leadership on the Line*, 13–20.

and be able to do a year after the course encouraged me to think about the integration of course material into their ministries.

Second, Fink's concept of forward-looking assessment is central to the integrating process. Forward looking assessment is formulated to approximate settings in which students will use the material of the course. It was never a matter of simply stating a concept but always of relating it to a particular situation. The case studies proved to be a valuable learning tool. My experience also demonstrated the validity of Fink's contention that significant continuity between the learning tools and the assessment is essential. So, for example, the midterm exam in the course was one of the most significant learning tools.

Effective integrating in theological education must happen in virtually everything the school does. The course design process provided by Fink provides a significant and helpful tool as one way to do so in the classroom.

Bibliography

Fink, L. Dee. *Creating Significant Learning Experiences: An Integrated Approach to Designing College Courses.* San Francisco: Jossey-Bass, 2003.

Heifetz, Ronald A., and Marty Linsky. *Leadership on the Line: Staying Alive through the Dangers of Leading.* Boston: Harvard Business School Press, 2002.

Mahan, Jeffrey, et al. *Shared Wisdom: A Guide to Case Study Reflection in Ministry.* Nashville: Abingdon, 1993.

15

The Pain of Racial Differences Emerges in the Introductory Integrating Course

——— Jeffery L. Tribble, Sr. ———

One distinctive feature of a theological education at Columbia Theological Seminary is its vision of being a large table—a rich environment of theological, cultural, ethnic, geographic, and denominational diversity.[1] However, living into this big-table vision of diverse community is taxing and downright painful at times. Thoughtful trustees, faculty, administration, staff, and students acknowledge the challenge. I find it significant that the school's current vision closes with the following reflection:

> "Big table" communities frequently cause distress, and sometimes significant pain, for those around the table. Most often it is unintentional. Sometimes it is far less innocent. We often don't know how to handle conflicting convictions, unsettling conversations, and confusing differences. The fact is that our own convictions, communication and differences are just as challenging to others as theirs are to us. But over time, like stones in a rock polisher,

---

1. *Moving toward Our Third Century*, 7. This document is an update of the Vision 2020 report of 1998. The aspiration of being a "large table" is one of seven distinctive factors of our theological education.

appropriate, intentional, loving relationships can be used by God to make more Christlike gems of us all.[2]

My teaching case study examines a painful slice of life in the flow of an introductory course in the master of divinity curriculum. The course addresses how faculty and students become theologically informed readers of the intersections of the gospel and diverse contexts of lived experiences—including differences of racial identity and sexual orientation as well as differences of theology and ecclesiology. At the time of the incident described here (spring semester of 2008), the Intersections course was the first of the three required integrative courses in the curriculum. The course description was as follows:

> Intersections is a multidisciplinary course which brings together a student's background and faith journey with the biblical, theological, historical, and ecclesiastical dimensions of the sacraments of baptism and Communion. The course introduces students to reflective contextual study of these topics, and begins to think about the implications of such study to the understanding of calling and mission—of identity and the meaning and purposes of God's presence in the world.

Hence, the course was intended to foster greater attentiveness to the mission of God in the world and our individual and collective vocations to participate in the mission and reign of God. The pedagogical interplay between missiological awareness and embodied ecclesiology is captured in the instructions for one paper where students reflect on the statement "It is not God's church that has a mission in the world, but the God of mission that has a church in the world."[3]

The teaching team discussed all parts of the syllabus in preparation for the course. Instructional methods included large group lectures and discussions that sometimes included media input and guest interviews with the teaching team. Students were assigned to small groups with one of the course instructors. Students were required to write short reflective papers, the purpose of which was to develop an integrated understanding of the essential elements of the course: developing one's credo, learning to analyze and engage an ecclesial and communal context, and deepened

2. Ibid., 27.

3. A discussion of the radical shift from the traditional understanding of Christian mission during Christendom is explained in one chapter in a textbook for the course. See "Mission Revisited Christendom and Missio Dei" in Cardoza-Orlandi, *Mission*, 31–48.

understanding of the mission and sacramental life of the church. During the latter half of the course students practiced the dynamic and ongoing integrating trajectory by reconsidering the essential topics in light of continuing input and reflection. The final exam consisted of a case study on the church, vocation, and sacraments. Reflecting the seminary's focus on ministerial education, the case studies were similar in type to those used for Presbyterian Church (USA) ordination exams.

The Issue Provoking a Redesign of Lesson Plans

Later in the second week of class an African American student approached two members of the teaching team (Mark, a white male ethics professor, and myself, an African American male ministry professor). He was concerned about "the necessity and utility" of class materials that he perceived as racially offensive in three consecutive weeks of the course. The student cited the use of Flannery O'Connor's short story "Revelation,"[4] comments made by church leaders at our site visit to Oakhurst Presbyterian Church, and a film clip of a baptismal scene from the movie *O Brother, Where Art Thou?*[5] as being racially offensive.

"Revelation" contains several references to "niggers" and "white trash," who, in the eyes of the main character, Mrs. Turpin, are identified as being on the bottom of the South's social structure. This short story had been chosen to help students to see the intersections of faith and context. Oakhurst is a diverse congregation, not only racially but also regarding sexual orientation, educational levels, physical abilities, and economic status.[6] At Oakhurst we discussed with church leaders the issue of racial inequalities and their praxis of intentionally building a multicultural congregation through dialogue, leadership selection, preaching and worship, pastoral care, and community activism. Provocative from the perspective of race and gender was the congregation's stated practice of baptizing their members, teaching that baptism into Christ "involves them in a new society, the church."[7] One student wrote the following description of Oakhurst's

4. O'Connor, "Revelation."

5. Coen et al., *O Brother, Where Art Thou?*

6. Oakhurst Presbyterian Church, http://www.oakhurstpresbyterian.org/?page_id=22181.

7. The expression that "baptism into Christ involves us in a new society, the church" is from Vander Zee, *Christ, Baptism, and the Lord's Supper*, 88–90. This understanding

baptismal practice: "With each child's baptism, they acknowledge the categories in which society will place that child based on race and gender. They acknowledge the inequality of a society that looks at white boys as future rulers, black boys as potential criminals, and girls as something men possess. By acknowledging what society does, they are then challenged to teach these children that they are all daughters and sons of the kingdom." The Oakhurst site was selected as a particularly rich context to consider the intersections of gospel and culture, giving students an opportunity for "cultivating an ethnographic disposition" in their church observations.[8] The film clip from *O Brother, Where Art Thou?* portrayed a baptismal scene, an African American musician, and a comment about white men as "devils." The film clip was selected to provoke questions about our baptismal theologies.

Mark and I engaged the student in dialogue about his concerns. The student asked that the entire teaching team respond to this perceived pattern of racially offensive content in whatever manner we deemed appropriate. We had considerable one-on-one dialogue after the student left to process our perspectives on race and pedagogy. Initial questions included these: Do we think that this is an isolated concern of one African American student or might this concern be shared by others? Would it have been disruptive to the flow of the film clip presentation to provide more context to interpret the explicit content that students were asked to engage? How does our racial identity formation as instructors influence our different perceptions of these classroom incidents? Based upon our separate interactions with African American students in the class, we agreed that they too had expressed discomfort with respect to racially related material in each of the three classes. One of the teaching team's African American students had been very vocal in small group discussion about concerns with the selection and use of O'Connor's short story. Others had expressed to me privately their concerns about the pattern of introducing but not discussing racial stereotypes in the first few weeks of the course.

Prior to the conversations, members of the teaching team had shared their own concerns about material introduced in the Oakhurst site visit and the need for space to process these concerns with the students. The

---

of baptism seems to capture the theology of baptism practiced at Oakhurst Presbyterian Church.

8. Frank urges congregational leaders to cultivate a set of skills that he calls an "ethnographic disposition." See *Soul of a Congregation*.

site had been selected precisely because of the multivalent nature of this congregation, which was seen as a creative context for a brief ethnographic study. Oakhurst is a context in which the issues of race, gender, class, and sexual orientation are live theological issues and are contested in their congregational practices. The teaching team, in selecting Oakhurst, was well aware of a controversy that had ensued two or three years prior when the church was used as part of a class assignment. Some students assumed that faculty members saw Oakhurst as a model Columbia was advocating—in that case, the ordination of practicing homosexuals, a contested issue in the denomination's polity. As site visits were a pedagogy used for the first time and members of the teaching team had discerned various student concerns about the site visit (not just African American students), the teaching team discussed how we might adjust the teaching schedule to better process issues raised by this challenging context.

The faculty continued to discern the problem of adequate time and space for student reflection and integration of the Oakhurst site. We asked at the outset, How do we create spaces for reflection and integration, not only of texts and lectures but also for other elements articulated in the Intersections syllabus? Does the course help students bring "who they are, where they've come from, and where they think they're going" in dialogue with course content?

Furthermore, we wondered if this critical incident might be reflected upon in light of our larger institutional goals articulated in Multicultural Organizational Change Development, a strategic initiative to help CTS move toward being an "anti-racist institution." We connected our incident with other situations, in particular the memory of two African American women who, several years before I joined the faculty, decided to leave Columbia. Though it was never clear why they left, many faculty were sensing something "below the water and in the mud" of the institution.[9] While acknowledging the possibility of a number of contributing factors besides

9. Thompson, "Maps and Compass." Thompson illuminates the "down in the mud" character of the cultural swamp of CTS: "What gives the swamp the support that it needs to exist is its massive, dark section layer, hidden below the water's surface: the mud. Although this enormous portion of the cultural swamp is deeply submerged, it holds the keys to the swamp's very character. What is submerged are beliefs, deeply held, hardly ever spoken aloud, hardly ever thought about by anyone. These deepest beliefs took their place in the mud during the group's (think "church's") earlier years, as it learned from experience what worked, what it could trust. Submerged parts of the culture do not see the light of day without some prompting. Most commonly, the prompting occurs when a new piece of stuff appears, one that does not seem to fit in with the other stuff," 78.

racially shaped perceptions and interactions both within and beyond the classroom, the teaching team felt there were strong similarities between our class and problems that had emerged over time. Could our response to the student's question about "the necessity and utility" of our teaching over these three weeks become a teachable moment for faculty and students alike?

The Redesign Process

At the next face-to-face meeting of the teaching team, we reached consensus to address the issue directly. We agreed to adjust the day's schedule to respond not only to the race-related issue raised by the African American student but also to process other emotional and intellectual concerns that we sensed might be felt more broadly. Anticipating that a conversation could, among other things, create space for discussing race and racism in the United States, teaching team members quickly agreed to adopt as ground rules for our discussion ideas articulated by Lynn Weber Cannon.[10] In her article "Fostering Positive Race, Class, and Gender Dynamics in the Classroom," Cannon describes herself as "a white, Southern, female sociologist who teaches about race to a racially and ethnically mixed population of students in the city where Martin Luther King Jr. was killed." The ground rules that she has practiced in her classes reflect her thinking about the ways that power and privilege, and the interpersonal dynamics that support them, are reinforced or challenged in group settings. We agreed that Mark would open up the discussion and that the rest of the teaching team would then join him on the stage, sharing our perceptions, particularly about the Oakhurst visit, across our differences.

Mark introduced the topic: intersections in our life together, deconstructing our points of pain. Making a connection to the opening class lecture in which students tossed a ball of string that resulted in a complex web, which illustrated the interrelatedness of reality, Mark asserted that when we pull on points in this web, tension or pain, is a likely result. As a way of acknowledging and addressing this, students were invited to share various points of pain caused by the course thus far. This invitation initially evoked a variety of reactions from students: concern about whether their pain should become the subject of open discussion, suspicion about whether the

10. Cannon, "Fostering Positive Race, Class, and Gender."

group should be trusted with their pain, wondering if pain and suffering can be redemptive, and asking if this was a breach of the syllabus objectives.

After some negotiation of how the question was framed, students warmed up to the idea and named some of their "points of pain." Reinforcement of negative culturally conditioned racial images of African Americans was named. The pain of white males "being blamed" for the pain of women and African Americans was named. One student suggested that there seemed to be inadequate time and space for processing content that was emotionally provocative for some members of the class. Another point of pain for one student was visiting Oakhurst, a church that was defying the Presbyterian Church (USA) policy on the ordination of gay, lesbian, bisexual, and transgendered people.

The teaching team then joined Mark on the stage and shared various critical perspectives with one another and in response to each other. Following that, the students were invited to join the discussion as they negotiated their thoughts and feelings about why such an exchange was taking place. The student who initially raised the question with Mark and me recognized this as a response to his concern and said to the class that he appreciated the discussion that went way beyond his expectations. Another student named the class time as an opportunity to witness how one might make adjustments in ministry when unexpected conflict arises. Students confessed their difficulty in talking about race and racism. Some did not see any theological underpinnings for such a discussion; they characterized it as a search for so-called politically correct ways to engage intercultural discourse. Over two hours were spent in exchange. The class ended with two members of the teaching team leading prayer.

A Critical Opportunity for Cocurricular and Broader Faculty Learning

Student discussion of this class session spilled out beyond the classroom. One place where it ended up was in the next meeting of the community life and discrimination and inclusiveness committee. The chair of the committee and dean of student affairs invited two members of the teaching team who were members of this committee to expound on the incident. The academic dean was present for most of this discussion and requested that I write this case study for broader faculty discussion. At the ensuing faculty evaluation day scheduled at the end of the semester, faculty members discussed issues raised by this case study.

Discussion of this case provided a critical opportunity for faculty members to reflect together on the challenges of teaching in racially and culturally diverse classrooms, to recognize that there are pertinent pedagogical resources, and to consider the next step or two that might promote institutional learning toward becoming a more multicultural institution. Furthermore, since the Intersections course was one of the three required integrative courses, this case helped our faculty to think together about the difficult work of integrating. The general sense from faculty who were familiar with the evaluation of the course over three years ago was that the course wasn't working. With the decision to review the curriculum, the Intersections course was jettisoned, with the understanding that some strengths of the course (especially the contextual experiences) would be maintained in other parts of the curriculum.

An Assessment of Strengths and Weaknesses of the Integrating Work of This Course

The Intersections course reflects the concern to make ministry education more integrative in a variety of ways. The integrating project is pursued across the theological disciplines at CTS: biblical, historical and doctrinal, and practical. The assumed makeup of the faculty is that it is not populated by hyperspecialists. Whatever the area of specializations, all faculty are presumed to be well grounded in biblical studies, historical theology, systematic theology, and ethics.[11] Further, the course recognizes diverse skills and competencies that are needed for effective ministry, including competencies in theological reflection as well as analyzing and engaging ecclesial and communal contexts. The faculty understanding of integration is broadly congruent with the Carnegie Foundation's approach, where all aspects of student learning are brought together to create a knowledgeable, competent practitioner with a deep sense of vocation, identity, and purpose who is attentive to social and cultural contexts.[12] The course design pursued a pedagogical strategy integrating learning objectives, learning activities, and formative as well as summative student assessment.

11. From addendum 1, "Character of Our Faculty," 28, in *Moving toward Our Third Century*.

12. Sheppard et al., *Educating Engineers*, 6.

This case study illustrates the importance of what this volume's authors understand as the communal character of integration based on a social understanding of the human person as well as the communal character of teaching and learning, which involves students and teachers alike. Teachers include not only the seminary "lead instructors" but also the teachers in contextual sites such as Oakhurst Presbyterian. The communal character of integrating work accentuates the dynamic situational factors of the large-table vision of CTS and other theological seminaries. Among the situational factors salient to this case are an increasingly diverse faculty and student body that heightens the institution's pedagogical challenge of helping students understand how the gospel and contexts shape individuals and communities through language, symbol, rituals, and diverse human experiences and hermeneutical work. The instructors' critically reflective and improvisatory response to the incident narrated here highlights the need for goals of integrative learning to include multiple ways of knowing (such as embodied and emotional ways of knowing), relating, and building significant relationships with God, self, and others.

Bibliography

Cannon, Lynn Weber. "Fostering Positive Race, Class, and Gender Dynamics in the Classroom." In *Women's Studies Quarterly* 18.1–2 (1990) 126–34.

Cardoza-Orlandi, Carlos F. *Mission: An Essential Guide.* Nashville: Abingdon, 2002.

Coen, Joel, et al. *O Brother, Where Art Thou?* Burbank, CA: Touchstone Home Video, 2001.

Frank, Thomas Edward. *The Soul of a Congregation: An Invitation to Congregational Reflection.* Nashville: Abingdon, 2000.

Moving toward Our Third Century: A Vision Frame. Decatur, GA: Columbia Theological Seminary, 2012.

O'Connor, Flannery. "Revelation." In *The Complete Stories*, 488–509. New York: Farrar, Straus, and Giroux, 1971.

Sheppard, Sheri D., et al. *Educating Engineers: Designing for the Future of the Field.* Preparation for Professions Series. San Francisco: Jossey-Bass, 2008.

Thompson, George B., Jr. "Maps and Compass: Swamp Culture and Power." In *Alligators in the Swamp: Power, Ministry, and Leadership*, edited by George B. Thompson Jr., 65–108. Cleveland: Pilgrim, 2005.

Vander Zee, Leonard J. *Christ, Baptism, and the Lord's Supper.* Downers Grove, IL: InterVarsity, 2004.

16

Online Teaching and the Challenges of Integrating

———— Edward Foley ————

My Digital Location

O ver thirty years ago I was hired by Catholic Theological Union (CTU) when the school was searching for an instructor in worship who could also direct the choir. Since I held graduate degrees in worship and music and was an ordained cleric in the Franciscan tradition—a strong presence at CTU since its inception—it seemed like a fit, and I was offered a contract. That academic year (1984–85) could be characterized as a time of low technology, when the dominant form of instruction was the faculty lecture, with liberal use of chalkboards and photocopied notes, and a physical reserve shelf limited to twenty books for each course in CTU's cramped library. Communication with colleagues or students was through face-to-face encounters, the occasional telephone call, or the busy in-house mail service. As part of a consortium of schools, CTU also was the beneficiary of a courier system that transferred library books and memos between the six schools that made up the Hyde Park Cluster. We certainly thought of ourselves as well-connected at the time.

CTU has gone through many changes over the years. It experienced a rich expansion of programs and student population during the 1990s and in the early years of the new millennium. It also was the recipient of various grants that introduced technology into teaching and learning, built a new academic facility with smart classrooms, and have a library that offers many digital sources and services. CTU also has gone through a series of online learning systems: first Blackboard, then Moodle, and most recently—because of an alliance with DePaul University—D2L (desire to learn).

A few years into the new century CTU's student population began to decline as a result of multiple factors. Chief among them was the broad downturn in vocations to ordained Roman Catholic ministry—the mainstay of the student population in "billable credit hours." CTU also moved from an eleven-week quarter system into a semester system in which each fifteen-week course was more expensive. A part-time student could take a three-credit course for $1,500 on the quarter system and maybe take two a year for $3,000; on the semester system that same three-credit course would cost $2,000, and she might take only one a year. Income began to decline noticeably, exacerbated by the global financial crisis of 2007. In that environment CTU began to develop an online teaching presence.

I purchased my first computer in the early 1980s when writing my doctoral dissertation. While digital is not my first language, I have become pretty savvy with technology over the years and even published on the topic.[1] Given my institution's push for mounting courses online from the core curriculum and the need for all academic departments to provide such offerings, I began a certification process for online teaching, becoming the first full professor in the school to acquire that credential in 2010.

Rethinking a Core Course

A foundational course for many of CTU's MA degrees—and a theological issue central to Roman Catholic belief—is one I have taught regularly over the past three decades: the history and theology of the Eucharist. It is a topic that has occupied much of my scholarship as well, including a well-received textbook. Over the decades, I had translated my many pages of photocopied notes, quotes, and images into other media. *From Age to Age* was a published version of my multimedia thinking. In its revised edition, it was a book with more than 360 sidebars and 240 illustrations.[2]

Converting images and texts, PowerPoint, and notes into an online course, however, was not so simple. As two-dimensional thinking does

1. See Foley, "'Theological Reflection, Theology and Technology."
2. Foley, *From Age to Age*; also in Spanish and Japanese.

not translate well into three-dimensional thinking, so classroom presenta-tions—even with PowerPoint, replete with animation and images—do not easily translate into an effective online learning environment. I thought new technologies would be sufficient, but instead it required new thinking.

One misconception about online teaching is that technology, in whatever new and improved form one can find it, is the answer. Early on I learned from my first mentor in the certification process that was not only an insufficient but a wrongheaded approach. She was a specialist in middle-school online learning, and at first I was a bit miffed by our pair-ing. How could someone supplying digital support for preteen students in a geographically fixed school, whose students lived in the neighborhood, help me negotiate learning with online graduate students spread across the globe?

We did not have an enduring fit, although she did teach me one quite valuable lesson that continues to inspire my online and face-to-face teach-ing. While I had harbored this unspoken instinct about both ministry and pedagogy for years, I had never heard it so blatantly articulated: *you are not the focus of learning.*

Since the beginning of my career as a graduate instructor I have em-ployed small group work in courses, but those groups were initially used as a technique to involve students more actively in the learning. An of-ficial feature of Roman Catholic worship, articulated by the Second Vatican Council, is the "full, conscious and active participation" of the assembly. I presumed that my teaching of worship should try to do the same. Through my exposure to practical theologies, however, it began to dawn on me that group-centered work is more than a tactical move for staving off boredom among students. Rather, it is a decentralizing pedagogy that more explicitly acknowledges students as responsible subjects in the learning process and properly confirms peers in their role as co-learners-teachers. It also redis-tributes some of the teaching-learning power in the process.

Often CTU's online learners—especially those in the master of arts in pastoral studies (MAPS) program—can be more anxious than face-to-face students. Frequently they are older and digitally less adept than some of their younger face-to-face counterparts. Sometimes they are more geo-graphically isolated (one reason they enroll with us) and may be lacking an environment broadly supportive of their pursuit of an advanced degree. Finally, they are often years away from their last experience in higher edu-cation and anxious about their ability to perform at the graduate level.

From a tactical perspective, creating an online environment in which students are not only encouraged but fundamentally required to engage with each other in a constant and rigorous way takes multiple pressures off of the salaried "lead-learner."[3] However, my albeit limited experience of teaching graduate students online also suggests that, beyond a pedagogical tactic designed to minimize demands on the lead-learner's time, developing this more horizontal type of learning environment must help to affirm that those who matriculate into this online environment are honored as experienced, insightful, caring, and invaluable learning partners.

It may seem odd to think about graduate theological pedagogies as concerned with care. Early in my career I had the privilege of teaching and writing with the Lutheran theologian and pastoral care specialist Herbert Anderson. Through my work with Anderson and subsequent reflection and study, I have begun to believe that teaching should fundamentally be an act of pastoral care. While sometimes that care requires various forms of tough love, it first seems to require an intention and design that provides a supportive learning environment for all participants. This seems particularly true for the online students that I have encountered for the reasons noted above.

The Design

The design of the Eucharist course is detailed in an eighteen-page syllabus. The student's first experience of the course, however, is not through the syllabus but through its Internet portal on the CTU website. I try to employ a good deal of art and attempt to make the design as attractive as possible. Besides a welcome text, I also post a short, informal video of myself—recorded with the program Camtasia—welcoming the students, assuring them that this is an adventure for all of us, and affirming my hope that we all stay connected and do well in this joint learning venture.

The digital space opens onto the welcome unit, containing my prerecorded welcoming video and text. There is an opening icebreaker called "Truth or Lies" in which participants post three statements about themselves, one of which is untrue. I initiate the process in a digital space that I first called the water cooler, a chat room in which people can post interesting

---

3. This is a term borrowed from Thomas Groome that I find particularly appropriate for referencing in various learning environments, especially in seminars in which students take primary responsibility for the teaching-learning.

resources or stories or discussion not directly related to the course content. Through the example of some colleagues, I have rechristened that room the atrium to provide some resonance with the physical academic and convocation center whose central feature is a large, three-story atrium. After noticing that students were e-mailing each other with prayer requests, I also created a prayer forum where students could share their concerns with one another.

The welcome unit also contains a chat room for each small discussion group: students are placed in one group that stays together for the entire semester. The welcome unit also contains various free Internet resources, links to the student handbook, the bookstore, and a digital clock that always displays the current Chicago time. Although students may matriculate into the course anywhere from mainland China to Ghana and thus engage in asynchronous learning, all assignments are due every Monday of the semester at 5:00 p.m. Chicago time. This opening unit is followed by fifteen instructional units arranged chronologically according to the fifteen weeks of the semester. Each week covers a discrete amount of material, videos, readings, and discussion topics on which the students will be quizzed.

The extensive syllabus operates as a manual for this online learning experience. The second half of the syllabus outlines the course topics, required and recommended readings, and links to the resources. Hyperlinks to over 130 such readings are embedded in each of the weekly modules. Because the course calendar and content are repeated in each of the weekly modules, it is really the first half of the syllabus that appears more important to me.

One extensive segment of this opening half of the syllabus is a detailed outline of the seven learning outcomes for students who complete the course successfully. The longest section in this opening segment, however, is the almost five pages on assessment points, grading, and evaluation. This includes a grading grid for MAPS and MDiv students showing the maximum of points (200) that can be earned for all work over the duration of the semester.

	Module Engage- ment	Small Group Work	Group Quizzes	An- notated Readings	Oral Exam	Extra Points
Week 1:	3	3	3	5		
Week 2:	3	3	3	5		
Week 3:	3	3	3	5		
Week 4:	3	3	3	5		
Week 5:	3	3	3	5		
Week 6:	3	3	3	5		
Week 7:	Reading Week	Reading Week	Reading Week	Reading Week	Reading Week	Reading Week
Week 8:	3	3	3	5		
Week 9:	3	3	3	5		
Week 10:	3	3	3	5		
Week 11:	3	3	3	5		
Week 12:	3	3	3	5		
Week 13:	3	3	3	5		
Week 14:	Catch-up Week	Catch-up Week	Catch-up Week	Catch-up Week	Catch-up Week	Catch-up Week
Week 15:					32	
Total	36	36	36	60	32	200

One key requirement is active engagement in the assigned small group. Each student needs to commit to a minimum of forty-five minutes of group asynchronous interaction each week, including ice-breaking exercises, postings, and working on quizzes. Each group also completes a weekly quiz, due on Monday at 5:00 p.m. (CST). The answers, negotiated through group discussion, are found in the assigned readings or in one of the thirty-three PowerPoint videos, with my voiceover, posted across the course. During the semester students are also required to alternate leading the group each week.

Small group work is so critical to the enterprise that, as noted in the syllabus, students must evaluate each person's contribution to their group over the course of the semester. They employ a peer evaluation form based on a five-point Likert scale, ranging from "superior engagement" to "very poor engagement." This feedback figures into the final grade (under the rubric of small group work) that can total up to 36 points or 18 percent of the final grade.

Each MAPS and MDiv student is also required to complete a minimum of one thousand pages of reading for the course, which achieves the minimum grade of B minus for that requirement. Each week students also must submit to me an annotation on each reading they have completed for that module according to a clearly defined formula. One of these annotations must be posted each week for review and comment by their colleagues. This interchange of postings and reviews goes beyond the small group and requires each student to interact with all the course participants.

Engaging in graduate online learning as outlined is taxing and complex. My task is to create clear and consistent portals so that each student and, in turn, each group stays on task throughout the whole of the semester and does not go missing in action. To help insure accountability, I require all students to complete a quiz on the syllabus so they at least initially understand the requirements and protocols. Also, each weekly module outlines all required tasks for that week and includes links to whatever videos accompany that segment of learning, hyperlinks to an ample amount of reading, and a weekly reading forum for postings annotations for their colleagues.

Once the course launches I am the head cheerleader for learning, attempting to provide affirmations for good work and recommendations for improvement. I try to respond to all postings and annotations within twenty-four hours. While the online course does have technical support and ways of reaching that support are listed in the syllabus and linked online, and there is a class forum for technical issues, I also end up as the de facto frontline techie who needs to confirm that links are working, videos operative, and readings accessible. While it is seldom possible to make any radical changes in such a course design once it is launched, it is my task to provide supplemental materials where necessary, especially if a student feels their needs are not being met. For example, one Episcopalian ordination candidate did not feel that enough attention was being given to Thomas Cranmer. We crafted special resources for him that, in large measure, substituted for virtually all optional readings for the last third of the course.

Integration and Online Learning

In writing about integrated course design, L. Dee Fink values a "backward design" approach that asks what I hope students will have learned and what will still have value to them several years after the course is over.[4] While I do want them to have a basic understanding of Roman Catholic sacramentality and official teaching on key issues such as real presence, those are not my primary goals. Theologically, I want them to understand that ultimately Eucharist is a God mystery that cannot be explained in human terms, and every explanation is incomplete and inadequate in the face of such mystery. Thus, the ability to do theological reflection on eucharistic practice and thinking is more important than being able to repeat dogmatic statements. For me, this is akin to Stephen Brookfield's characterization of critical thinking as an exploration and evaluation of one's presuppositions, the need to consider things from new and different viewpoints, and only then take informed action.[5]

Theological reflection, even as it evolves into interfaith forms, is best understood as a communal enterprise.[6] It requires fundamental trust that there is wisdom in the group, and that reflection is for the sake of community. For present or future ministers, it also models a collaborative form of ministry that (in my opinion) is essential. If I can construct a digital learning environment in which participants thrive in interactive learning, develop close bonds in their group, discover that group wisdom is more than the sum of the parts but a gifted symbiosis, and support each other as practical theologians who can interface experience with the appropriate theory, then I am extremely satisfied.

It is not clear to me that the integrating project is more difficult or complex with online learners. Maybe this brace of unexpected learners only allows me to see the enterprise more clearly. They live in multiple time zones and contexts: I hope that they can integrate their own contextuality into a shared environment of respect and learning. They live in very different ecclesial contexts: some of them have leaders who support their efforts with personal and fiscal affirmations, others do not. I hope that in this digital community they digest something of the ecclesial vision of CTU and allow that to nourish themselves as they, in turn, nourish the institution.

4. Fink, *Creating Significant Learning Experiences*, 63.

5. Brookfield, *Teaching for Critical Thinking*, especially 11–13.

6. See Foley, *Theological Reflection across Religious Traditions*, especially 93.

Ironically, this digital environment provides a praxis that has great potential for pondering mysteries from new angles. Digital presence itself is a kind of mystery: one analogous to eucharistic presence. I am hoping that in their interactions, students have an experience of "real presence" with each other and me, even though we do not share a physical space and have no contact with each other's DNA.

The integrating journey for online students does not redefine but, in my view, crystallizes the integrating mission of an institution like my own in stark and challenging ways. Lead-learners such as myself need to craft a formative loop in which the resources and vision of a school of ministry equip students on their integrating journey, even deploying digital technologies as a unique resource on this journey. At the same time, the needs, contexts, and visions of such students must prod the institution and its faculty to think and act more effectively in service to them, the church, and the world.

Bibliography

Brookfield, Stephen D. *Teaching for Critical Thinking: Tools and Techniques to Help Students Question Their Assumptions.* San Francisco: Jossey-Bass, 2012.

Fink, L. Dee. *Creating Significant Learning Experiences: An Integrated Approach to Designing College Courses.* San Francisco: Jossey-Bass, 2003.

Foley, Edward. *From Age to Age: How Christians Have Celebrated the Eucharist.* Rev. ed. Collegeville, MN: Liturgical, 2008.

———. *Theological Reflection across Religious Traditions: The Turn to Reflective Believing.* Lanham, MD: Rowman & Littlefield, 2015.

———."Theological Reflection, Theology and Technology: When Baby Boomer Theologians Teach Generations X and Y." *Theological Reflection* 41.1 (2005) 45–56.

17

Harvesting Insights

——— Gordon S. Mikoski ———

The five cases provided in part 3 illustrate a variety of ways in which instructors can make integrating work a focal concern in courses at the master's level of theological education. If we now zoom out from the specifics of the cases, we can identify several insights about integrating at the course level that will transfer to other contexts.

Each of the courses represents a successful effort at course redesign based on insights, questions, or concerns that arose from paying attention to the way previous incarnations of the courses played out in practice. The feedback provided by learners and by the reflection of the instructors with respect to learning outcomes provided the impetus for course redesign. Though many in academia today dread assessment, disciplined and reflective use of assessment data can prove to be an invaluable asset for improving the effectiveness of courses in relation to integrating work. Sometimes the usable assessment data comes at the end of a course. Often it arises in midst of executing or implementing a course. Sometimes, as in the case offered by Tribble, the essential assessment data appears as an interruption to the flow of the course. How the instructor responds to interruptions and surprises can teach as much about integrating work as does the explicit content of the course. Whether the feedback related to integrating work comes in the middle or as a postmortem reflection, the wise instructor will use assessment data to make changes to the course either as it continues to unfold or for future versions.

Assessment data can also aid in the design, development, and implantation of new courses. The lessons learned by attending to what actually occurred regarding learning connected with integrating work can serve as a resource that funds the educational imagination on the front end of developing new courses.

The five cases highlight the need for certain dispositions of the instructor in course design and execution. For learners to maximize their understanding of and ability to make meaningful connections between different kinds of knowledge, the instructor has to be willing to take several kinds of risks. First, the instructor has to be willing to risk sharing control and power with learners by establishing a learning community in which the learners have some say in the way in which the course unfolds, as we saw with particular poignancy in Tribble's chapter. Second, the instructor has to legitimate and make space for the prior experiences learners bring into courses, as was a key dynamic in the travel seminar to borderlands led by David Jenkins. Third, the instructor has to establish space and opportunity for learners individually and in groups to reflect on their interaction with course-related subject matter and experiences, as in Click's and Jones's cases. Instructors function somewhat as an artist or jazz improvisationist who responds creatively to substantive contributions that lie outside their direct control.

Fourth, related to giving up some control in order to establish a reflective and dialogically oriented learning community, these five instructors had a commitment to a constructivist orientation to learning, which means they have faith in the ability of learners to construct meaning for themselves and with others. Such a commitment implies that the instructor may have to let go of anxious commitments to cover a certain range of content. Instead, the courageous instructor attends to the learning of the learners and seeks to establish connections and meaning relevant to the learners. As Foley states, the effective instructor often functions as "the head cheerleader for learning." Particularly since integrating work can never come to complete fulfillment as a result of having participated in a single course— even one that foregrounds integrating work—the effective instructor will aim for depth and help students see the relevance and pursue it long after the conclusion of the course.

Fifth, the effective instructor also has to track several levels of a course simultaneously, which takes a fair amount of mental work. The instructor has to track multiple levels of content, processes, individual student and small group engagement, as well as the instructor's own personal and intellectual functioning in the course. Teachers cannot hide behind lectures as a way to avoid engaging the learners and the subject matter in a holistic manner. The instructor has to risk a degree of appropriate self-disclosure that may go beyond that which is required in other courses. Often, the most effective learning arises in direct proportion to the modeling of engagement, reflection, and subsequent action provided by the instructor herself.

A sixth way that the effective instructor risks integrating involves the management of risk to students. The work required of learners in such courses can prove challenging, particularly for those who have not had much experience in courses that call upon them to take part actively through collaborative, experiential, reflective, or holistic pedagogies. The instructor has to foster a learning environment in which learners can feel safe enough to take some risks of self-disclosure and reflective construction of meaning.

Though the risks are real, they pale in comparison to the rewards. Each of the instructors in the five cases have a deep and abiding commitment to this work because it provides them with an enormous sense of satisfaction intellectually, pedagogically, personally, and ethically. They have a sense of contributing to the maturation, professional competence, and spiritual development of learners. They have also benefitted from engaging in such pedagogical work for their own intellectual, professional, and spiritual development. It would not be a stretch to say they have a palpable sense of having contributed to the development of theological knowledge, the strengthening of the church and other contexts of ministry, and, in some way, the repair and transformation of the world for the sake of the reign of God.

Though the instructor in courses that effectively promote integrating work has to take some important and predictable risks, other factors also matter a good deal. For example, instructional methods like case studies, collaborative instruction, field trips or travel seminars, and portfolios each played a major role in helping learners make meaningful connections between various kinds of knowledge and experience.

Different rhythms also exist for integrating work in courses. Jenkins's travel course to the US-Mexico borderlands involves a clear interplay between disintegrating and integrating work. Learners never begin with a blank slate; they always bring with them the fruits of prior learning, certain experiences, and particular conceptual understandings. Integrating work in courses involves more than simply constructing meaningful connections; it also involves destabilizing, challenging, or questioning existing structures of knowledge. Perhaps all courses that foster integrating work have to manage the work of disintegration to some degree. In this regard, instructors are attune to multiple levels of the course as it unfolds, particularly with respect to the interplay between the intellectual, emotional, spiritual, and social levels of the course.

The cases here also highlight the rhythm involved in the dynamic movement between action and reflection. In the travel seminar and in the visitation reports featured in Jeffrey Jones's course on leadership for the small church, learners engaged actively in a variety of ways, stepping back to reflect on and discuss what such engagements might mean. Aiming for an optimal balance and sequencing of action and reflection in these courses makes a difference pedagogically. Integrating work has an iterative, recursive, or spiral trajectory through a course rather than a strictly linear pathway; there is not a single pathway but at least as many pathways as there are learners (and instructors) in the course.

Several cases highlight the value of using course (re)design resources. Click and Jones closely followed Fink's framework as a way to strengthen integrating work in their courses. While Fink's model is not the only tool available, it has a proven track record and instructors generally find it user-friendly. These teachers would, however, be the first to say that Fink's approach does not do the work for the instructor; it does make the imaginative process of design and implementation easier, because key elements are not overlooked and all elements must be connected to each other.

Finally, the five case studies illustrate that effective integrating work can never occur solely within a course. Learning spills over into other parts of a theological school, particularly in relation to other courses and the larger curricular framework. Administrative structures, cocurricular activities, and the ethos of the school are affected as well. Here again there is no single linear movement between courses and other learning environments.

Integrating work also cannot be contained or accomplished in a course or even within the parameters of a theological school, because this work has a forward-looking and ever more expansive trajectory. Ultimately, it has an eschatological horizon. In a sense, this work entails thinking globally and even eschatologically while acting locally and immediately. Perhaps instructors who teach courses that emphasize integrating work should see such courses as important stops along a long journey rather than a short hop to a final destination.

PART 4

Frameworks

18

Conceptual Models and Theological Frameworks for Thinking about Integrating Work

—— Gordon S. Mikoski ——

Several metaphors for integrating come readily to mind: building bridges, making connections, weaving together, or establishing networks. Whatever the guiding metaphor, integrating work at its most basic level involves communities of learning that are establishing, reforming, and strengthening connections between experience, knowledge, skill, self-understanding, and community, which, in turn, allow for capacious, flexible, and life-affirming patterns to emerge.

Every year graduating students at Princeton Theological Seminary (PTS) participate in focus groups conducted by the curriculum assessment committee. They repeat the same critique: "You did a great job of taking things apart, but you did not do much to help us put the pieces back together again." Students regularly affirm that PTS's curriculum effectively moves people from a precritical to a critical posture toward scripture, doctrine, the church, and culture. We are quite adept at providing students with opportunities to disintegrate the often tacitly held assumptions they bring to theological education. One of PTS's curricular vulnerabilities is providing equally strong opportunities for students to revise or to establish new connections among their faith experiences, insights obtained from the study of scripture, history, practical and systematic theology, field education assignments, professional identity, and informal social interaction with peers and faculty in the seminary community. As we encountered this same critique repeatedly from graduating students over the past several years, the faculty began to consider new ways to promote the integrating work that is necessary once students have gained critical perspective on the assumptive worlds they bring to theological education.

One approach we have taken over the past five years is voluntary in character. We formed student cohort groups that are facilitated by one or two faculty members. Fifteen students meet with faculty from different departments and an area pastor for two years. In the group I facilitated we explored Christian vocation in relation to the theme of liturgy and social witness. The students who participated in this high-commitment extracurricular group had opportunities to engage in integrating-trajectory activities such as offering ashes at the local train station on Ash Wednesday during rush hour, having a retreat at a community worship and arts center in Philadelphia, as well as leading discussions about the interrelatedness of liturgy and social witness. Through such experiences, participants made meaningful connections among the various aspects of their otherwise fragmented seminary experience.

When these students were assessed just prior to graduation, the curriculum assessment committee discovered a striking contrast between students who had participated in cohort groups like the one I co-led and those who had not participated in any such group. Those who had participated in a cohort group expressed a higher degree of overall satisfaction and indicated they had ample opportunities to make meaningful connections between faith, learning, and field education experiences. These assessment results further piqued my interest in what needs to happen in integrating work in order to make meaningful connections among the otherwise fragmented dimensions of many students' experience.

As a professor of Christian education, I began to reflect on how integrating can be fostered intentionally. As with most educational theory, no one model, explanation, or diagram captures it completely. In this chapter, I propose several models as ways to conceptualize what is happening in integrating work: the various elements, types, processes, and theological valences.

The Synthetic Nature of Integrating Work in Theological Education

One student from the liturgy and social witness cohort group stands out in my memory. Upon graduation from seminary, she was called to serve as pastor for a Presbyterian Church (USA) congregation in the Saint Louis area. Her ministry in that congregation began a month before the racially charged events in Ferguson unfolded. In the midst of the political and civil conflict, she participated actively and regularly in events coordinated by area clergy to provide constructive social witness in the face of pervasive racial injustice. Though this student brought many resources to her ministry from theological education, I would like to think that her participation in the liturgy and social witness cohort group played a role in equipping her to make meaningful connections—both for herself and for her congregation. Somehow, this student moved beyond the fragmenting character of theological education toward making synthetic judgments.

Unfortunately, many theological educators assume that the reassembly or reintegrating process for learners who have come through the fires of higher criticism will take place rather easily and mainly at the student's initiative. Intentional and explicit attention to the development of synthetic judgments is often significantly underdeveloped in the curriculum. While theological schools make some gestures (such as field education reflection or capstone courses) toward forming synthetic judgments, students usually have to do the work on their own without much pedagogical scaffolding or guidance.

Elements and Patterns of Integrating Work

Integrating work focuses on a range of elements that require meaningful interconnection in order for responsible ministerial leadership to occur. Oftentimes theological educators have a particular set of elements in mind, such as theory and practice or head and heart. Bringing together two kinds of disconnected material can have great value, even if the scope is limited. By its very nature the integrating cuts against the grain, presents pedagogical challenges, and continually opens out to larger and more comprehensive realities. While integrating two elements—for example, theological concepts and personal biography—can suffer from reductionism, it is the most common way we speak about integrating.

For the sake of illustration, several thematic elements can be listed as commonly-linked pairs:

- Theory and practice
- Understanding and skills
- Cognition and affect
- Inductive and deductive methods of inquiry
- Individual and group processes
- Ideal aspirations and contextual realities
- Intentionality and effects of action
- Classroom and field education
- Intra- and interreligious perspectives
- Distinctive identity markers and group cohesion
- *Intra*disciplinarity (relating topics or skills within the same knowledge domain)
- *Inter*disciplinarity (relating topics or skills across knowledge domains)

The first step in becoming intentional about integrating work often begins with identifying such pairs, partners, or opposites. This does not mean, however, that integrating work only involves negotiating binary oppositions or tensions; we can also aim to establish connections among three or more thematic elements (for example, a course on the Psalms can focus on biblical interpretation, developing sermons, and leading worship as a chaplain in a psychiatric hospital). In reality, the various thematic elements and paired groups listed above often overlap, interrelate, and function in significant tension with one another. Many of these elements have a tendency not to park neatly in their designated spaces. Integrating processes always involves attending to multilayered complexity and richness.

Beyond working with combinations of various elements, integrating occurs in relation to a variety of predictable patterns or relations. I have developed a description and visual representation of five common patterns: linked or connected, fusion, mutual influence, networked, and complex open systems.

Pattern	Description	Symbolized Relations
Linked or connected	Elements retain their inherent integrity and are connected in some ways to other elements; ad hoc union.	Concept A → Concept B; Concept C; Concept D; Concept F; Concept E (arranged in circle with arrows)
Fusion	Elements are brought together in a way that establishes a new reality that is co-incident with the prior elements; union without differentiation.	Skill A + Skill B → Skill AB
Mutual influence	Elements influence and are influenced by one another in some reciprocal fashion.	• Skill A (Influenced by C and influences B); • Skill B (Incluenced by A and influences D); • Skill C (Influenced by D and incluences C); • Skill D (Influenced by B and influences D)

Pattern	Description	Symbolized Relations
Networked	Elements coordinate in multiple and complex ways in service to some particular end; end products are not identical with original elements nor with transitional schemas.	 Photo: Colourbox.com
Complex open systems	Elements are networked configuration of networks.	 Photo: Colourbox.com

Linked or connected integrating work involves helping learners bring together different kinds of knowledge or experience and fostering the development of a framework that can coordinate the various kinds of knowledge. The change to the thematic elements in play has to do primarily with external linkages and may not have a substantial impact on the thematic elements themselves. In this pattern, new insights arise from having a way to see formerly disparate elements in a larger, coordinated frame of reference. For example, a course on Cappadocian theology might include materials on Gregory of Nazianzen's biblical hermeneutics, a treatment of the shape of higher education during the period in which Gregory and Basil studied together in Athens, and analysis of the social and economic context among the privileged class in central Asia Minor during the middle of the fourth century. The perspectives from various fields of study could be linked or coordinated in order to shed light on Cappadocian theology in the cultural context of its origin.

Fusion involves bringing thematic elements together into a unity that contains most or all the dimensions of the component pieces. Much like harmonics in music, the whole here is greater than the mere summation of the parts. For example, an introductory course in speech for ministry would help presiders in corporate worship learn to bring together exegetical practices and speech techniques in order to begin developing skills for public reading of scriptural texts as oral performance. Or, an educational ministry course focusing on educational psychology might feature the "interpersonal neurobiology" perspective on learning as articulated by Daniel J. Siegel in his book *The Developing Mind: How Relationships and the Brain Interact to Shape Who We Are.*[1] In this framework, the biology of the brain and the dynamics of attachment in social relationships are fused into a larger whole for understanding how learning works; it would no longer make sense for students and teacher to talk about learning solely in relation to either the brain or social relations.

The *mutual influence* pattern for integrating work allows the component thematic elements to remain intact while emphasizing or exploring ways in which the juxtaposition of the elements can enrich or challenge one another. For example, a course on baptism and Christian formation could consider the ways in which liturgical practice has been influenced by differing theologies of the Trinity and vice versa.

In a *networked* pattern, the elements retain their own integrity while simultaneously contributing to and being influenced by other elements in a dynamic system of influence. For example, a course on practical ecclesiology could explore the complex phenomenon of a parish through a practical theological lens that connects theology, church history, studies of nonprofit corporations, congregational studies, sociology, and leadership theory. Here, each of the informing disciplines are made up of complex and differentiated knowledge fields; while each explains a parish in its own way,

1. Siegel, *Developing Mind*.

connections could be made across the networks, establishing similar and unique perspectives on distinct issues or common threads.

A *complex open systems* model functions as a system of systems or a network of networks. Well-defined and interconnected systems link with other such systems in order to establish larger and larger frames of reference. The deep learning associated with developing expertise could be seen as establishment of several overlapping and interrelated networks of complex knowledge and skill. In this pattern, insight and skill developed in relation to a particular cluster of integrating concerns would connect dynamically with other clusters of integrating concerns. For example, a course on critical race theory would open out to feminist and eco-justice concerns. A larger pattern of networked concerns could, in turn, provide the occasion for establishing further connections with public theology, communications studies, globalization studies, and interfaith dialogue.

Each of the patterns described here can fulfill a productive pedagogical purpose related to integrating work in theological education. Depending upon the pedagogical goals, context, subject matter, methods, and learner profiles, any one of these patterns could serve a useful pedagogical purpose. No one pattern need be adopted as normative for every course or the curriculum as a whole. Rather, a range of models exist that can be used in enhancing integrating work in classrooms, curriculums, and schools.

Rhythms of Integrating Work

Developing facility with integrating work does not occur in a single session of learning, nor does it take place through the use of a single method or in relation to a particular area of curriculum. Instead, it develops over an extended period of time and requires intentionality, dialogue, reflection, and instructional scaffolding. It also requires a rhythm of engagement, reflection, consolidation, communication, and expression. To engage in integrating work, there must be enough rich and textured experience, knowledge, and skill for learners to make new and dynamic connections among disparate aspects of their experience in theological education.

New connections, once established, need testing through expression in words, symbols, or action in order to become fully integrated into the learner's frame of reference. Because integrating remains an open-ended and fluid process without reaching an ultimate stasis, learners need opportunities to express and consolidate their learning as signposts or enting markers along the way.

A key part of the rhythm of integrating work also involves, as this book has demonstrated, disintegration. Disintegration has a positive role to play in the integrating project. In fact, preexisting forms of integration must be challenged, reframed, or even broken down in order to create conceptual space for more adequate, flexible, life-giving, and open-ended patterns of meaningful connection. Integrating work frequently involves retrogression in order to progress. The processes of integrating work are more iterative and messy than strictly linear and straightforward.

Theological Perspectives

Many theological issues come into play when exercising pedagogical imagination in relation to the various elements and patterns associated with integrating work. In fact, integrating always carries some degree of theological valence. While in some sense all the major loci or theological doctrines have something important to contribute to the theory and practice of integrating work in theological education, a handful of theological themes from the Reformed tradition in which I teach and practice stand out in bold relief: God as Trinity, creation, sin, Christology and soteriology, sanctification, and eschatology. I offer a brief consideration of theological themes that draw further insight into the elements and patterns discussed above.

The theological affirmation of God as triune suggests that all integrating work finally takes its cues from the mystery of God as revealed in Jesus Christ by the power of the Holy Spirit. In some profound way, ultimate Truth has the character of both differentiation and unity. Christians can easily distort the Trinity by stressing either too much unity or too much diversity. The mystery of God as three in one stands as the norm for understanding the mystery at the heart of integrating work.

Considered from the doctrine of creation, the whole cosmos exists as a panoply of particulars that have their own beauty and integrity and are simultaneously and necessarily elements of interrelated systems and increasingly more comprehensive frameworks. Today we increasingly see the creation as a series of interconnected, overlapping, and mutually influencing networks of energy and power.

Despite God's glory and the interrelated beauty of the cosmos, the reality of sin is pervasive and persistent. In short, individually and collectively we have disintegrated and are disintegrated by things inside us, between us, and around us. The character of sin and its wretched consequences has everything to do with disintegrating the original order and beauty intended by the triune God.

Christian theology reframes sin through soteriology. From beginning to end, the witness of scripture points to divine action in history to repair the damage humans have inflicted on each other and the created order. The story of divine redemption in history is a story of integrating work initiated by and carried out by the triune God. For Christians, the central divine act of salvation involves the coming, ministry, death, resurrection, ascension, and reign of Jesus Christ—who in his person manifests the mystery of integrating work between God and creation. God's integrating work in human history culminates in the death and resurrection of Jesus Christ, which manifests the integrating power of divine love:

> He is the image of the invisible God, the firstborn of all creation; for in him all things in heaven and on earth were created, things visible and invisible, whether thrones or dominions or rulers or powers—all things have been created through him and for him. He himself is before all things, and in him all things hold together. He is the head of the body, the church; he is the beginning, the firstborn from the dead, so that he might come to have first place in everything. For in him all the fullness of God was pleased to dwell, and through him God was pleased to reconcile to himself all things, whether on earth or in heaven, by making peace through the blood of his cross. (Col 1:15–20)

Based on the integrating power of trinitarian love manifest in Jesus Christ, human efforts at integrating resonate with sanctification, the processes of transformation from one degree of Christ's glory to another (2 Cor 3:18) brought about by the work of the Holy Spirit in the church. To become conformed more and more to the image and likeness of Jesus Christ, by the work of the Holy Spirit, means to become more loving toward God, ourselves, one another, and the rest of creation. For Christians, love functions as the driving force and the destination for all integrating work, as Rebecca Slough noted in her chapter in this book.

Ultimately, our sanctification has an eschatological horizon. As has been stated at various points in this book, integrating work has more to do with verbs than nouns. It involves ever-widening processes and concerns. In fact, integrating work eventually moves toward the final act of the divine drama of redemption in history when all things in heaven and on earth will be brought together into a dynamic and differentiated unity of praise and thanksgiving. The trajectory for integrating work in theological education concerns the divine fulfillment of love that will reverberate through all things in the future that God will bring about. Only eschatologically does it make sense to speak of integrating work in a proper theological sense; yet even then it exists not as a static and lifeless end state but as a dynamic symphony of doxological praise lifted up by all God's creatures.

A Concluding Unscientific Postscript

Integrating work in theological education involves putting into play a range of thematic elements in relation to particular patterns of interconnection for purposes of fostering faithful and effective ministerial leaders who will participate in the triune God's ongoing work of bringing all things into loving fulfillment and the fulfillment of love in the future. Though this work starts as small as a mustard seed, it eventually grows by God's grace and by our pedagogical imagination into a large and life-giving enterprise. For this reason, integrating work is one of the most exciting, challenging, and rewarding aspects of the entire enterprise of theological education.

Bibliography

Siegel, Daniel J. *The Developing Mind: How Relationships and the Brain Interact to Shape Who We Are.* 2nd ed. New York: Guildford, 2012.

19

Integrative Knowing
and Practical Wisdom

—— Kathleen A. Cahalan ——

I drove to my aunt's funeral with a heavy heart. The last family funeral I had attended in my family's rural parish was for my cousin's son who died in the Iraq war. It was crushing for so many reasons, but one key reason was the presider. His ministry was ineffective (cool, distant, and unemotional), rule bound (arguing with the family over their request for popular music outside the liturgical tradition), and rigid (he clung to the book and read the scripture and prayers in a monotone). Actually, for pastoral care, the National Guard trumped the church. They sent a caregiver who provided continual help and presence to the family (including meeting the family and the body at the airport and standing with them through hours of visitation); their symbols and rituals were dominant throughout the funeral and burial; and the narrative of the brave soldier had more weight than the gospel.

At my aunt's funeral, I was taken by surprise. The new pastor was pastorally and liturgically in another league than his predecessor. He led the wake service with a brief catechesis, explaining what we could anticipate that night and the next day, as he leaned into the narrative of Jesus's death, burial, and resurrection. He led the service with the standard rituals but augmented them with a time for storytelling. The next morning he met the extended family and invited each one of us to come to the casket, offer a prayer, and say good-bye. He then formed us into a line and we processed from the school chapel to the main church, evoking Thomas Long's admonition that Christians accompany their dead all the way to their graves.[1] The burial, a few plots away from our fallen soldier, drew together the baptismal images with our hope in the resurrection. At the luncheon I asked this priest, "Where did you learn to preside like that?" "I try to pray the liturgy," he told me. "And not just read the words from the book."

This tale of two funerals illustrates the integrative work at the heart of ministry, what Robert Hovda describes as "strong, loving, and wise" presence.[2] How did this priest learn to be this kind of minister?

The Intelligence of Practice

There is an intelligence to practice. That intelligence is the knowing that emerges from intentional practice over time. That intelligence is multiple in regard to both what one knows and how one comes to know. Yet, it is not cumulative but integrative, drawing together how one comes to know and that which one knows. In philosophical and theological traditions, this kind of intelligence is referenced in many ways: *phronesis*, prudence, practical reason, and practical wisdom.

For Aristotle (384–322 BCE), phronesis is an intellectual virtue that relates the highest truths and moral *telos* to everyday actions and decisions, an intelligence that draws insights from many situations in order to judge what to do in a particular instance. Phronesis is neither scientific (*episteme*) nor craft (*techne*) knowledge but is a distinctive kind of integrative knowing, taking account of multiple sources of information and combining them in ways that render insights into action, information into judgment.[3]

Similarly, for Aquinas (1225–1274 CE), prudence is the highest moral virtue, because it integrates other virtues and comprises eight elements that coalesce in a prudent person who is wise in action. To be prudent and make wise decisions requires drawing upon memory, understanding, and reason; it demands dispositions of docility (learning from others) and shrewdness (learning from one's self); and it exercises imagination regarding various courses of action and their consequences—what Aquinas called foresight, circumspection, and caution.[4] This highest moral virtue reckons multiple

1. Long, *Accompany Them with Singing*.
2. Hovda, *Strong, Loving and Wise*.
3. Aristotle, *Nicomachean Ethics* 1139a–42a.
4. See Thomas Aquinas, *Summa Theologica*.

ways of knowing that combine rational thought with imagination and dispositions toward knowledge.

Scholars of professional education—for example, Don S. Browning (1934–2010) in practical theology, Patricia Benner in nursing, and William Sullivan and Matthew Rosen in higher education—advocate retrieving Aristotle's practical reason as a distinctive kind of knowing. Practical reason for such thinkers also includes narrative, imagination, discernment, perception, communal wisdom, and moral vision as indispensable aspects of the human knowing that informs intention and action. Hence, it is a deeply integrative way of knowing and living. The value placed on abstract, objective, theoretical knowledge—central to the Enlightenment project and the backbone of higher education—is too limiting. Neither theory nor critical thinking is rejected, but they are not ends in themselves; rather, they are integral to practical knowing. Educators mistakenly conceive of theoretical knowing as the highest knowledge and reject or deem lesser other kinds of knowing.[5]

Why is "the very kind of knowledge that people need to live well— what we call *practical wisdom*—the least understood, the hardest to learn, and often the most devalued kind of knowledge?"[6] This essay will explore the second question: Why is practical wisdom the hardest kind of knowledge to learn? My answer is because practical wisdom is integrative knowledge that encompasses the full dimensions of human being, knowing, and acting.[7] In the context of professional education, it requires intentional practice over time with attention to multiple kinds of knowing and learning. In studying practical wisdom and integrating work in theological education for ministry, I have identified eight ways of knowing that are essential to wise practice:

1. *Situated awareness* is noticing and describing contextual factors.

2. *Embodied realizing* is developing skilled competence in bodily action.

3. *Conceptual understanding* is comprehending and remembering key information.

4. *Critical thinking* is analyzing and evaluating concepts and actions.

5. Schön, *Educating the Reflective Practitioner*, 3.

6. Bass et al., *Christian Practical Wisdom*, 1.

7. See Cahalan, "Reframing Knowing, Being, and Doing"; Cahalan, "Integration in Theological Education"; Foley, *Theological Reflection across Religious Traditions*, 65–90.

5. *Emotional attunement* is identifying and using awareness of feelings and affective states.

6. *Creative insight* is developing imaginative and creative responses.

7. *Spiritual discernment* is perceiving what is of God and not of God.

8. *Practical reasoning* is problem solving, forming judgments, gaining a sense of salience, and acting wisely.

Professional education aims at forming persons who are knowledgeable, skillful, moral, and competent practitioners—a difficult task in any field. Yet, we know practical wisdom when we see it: "It shows up in a kind of good judgment they are able to put into play in a particular time and place, sometimes as if by second nature . . . [T]hey are engaged, flexible, attuned, and attentive on many levels—cognitively, emotionally, relationally, morally, and spiritually."[8] Thus, practical wisdom is not a ninth way of knowing but rather what emerges from drawing together these multiple kinds of knowing. Such learning and knowing take place over time, although the process is not linear or simple; it is not mastering a body of ideas or the interpretation of texts but rather the kind of knowing that emerges from engaged, embodied practice. It develops through what Christian Scharen and Eileen Campbell-Reed call the "long arc of learning ministry," which is when a leader knows what to do, why to do it, and how to do it for the sake of God's people.[9]

Initially I viewed the first pastor, whom I will call Jamie, as a failed or deficient practitioner until I came to see that he was a novice at funeral ministry.[10] To be fair to him, burying a twenty-two-year-old man killed in action is not the same as burying a ninety-year-old woman. With more experience combined with opportunities for reflection on practice with mentors and peers, he will have the chance to embody the presence, knowledge, skill, and wisdom that were apparent in the second pastor.

8. Bass et al., *Christian Practical Wisdom*, 1.

9. Scharen and Campbell-Reed, "Learning Pastoral Imagination," 2.

10. See Dreyfus and Dreyfus, *Mind over Machine*; Scharen, "Learning Ministry over Time," 265–89; Cahalan, *Introducing the Practice of Ministry*, 118–48; Foley, *Theological Reflection across Religious Traditions*, 80–82.

In the Beginning

Jamie was like many seminarians in his class: bright, with good grades from his undergraduate study, active in church activities, and possessing a felt call to ministry. He was not a novice to ministry, since he had participated in church life, but he was a novice in the sense that he lacked practical know-how. Novices are students at the beginning of professional practice. They are not incompetent; rather, they lack the experiential background to know what to do. Novices generally (1) rely on theoretical models, preferring to follow a set of rules or steps; (2) mimic the practice of exemplars; (3) are physically and emotionally self-conscious; and (4) have limited ability to read the dynamics of the context beyond their own actions. Jamie was doing his best to follow the rubrics of the funeral liturgy and read correctly from the book; he was undoubtedly nervous about standing before a crowd of people in this emotionally charged situation; and he had little experience to help him understand what was happening to the family, town members, media, military personnel, and himself.

To learn a skilled practice, beginners begin with parts of a practice. In learning to teach a children's catechetical lesson, for example, novices need to understand the basic elements of teaching: lesson planning, public speaking, age-appropriate activities, and classroom management. They need basic guidelines in order to carry out each of these parts of teaching. Musically speaking, they must start by learning the basic scales of practice. John Witvliet notes, "As any veteran athlete or musician knows, these drills and scales are a critical part of the work, an activity from which one never graduates."[11]

Practicing a skill repeatedly is important because the actions become inscribed in the body as muscle memory. "Such skills 'literally get sedimented' in the 'embodied know-how' of the mature practitioner."[12] Expert practice is built upon innumerable hours of habit formation. Novices require intense concentration when practicing, even to the extent that their capacity to talk or to hear advice is severely limited.

Practicing scales, building muscle memory, and acquiring focused attention are the foundations on which a practitioner can build the scaffolding of practice. Having specific steps to guide their actions helps novices know what to do. Their practice is generally limited and inflexible, but over

11. Witvliet, "Teaching Worship as a Christian Practice," 140.
12. Miller-McLemore, "Practical Theology and Pedagogy," 181.

time these steps become less clunky and artificial and more fluid. Jamie may have presided at only a few funerals, and thus he needed to rely on the book. As Eugene Walsh notes, however, "There is no way for one to think oneself into being a good presider. One has got to get it into one's muscles and bones, just like dancers, actors, and ballplayers."[13] Only through reflective practice over time will Jamie feel the movement of the liturgy as part of his embodied presence. He will become less concerned with following external rules because they will have become more internalized.

Novices also pattern themselves after the actions of exemplars. In their study of how a vocation emerges among ministers, health care workers, and humanitarian workers, Matt Bloom and associates underscore the importance of exemplars in the first stage of discerning a calling. Such exemplars provide people with a living example of someone who embodies a high level of competence as well as personal integrity and a sense of calling.[14] When students engage with an exemplar in practice, they begin what Bloom and colleagues calls the "mapping" of their identity onto an exemplar, comparing and contrasting themselves to this practitioner. Mapping one's self onto another eventually leads people to be able to imagine themselves as enacting the role.

Jamie may well have had exemplars of ministry, but in this crucial moment he needed to know how a wise pastor would perform this funeral. It might have been better if another pastor had been present that day to help him. Exemplars of practice provide novices with models to follow. Mimicking exemplars is fairly normal for beginners, since it takes time and practice to find one's own style.

A beginner has low contextual awareness, emotional attunement,[15] and relational perception of others. Much of Jamie's focus was on his performance. Reflection on that performance is an essential part of learning, but novices often judge their performance by how well they followed the rules. Their critical perspectives widen when they can reflect on their practice with peers with whom they can share their vulnerability, mistakes, and joys.[16] To learn a practice means to "experience the practice, practice it,

13. As cited in Hovda, *Strong, Loving and Wise*, 92–93.

14. Bloom et al., "Work as a Calling," 23–27.

15. Emotional intelligence is a "subset of social intelligence that involves the ability to monitor one's own and others' feelings and emotions, to discriminate among them and to use this information to guide one's thinking and actions." Salovey and Mayer, "Emotional Intelligence."

16. Brookfield, "Adult Cognition," 100.

tell about it, ask questions about it, read about it, write about it, practice it, do it, empower others to do it."[17] The ability to respond in a given situation, strategize what to say, and work with individuals or groups develops over time as novices compare their capacities to basic rules, standards, exemplars, and other novices.

Although novices generally are not highly attuned toward others, many feel vulnerable, artificial, and even fraudulent in their roles.[18] These emotions are quite normal, since the actions and decisions are not yet their own. As Bonnie J. Miller-McLemore writes, "One may feel artificial and forced in making these moves at first, but over time, as one experiments with particular gestures and phrases, practices them over and over, and considers their theological implications, these actions and decisions can become a more reliable and authentic part of one's own pastoral repertoire."[19] Jamie's lack of emotional connectedness to the people at the funeral may have stemmed from his feeling inauthentic.

Adult learners learn in "incremental fluctuations," which can be frustrating. They take "two steps forward, one step back, followed by four steps forward, one step back."[20] Because learning new ideas and skills requires taking on new perspectives, challenging personal and cultural assumptions, and tolerating ambiguity, it is common for novices to vacillate between feelings of failure and moments of exhilaration.

Other features of practical wisdom are limited for novices entering new situations. Most cannot fully read a context because they have a limited ability to imagine different options and their consequences. Thus, novices do not execute a high degree of practical reasoning since they lack the experience of multiple situations to help them discern what to do. Learning ministry in seminary and the first few years of a call requires a range of experiences in order build a repository of similar cases on which a practitioner can draw. As Bent Flyvbjerg notes, "Common to all experts is that they operate on the basis of intimate knowledge of several thousand concrete cases in their areas of expertise."[21] Jamie is not going to become better at funeral ministry after a few liturgies; rather, he needs to preside at many in order to build up a repertoire of insights upon which he can later rely.

17. Miller-McLemore, "Practical Theology and Pedagogy," 178.

18. Brookfield, "Adult Cognition," 96–100.

19. Miller-McLemore, "Practical Theology and Pedagogy," 180.

20. Brookfield, "Adult Cognition," 98.

21. Flyvbjerg, "Five Misunderstandings."

Regarding spiritual discernment, the tradition has a similar approach to novices as do today's professional educators; a particular kind of knowing emerges from spiritual practice.[22] After traveling through Egypt and Syria as a novice learning what he could from monastic practitioners, John Cassian (ca. 360–435 CE) then returned to the West to found monasteries in Marseilles. In his two major works, Cassian is writing for new communities embarking on the monastic life and is particularly attentive to beginners.[23]

One key aspect of practical wisdom for Cassian is discernment. To learn the way of desert monasticism, novices had to follow some rules. The rule concerning eating and fasting that governed choices was not quantity but moderation (not eating too much or too little). A second discernment that also needed to be learned was of thoughts, or identifying what is from God and what is not. Cassian wanted to learn how to pray ceaselessly but found that in prayer he was attacked by his own thoughts. In learning to pray, Cassian was taught and passed on a simple practice: if one is prone to afflictive thoughts during prayer or work, replace them with a word or phrase from scripture. In this way, a scriptural consciousness came to replace the afflictions that plagued monks' inner life and transformed their ordinary consciousness. Novices learned spiritual practices that shaped body, mind, and heart through repetition, simple actions that focused the mind, gentle encouragement from exemplars, and support in a community of learners.

Advancing in Practice

Ministry students eventually become less reliant on theories, models, and rules as their contextual awareness grows. They gain the ability to recognize elements in situations because they perceive similarities with prior examples. Practice builds intuition; reflection on practice builds judgment. Students grow in their ability to assess situations and make nascent decisions about how to proceed. Most tend to focus on immediate details, and thus their narratives about a situation can be partial, abstract, or generalized; they may not yet see the whole situation.[24]

Students need to practice alongside a mentor whose practice they respect. They can both observe and be observed by them in practice.

22. See Cahalan, "Unknowing," 275–321.

23. See *John Cassian: Conferences*; and *John Cassian: The Institutes*.

24. Benner, *From Novice to Expert*, 23.

Mentors become dialogue partners, explaining the thinking behind their practice as well as guiding a student in his or her own performance and skill development. Advanced beginners are practicing "at the border of their own skill," are continually dependent on others, and may have difficulty understanding where their responsibility lies.[25] They act in ways that are largely external to the situation or are guided by factors external to the immediate situation, and may not always feel responsibility for the outcome. "Advanced beginners demonstrate extraordinary dependence on the expertise of others, striving to assert their own independent practice, and continually questioning their capacity to contribute."[26] They define success as the completion of tasks, everything being okay, and the fact that they are not failing. At this point, though, failure and mistakes are pivotal to learning. If the learner has a wise guide, missteps can become opportunities for creative insights about alternative courses of action with different consequences. Failure becomes the gateway to greater emotional attunement.

As practitioners assume roles, their identity and sense of calling is shaped by what Matt Bloom and his colleagues term "acknowledgement." When their skills and knowledge are acknowledged by others in a professional setting, they begin to embrace the responsibilities and expectations of the position. For ministry students this occurs when they preach for the first time, offer counsel, or accompany the dying. "Acknowledgement occurs when informants made a psychological commitment to the certainty that there was some distinctive and important work for which they are specially endowed and therefore to which they are called. In acknowledgement, individuals fully accept and affirm to themselves the reality of their call. During acknowledgment, intuitive awareness becomes self-declaration about one's future."[27] Students require affirmation by mentors who confirm their intuitive sense of vocation. When they make their call public, they begin to profess who they are.

Another feature of practical wisdom and emotional maturing is docility—the capacity to learn from others. For example, after several years of ministry, Emily was asked to preside at a funeral for a two-year-old. Knowing this was beyond her present experience and competence, she called three other pastors whose judgment she respected. These experiences are

---

25. Tanner and Benner, *Expertise in Nursing Practice*, 49.

26 Ibid., 26.

27. Bloom et al., "Work as a Calling," 30.

crucial moments in which either a door into deeper, more reflective practice opens or a person becomes too intimidated and the door to learning closes.

Humor, or the ability to not take oneself too seriously, is another important sign of emotional maturing. For example, as a student pastor in field education in a poor inner-city neighborhood, Heidi B. Neumark created a flyer for a Sunday school program, which she wanted to deliver to every door in a twenty-one-story building. Her supervisor suggested that she wait until someone could accompany her, but Neumark became impatient and headed into the building in August, confidently wearing her "black shirt with its white clerical collar." She got stuck in a stairwell when the electricity went out. When she began sweating profusely, she "pulled out the white collar tab and opened a few buttons," losing her "pastoral identity" in the dark.[28] Some children eventually found her and helped her out of the building. In retrospect, she could see and share the event in a humorous light.

Cassian taught that humility, like discernment, is a virtue that emerges from practice. As the desert monastics practiced moderating their desires and turning their attention toward God, they acquired humility regarding who they were in the sight of God: both sinful and graced. They realized that their attempts to improve their practice and become more competent and skilled largely led to complete failure—similar to the foolishness of human wisdom that Paul wrote about.[29] Humility is knowing that one's life and practice entirely depend upon God.

Regarding practical reasoning and decision-making ability, advanced beginners are gaining what Benner and colleagues call "a sense of salience." They know what to do and when and why to do it, and they can give reasons for their actions. She notes, "Deep background knowledge is the heart of practical reason."[30] Building up their humility, intuition, and judgment over a thousand cases, the student is learning practical or ministerial reasoning in context.[31]

28. Neumark, *Breathing Space*, 20–22.

29. See 1 Cor 1:18 and 3:19.

30. Benner et al., *Educating Nurses*, 30.

31. Ibid., 46, on clinical reasoning.

Competence in Practice

Over the first ten years, most practitioners become competent as they take on the full identity, role, and responsibility of their profession.[32] They have an array of experiences they deploy in practice as they encounter both familiar and new situations. Over time, conceptual thinking moves to the background as practical thinking moves to the foreground. They do not need to mimic others as their own style emerges. Competence moves ever closer to practical wisdom when ministers discern the contextually salient features of a situation, are emotionally attuned to themselves and others, can think creatively, are relationally present, and decide how to act in a skilled way.

The third phase in the development of a "called professional" in Bloom's study is integration, in which there is an "integration of self and calling that leads to an identity as a called profession." Integration involves both competency and authenticity. A sense of competence is gained by knowing that "one is skillful in what one does." A practitioner can see immediately the positive impact of his or her work and experience positive emotions during and after situations. Further, the experience of authenticity and integrity emerges as the gap between one's self and the professional role narrows. Bloom and colleagues states that "authenticity is the experience of work as an expression of one's true self and therefore as a life calling." A person is "no longer playing the role of a professional, they have become a professional."[33] In addition, important people and institutions have endorsed, verified, and validated their work.

Competent ministers are able to predict situations more effectively, discern the salience of possible actions, and put the particulars of a situation in dialogue with what they know. According to Benner, "The competent stage of skill acquisition is typically a time of heightened planning for what are now more predictable immediate futures."[34] The ministers are better able to handle familiar situations and can ponder how to respond to likely events in the near future. They cope in stressful situations by adopting a process of decision making, evaluating what is most important to act on now and what can be delayed.

32. Dreyfus and Dreyfus, *Mind over Machine*, 16–51.
33. Bloom et al., "Work as a Calling," 38.
34. Benner, "Using the Dreyfus Model," 193.

Practical reasoning emerges over time. It is akin to problem solving and is a kind of "calculative rationality." Pastors can feel responsible for and are emotionally involved in their choices, but they can also step back to decide in a more reflective, even detached way. They are emotionally attuned but are not derailed by their own emotions in this difficult ministry. They can experience both joy at effective service and sadness when it does not go as planned.[35] Emotions serve to screen and alert practitioners rather than impede them; they become informative and trusted guides. As pastors gain insight into their emotions, they can become more emotionally available to others, embodying what Benner calls the "skill of involvement" in appropriate ways.

Competent ministers develop the ability to think on their feet as the theoretical material they learned moves into the background and their own experience-based knowledge moves to the fore. Because ministers have increased experience in different contexts, they can more immediately sense the needs and responses of people. They know when breaking the rule is the right thing to do because it serves a larger good—for example, when popular music might be warranted in a funeral even though it breaches the norms of a tradition.[36] Spiritual leaders can think creatively by identifying several options, imagine scenarios for each, and perceive the consequences of different courses of action. Their ministry has evolved beyond understanding theories about becoming a spiritual leader. Pastors move beyond attempts to find the right program and toward authentic interpersonal relating.

Becoming competent in professional practice is a way of being faithful to one's vocation, gifts, and capacities. According to Roman Catholic theologians Francis Nemeck and Marie Theresa Coombs, the focus of the first half of life is rightly on developing the self: "I must increase so that Christ may increase."[37] Nemeck and Coombs recognize that spiritual growth and development occurs when a person's sense of self is strong enough that one can surrender one's own desires in service to another.

35. Ibid., 194.
36. Taylor, "To Follow a Rule," 165–80.
37. Nemeck and Coombs, *Spiritual Journey*, 41.

Another Kind of Competence: Expertise or Unknowing?

Expertise in a particular field is not widespread.[38] In fact, most practitioners in most professions remain competent in their practice and do not strive for greater skill or knowledge. Furthermore, their domain of expertise is quite particular and not necessarily transferrable to other domains. Thus, being a US Open golf champion does not mean one can become a top-rated baseball player.

Several insights from expertise studies are applicable to ministry. First, expertise requires hours of practice to hone one's skill, but it also requires taking the time to focus on discrete aspects of one's practice and become more accomplished in these. For example, if a sermon at a funeral lacked imagination and insight, a pastor could take six months to study funeral preaching, examine what other pastors are doing, and rewrite his or her sermon. Second, experts go back to theory. They learn new ideas, frameworks, and ways of understanding their practice. A pastor might improve by reading recent research on grieving or homiletic theory, both of which have changed since his or her time in seminary. Third, experts learn from people who are better than they are and accept coaching. A pastor might identify some of the best preachers in the area, observe them, and identify a potential coach. Experts then have the ability to go back to the beginning and, in some ways, become a novice again.

The problem with the current state of expertise studies is that the majority focus on athletes, musicians, professional game players (for example, chess masters), or scientists. In these cases, the virtues of practice are related to speed, efficiency, accuracy, and often individual effort. But ministers who are expert practitioners require something very different: the ability to slow down and contemplate what God is doing.

The traditions of spiritual practices reveal a dimension of practical wisdom quite distinct from expertise studies. Besides discernment and humility, long engagement in spiritual practice also leads to unknowing.[39] Unknowing is a kind of knowledge that comes from spiritual practice, but was largely lost in the Christian tradition, becoming a doctrine of God rather than a practice. At a certain point in the spiritual journey, practitio-

---

38. Anders Ericsson, "Enhancing the Development of Professional Performance," 405–31.

39. See my discussion of unknowing in Cahalan, "Unknowing," 302–14.

ners recognized that the goal of achieving a loving relationship with God cannot be acquired through more knowledge, as traditionally understood. As the anonymous author of *The Cloud of Unknowing* teaches, they must leave behind book knowledge to receive and embrace unknowing.[40]

Unknowing relates to perceptions we have of the self, the world, and God. We can never know all there is to know, completely know ourselves, or ever completely comprehend God. Of course, unknowing is acquired through a life of discernment and humility. It becomes a stance in relationship to human knowledge; it is comfortable with ambiguity and doubt and can surrender to the one who cannot be known. This paradoxical knowing is grasped in relinquishing the self we have constructed. Nemeck and Coombs state that the practitioner's self-awareness shifts (in Christian terms) to an awareness captured in the words of John the Baptist: "I must decrease so that Christ may increase." Unknowing is kenotic knowledge; it is the experience of living by way of the imitation of Christ.[41]

Funeral ministry is one place for witnessing the integrative practical wisdom of the presider and its impact on the community. I recognized such wisdom the day of my aunt's funeral—that presider was cognizant of the situation and emotionally attuned to our loss. He was also able to interpret our experience from biblical and theological perspectives, embody with grace the ritual actions, and be creative and salient in how he led us. He also demonstrated to me spiritual discernment and humility. I was invited to serve as a eucharistic minister, and when he handed me the plate he asked, "Would you like to give Communion to your family?" My family consisted of a rather large group of people sitting on the left side of the church. I was overcome with joy and grateful for his offer; he served a few people sitting on the right side of the church.

Bibliography

Aquinas, Thomas. *Summa Theologica*. Translated by Fathers of the English Dominican Province, I–II, q. 55–67. New York: Benziger Brothers, 1947
Aristotle. *Nicomachean Ethics*. In *Introduction to Aristotle*. 2nd ed., edited by Richard McKeon. Chicago: University of Chicago Press, 1973.

40. *The Cloud of Unknowing*. The author is writing a letter to a twenty-four-year-old disciple who is beginning to learn contemplative prayer.
41. Nemeck and Coombs, *Spiritual Journey*, 41.

Bass, Dorothy C., Kathleen A. Cahalan, Bonnie J. Miller-McLemore, James N. Nieman, and Christian Scharen. *Christian Practical Wisdom: What It Is, Why It Matters.* Grand Rapids: Eerdmans, 2016.

Bass, Dorothy C., and Craig Dykstra, eds. *For Life Abundant: Practical Theology, Theological Education, and Christian Ministry.* Grand Rapids: Eerdmans, 2008.

Benner, Patricia. *From Novice to Expert: Excellence and Power in Clinical Nursing Practice.* Menlo Park, CA: Addison-Wesley, 1984.

———. "Using the Dreyfus Model of Skill Acquisition to Describe and Interpret Skill Acquisition and Clinical Judgment in Nursing Practice and Education." *Bulletin of Science, Technology and Society* 24.3 (2004).

Benner, Patricia E., et al. *Educating Nurses: A Call for Radical Transformation.* San Francisco: Jossey-Bass, 2010.

Bloom, Matt, et al. "Work as a Calling: Integrating Personal and Professional Identities." Unpublished manuscript, 2015.

Brookfield, Stephen D. "Adult Cognition as a Dimension of Lifelong Learning." In *Lifelong Learning: Education across the Lifespan,* edited by John Field and Mal Leicester. New York: RoutledgeFalmer, 2000.

Cahalan, Kathleen A. "Integration in Theological Education." In *The Wiley-Blackwell Companion to Practical Theology,* edited by Bonnie J. Miller-McLemore, 386–95. London: Wiley-Blackwell, 2011.

———. *Introducing the Practice of Ministry.* Collegeville, MN: Liturgical, 2010.

———. "Reframing Knowing, Being, and Doing in the Seminary Classroom." *Teaching Theology and Religion* 14.4 (2011) 343–53.

———. "Unknowing: Spiritual Practice and the Search for a Wisdom Epistemology." In Bass et al., *Christian Practical Wisdom: What It Is, Why It Matters,* 275–321. Grand Rapids: Eerdmans, 2016.

The Cloud of Unknowing. Edited by James Walsh. Mahway, NJ: Paulist, 1981.

Dreyfus, Hubert L., and Stuart E. Dreyfus. *Mind over Machine: The Power of Human Intuition and Expertise in the Era of the Computer.* New York: Free, 1986.

Ericsson, K. Anders. "Enhancing the Development of Professional Performance: Implications from the Study of Deliberate Practice." In *Development of Professional Expertise: Toward Measurement of Expert Performance and Design of Optimal Learning Environments,* edited by K. Anders Ericsson, 405–31. Cambridge: Cambridge University Press, 2009.

Flyvbjerg, Bent. "Five Misunderstandings about Case-Study Research." *Qualitative Inquiry* 12.2 (2006) 222.

Foley, Edward. *Theological Reflection across Religious Traditions: The Turn to Reflective Believing.* Lanham, MD: Rowman & Littlefield, 2015.

Hovda, Robert W. *Strong, Loving and Wise: Presiding in Liturgy.* Collegeville, MN: Liturgical, 1983.

John Cassian: Conferences. Translated by Colm Luibhéid. Mahwah, NJ: Paulist, 1985.

John Cassian: The Institutes. Translated by Boniface Ramsey. Mahway, NJ: Newman, 1997.

Long, Thomas G. *Accompany Them with Singing: The Christian Funeral.* Louisville: Westminster John Knox, 2009.

Miller-McLemore, Bonnie. "Practical Theology and Pedagogy: Embodying Theological Know-How." In *For Life Abundant: Practical Theology, Theological Education, and Christian Ministry,* edited by Dorothy C. Bass and Craig Dykstra. Grand Rapids: Eerdmans, 2008.

Nemeck, Francis Kelly, and Marie Theresa Coombs. *The Spiritual Journey: Critical Thresholds and Stages of Adult Spiritual Genesis*. Wilmington, DE: Michael Glazier, 1986.

Neumark, Heidi B. *Breathing Space: A Spiritual Journey in the South Bronx*. Boston: Beacon, 2004.

Salovey, Peter, and John D. Mayer. "Emotional Intelligence." *Imagination, Cognition, and Personality* 9 (1990) 185–211.

Scharen, Christian. "Learning Ministry over Time: Embodying Practical Wisdom." In *For Life Abundant: Practical Theology, Theological Education, and Christian Ministry*, edited by Dorothy C. Bass and Craig Dykstra, 265–87. Grand Rapids: Eerdmans, 2008.

Scharen, Christian B., and Eileen R. Campbell-Reed. "Learning Pastoral Imagination: A Five-Year Report on How New Ministers Learn in Practice." *Auburn Studies* no. 21 (Winter 2016).

Schön, Donald. *Educating the Reflective Practitioner: Toward a New Design for Teaching and Learning in the Professions*. Jossey-Bass Higher Education Series. San Francisco: Jossey-Bass, 1987.

Tanner, Christine A., and Patricia Benner. *Expertise in Nursing Practice*. New York: Springer, 1996.

Taylor, Charles. "To Follow a Rule." In *Philosophical Arguments*. Cambridge: Harvard University Press, 1995.

Witvliet, John D. "Teaching Worship as a Christian Practice." In *For Life Abundant: Practical Theology, Theological Education, and Christian Ministry*, edited by Dorothy C. Bass and Craig Dykstra, 117–49. Grand Rapids: Eerdmans, 2008.

20

The Integrating Task

A Theological Reflection

EDWARD FOLEY

T he students I have had the privilege to teach at Catholic Theological
Union come from around the United States and around the globe.
Among other things, they are culturally attuned and instinctively take to
social analysis and contextual theology. Often I find myself asking them as
they are preparing a class presentation or some written submission, "What
makes this theological?" Just because someone is talking about a ministry
incident, a pastoral concern, or even some religious concept does not mean
that the discourse at its heart theological. Often it is simply political or so-
ciological or the opportunity to narrate a personal concern or experience.

As a theological educator, I experience something similar with my
peers. While we employ a wide range of pedagogical theories, principles of
appreciative inquiry, and various other learning tools in crafting curricula
and academic policies, it is theology that distinguishes our vocation. To
that end, I offer this essay as one attempt by a Caucasian, Roman Catholic cleric and senior citizen who is trained in liturgics and a self-professed
practical theologian to illustrate how such theologizing is possible and may
be useful from one social location.

The Turn to Jesus

As a Christian it is difficult for me to theologize about anything without reference to Jesus Christ. Sometimes that turn can be off-putting to those who do not hold for his divinity or the value of his message. Some have suggested that in this era of interfaith and interbelief dialogue it may be more effective to begin a conversation with the Spirit, a more ubiquitous and liquid concept that finds resonance across multiple religious boundaries.[1] In view of these concerns, I wish to lower the toll for entering this discussion by focusing on what we know of the pedagogical prowess he demonstrated. I do this because I am continuously fascinated and inspired by the life of the historical Jesus. Thus, his legacy can similarly inspire theological educators today regarding the integrating process.

The Data

The New Testament, particularly its Gospels, were not written as histories of Jesus or to chronicle the emergence of the Christian community. On the other hand, they contain much historical information.[2] Jesus was consistently remembered as a teacher in this literature. Some form of the teacher designation (*didaskale, didaskalos, epistata, epistatēs, rabbi,* and *rabboni*) is predicated of Jesus (fifty-six times) therein more than virtually any other title; only Lord is utilized more often (eighty-three times).[3] In the Gospel of Mark, for example, he is called a teacher by disciples (Mark 4:38), by those outside his immediate circle (Mark 1:21), and even by critics (Mark 12:18).[4]

The title is affirmed outside the New Testament by both Christians and non-Christians. The Jewish historian Josephus (ca. 37–100 CE) characterized Jesus as "a teacher of such people as accept the truth gladly" (*Antiquitates Judaicae* 18.3.3§63). The Greek philosopher Galen (ca. 129–216 CE) speaks about Christianity as a kind of philosophy (*De pulsuum differentiis* 2.4), and Jesus is thus construed as the de facto founder of this

1. See Johnson, *Quest for the Living God*, especially 181–201.

2. See Aslan's bestselling *Zealot*. Informative is Mitchell's critique of his work in "L'affaire Aslan," 10–17. I am grateful to Laurie Brink for this reference.

3. Keller, "Jesus the Teacher," 450–51.

4. See Graudin, "Jesus as Teacher in Mark"; more important, Robbins, *Jesus the Teacher*.

philosophical movement. While Christianity is defective for him, Galen is yet impressed by Christians' attempts to educate the masses regarding ethical issues.[5] Similarly, the Syrian apologist Tatian (120–173 CE), argued that Christianity was a philosophy superior to any of the Greeks (*Oratio ad Graecos* 31.1). The Greek satirist Lucian (ca. 120–180 CE) refers to Jesus as "that crucified sophist" (*Peri tes Peregrinou teleutes* 13) or one who taught only for money.[6] Thus sources both inside and outside the New Testament demonstrate that Jesus was understood to be some kind of teacher. Christians who choose a teaching vocation can revel in this celebrated ancestry.

Jesus's Preparation for Teaching

Numerous biblical scholars contend that Jesus was irregularly prepared to be a rabbi and, according to the standards of the era, "unqualified" to be a rabbi.[7] "There were strict regulations for the course of scribal education in the time of Jesus. From about the age of 7–10 the budding rabbi first lived permanently with a scribe, as a pupil. He heard his lectures and observed him exercising his profession and fulfilling the precepts of the Law in practice. When his pupil had mastered the substance of the tradition and knew how to apply it, he was ordained and entrusted with an office. There is no indication that Jesus underwent an education of this kind."[8] This lack of proper preparation becomes evident in Jesus's nonconformist approach to teaching his own disciples. As Gerhard Lohfink explains, Jesus shatters most of the traditional parameters observed by the rabbis of his era.[9] For example, the fundamental task of a disciple was to study Torah; however, disciples do not follow Jesus to learn Torah but to become fishers of people (Matt 4:19). Rabbinic tradition expects disciples literally to serve their teacher, such as waiting on him at table, cleaning his house, and going to market. Because of this, rabbinic students chose their teachers in whose service they would be enrolling. Conversely, Jesus selects his own disciples (Matt 8:22)—unprecedented in the rabbinic traditions. He also does not allow himself to be served but instead is the one who serves (cf. John 13). Finally, in order to teach Torah and have a stable of dependable disciples,

---

5. See Walzer, *Galen on Jews and Christians*, 63–64.

6. See van Voorst, *Jesus Outside the New Testament*, 62.

7. Kealy, "Jesus the Unqualified Teacher," 229.

8. Jeremias, *New Testament Theology*, 77.

9. What follows is condensed from Lohfink, *Jesus of Nazareth*, 73–77.

it was essential that the rabbi had an established house of studies an craft that would insure an income. Jesus, however, was a committed itinerant who touted his lack of home (Matt 8:20) and expected his disciples to be on the move with him (Matt 4:19–20). Lohfink surmises from this mobility that the petition for "daily bread" in the prayer Jesus taught his disciples was the expression of an existential need. This informal credentialing may be reassuring, especially when our teaching moves into fields in which we have no formal training.

The Jesus Pedagogy

A serious reading of the Gospels reveals that Jesus's most characteristic form of speech is the parable.[10] As a rhetorical device, parable does not so much convey information as much as it challenges the imagination. A decidedly poetic form of discourse, parables do not yield a predetermined answer but rather shock the hearer into envisioning what was previously thought to be if not impossible at least unlikely. Thus, Søren Kierkegaard (1813–1855) considered them an indirect form of communication.[11] Parables are characteristic of a pedagogy that does not so much shape students to parrot established learning but invites them into new ways of knowing. This could be considered a constructivist approach to teaching and learning that—especially through dialogue—invites students (or disciples) to imagine new possibilities or truths.[12] An example is Jesus's celebrated conversation with Simon Peter (Mark 8:27–29), an interchange that leads the disciple to declare something new about the identity of Jesus. Because Jesus believed he had been granted a unique epiphany about God, this maverick teacher required a provocative pedagogy if he was going to invite his disciples into the mystery of God's reign (Luke 8:10).

While inventive and constructive, Jesus's pedagogy yet seemed grounded in his present reality. Decades ago Amos Wilder (1895–1993) emphasized the extemporaneous nature of Jesus's speech: not carefully crafted or methodically thought-out beforehand but ingeniously improvised in a specific context. Jesus's speech was "directed to the occasion, it is not calculated to serve some future hour. This utterance is dynamic, actual,

10. See Theissen and Merz, *Historical Jesus*, 316.

11. Kierkegaard's thinking about indirect communication is well summarized in Cates, "Christianity and Communication."

12. Anuarite Wasukundi, "Pedagogy of Jesus," 266.

immediate, reckless of posterity; not coded for catechesis or repetition."[13] This thoroughly contextual yet ephemeral form of pedagogy—effective for immediate hearers—poses some problems for future generations. As George Riley remarks, "Very few of [Jesus's] sayings were preserved, and even these few survived only in forms that were either malleable or subject to rough handling and frequent neglect."[14] While a potential difficulty for future disciples, this daring form of instruction does encourage me in my own teaching to abandon some preset plan and on occasion follow the group energy, even if it seems to stray far from the syllabus.

Jesus's Assessment Goals

Jesus did not have to adhere to the language and frameworks of contemporary assessment requirements. Yet, viewing his ministry through some of these lenses might be enlightening. He clearly was a man on a mission and his mission statement appears early in Gospels: "The time is fulfilled, and the kingdom of God has come near; repent, and believe in the good news" (Mark 1:15). The motivation for this mission was a deep love of God and neighbor (Matt 22:36–40). Such is achieved through basic program goals for this Jesus school of discipleship.

Personal Transformation

While there is some information that Jesus communicates to his disciples about the in-breaking of God's reign and the need for repentance, a fundamental goal of his teaching ministry seems to be transformation.[15] As an apocalyptic teacher-prophet, engaging in God's unfolding reign requires "something more than an external and conventional righteousness based on observance of . . . Torah. Because the kingdom is at hand, Jesus regards merely external and legal observance as insufficient. The imminent sovereignty of God demands a response of the whole person . . . Accordingly, Jesus shifts the emphasis from *halakah* to *haggadah*, from rules for conduct to the formation of character by the story."[16] Resonant with Jack Mezirow's

13. Wilder, *Early Christian Rhetoric*, 15.

14. Riley, "Words and Deeds," 429.

15. Troftgruben, "Lessons for Teaching," 392. Parker Palmer famously noted that confronting transformation is of the essence in learning. *To Know as We Are Known*, 40.

16. Verhey, "Should Jesus Get Tenure?," 11.

concept of transformative learning as a "deep, structural shift in basic premises of thought, feeling, and actions,"[17] Jesus employed his parabolic gift to invite disciples into a fundamental reimagining of God and neighbor that was at odds with much of the religious thinking and accompanying religious practices of his context.

Societal Change

Stephen Spear believes that Jesus was self-conscious of his attempts to transform the thinking and acting of his disciples. As Spear imagines it, this transformative Jesus pedagogy was not simply for the sake of helping individuals progress in their personal spiritual journeys. Rather, it was a strategy for moving people from a sociocentric to a worldcentric view: "Sociocentric people love their neighbors. Worldcentric people love their neighbors, strangers, and enemies."[18] Thus, akin to the emancipatory approach of Paulo Freire,[19] instead of a focus on personal transformation á la Mezirow, Jesus seemed more concerned about the transformation of society into a more just and equitable reality.

Integrity

The Gospel of Matthew is often identified as "the teaching gospel."[20] Unlike Mark, Matthew has a keen interest in gathering and arranging the teachings of Jesus in five great discourses. The first of these is the Sermon on the Mount (5:1–7:29). In his analysis, Troy Troftgruben suggests that the conclusions of each of these pericopes contain a distinctive lesson about the ministry of teaching.[21] The finale of this first discourse (7:24–27) underscores the essential link between knowing and doing, between teaching and praxis for both teachers and students. As Troftgruben notes, the "cardinal sin of those explicitly condemned by Jesus is to know the good and yet not act upon it," and the harshest judgment is for teachers "who do not translate

---

17. Transformative Learning Centre (2004), as cited in Kitchenham, "Evolution of John Mezirow's Transformative Learning Theory," 104.

18. Spear, "Transformation of Enculturated Consciousness," 365.

19. Freire, *Pedagogy of the Oppressed*.

20. This is how Barclay characterized Matthew in his 1956 *The Daily Study Bible*, recently revised and updated as *The New Daily Study Bible*. Vol. 1, 9.

21. Troftgruben, "Lessons for Teaching," 390.

teaching into practice."[22] Conversely, Jesus's hearers seem impressed that, unlike the scribes, he teaches with a marked degree of authenticity. "Jesus embodies the ideals of blessing the poor in spirit, fidelity to God, and righteousness. The implication is that Jesus's disciple-teachers are called to do the same."[23]

In any era, calibrating pedagogies for personal and social transformation with integrity seems both right and just. This is a legacy that is both compelling and contemporary.

From the First to the Twenty-First Century

It does not seem plausible to replicate the practices of this itinerant, prophetic maverick within brick and mortar seminaries, divinity schools, and other institutions cued to ministerial preparation. Even as our institutions launch out into cyberspace with online courses and digitally enhanced educational strategies, we still are connected to physical campuses and postal addresses that never weighed down Jesus. We are also beholden to many a donor and judicatory, something he seemed to eschew. While we cannot mimic Jesus's pedagogy or hope to attain his integrating vision, those of us who honor Jesus as a gifted pedagogue can yet theologize from this pivotal revelation to shape our pedagogies for an integrating vision, grounded in love, for personal and societal transformation. This seems resonant with his constructivist approach to teaching and learning that invited disciples to imagine new possibilities or truths.

Since the goal of this essay is not only theologizing about ministerial training and pedagogies but also the integrating task in particular that should permeate these, the remainder of this chapter will lift up three frames of Christian theology. Doing so requires stepping out of the humanistic framework employed in the first part of this essay and entering into my theologizing as a Christian who holds for the divinity of Jesus.

22. Ibid., 392.
23. Ibid.

Wisdom Christology

One common way to envision Rabbi Jesus is as a sage or wisdom teacher.[24] It is true that, apart from Paul in 1 Cor 1:14, scant New Testament evidence explicitly identifies Jesus with the Wisdom of God. On the other hand, Elisabeth Schüssler Fiorenza contends that "the diversity of Christological discourses that developed in a time span as short as twenty years after Jesus's death can be plausibly explained if we assume Jewish Wisdom theology as the generative matrix."[25] The influence of this Wisdom theology can be detected in many strata of the Gospels. Pheme Perkins, for example, has demonstrated how the Gospel of Matthew makes a strong connection between Jesus and Wisdom, concluding that "the evangelist identifies Jesus's words and deeds with Wisdom."[26] Especially in the Gospel of John Jesus is presented as the very personification of Wisdom.[27]

From the viewpoint of the Hebrew scriptures wisdom is both a style and a content, ultimately concerned with living a good life in the here and now. As Roland Murphy notes, "The sages reflect on a wide area of life in order to provide insights into the way things are and the way they should be . . . Compared to the commandments of the Torah, their teaching deals with the grey area of life which has to do with formation of character."[28] As Jesus is remembered as appropriating this tradition, Murphy can consider Jesus as a source of "practical wisdom" in the New Testament.[29]

In some ways, the journey into integration could be consider one into practical reasoning or practical wisdom. Akin to Aristotle's concept of *phronesis* and its complementary form of action (praxis), practical wisdom is not some abstract form of reflection that might be fruitfully applied in the future. Rather, phronetic thinking is "our ability to *perceive* the situation, to have the appropriate *feelings* or desires about it, to *deliberate* about what was appropriate in these circumstances, and to *act*."[30] Acquiring a habitus of practical reasoning requires cultivating critical thinking skills in a highly

24. Murphy, "Wisdom," 1083.

25. Schüssler Fiorenza, *Jesus*, 139.

26. Perkins, "Jesus," 276.

27. See the overview of the literature on this topic in Kling, "Wisdom Became Flesh."

28. Murphy, "Introduction to Wisdom Literature," 448.

29. Murphy, "Wisdom," 1084.

30. Schwartz and Sharpe, *Practical Wisdom*, 5. I am grateful to Kathleen Cahalan for this reference.

contextual manner that guides and is guided by our doing in a heartfelt and ethical way: a combination of orthodoxy, orthokardia,[31] and orthopraxis.

From a Christian perspective, being formed in practical reasoning anchored in the Jesus revelation takes on particular nuance. Phronetic reason by its nature is ethical and concerned about acting for some common good. It is, in a word, prudent. Entering into a habitus of practical wisdom from a Christian lens, however, means reflecting and acting in service not only of the common good but also of the in-breaking of God's reign that Jesus announced. As Allen Verhey insisted, "The authority of Jesus calls us not only to hope for God's good future and not only to lament that it is sadly still challenged by the violence and poverty and prejudice that beat down and oppress our neighbors," but to embrace a spirit of justice and shalom that will sometimes shock and challenge our own contexts.[32]

Seminaries, divinity schools, and other institutions for ministerial training are called to be schools that not only teach but also rehearse in their own confines this practical wisdom. A learning environment imbued with such prudence of thinking, feeling, and doing is a promising and graced environment for shaping disciples committed to the pursuit of practical wisdom in their personal and ministerial lives.

Contextual-Incarnation Theology

Jesus exercised what could be considered an improvisational and extemporaneous style of pedagogy. His many references to the ordinary items that inhabited the lives of his hearers are striking. In the early twentieth century, Alban Goodier captured this unique texture of Jesus's teaching when he mused:

> He speaks of their everyday joys and sorrows; the salt of their everyday meal . . . their daily conversation with its oaths and loose language; their daily bickering before the local judge; their household quarrels; the local thief; the local borrower of money . . . their daily toil and their daily wages, carefully stored and hidden away in their money-bags at home; the rust and the moth, which were a constant trouble; the raven at that moment hovering above them; the flowers flourishing abundantly around them . . . their food,

---

31. This term is borrowed from Wesleyan scholar Gregory Clapper, "*Orthokardia*." Alternate language is the more common orthopathy.

32. Verhey, "Should Jesus Get Tenure?," 18.

their drink, their clothing, their need of daily sustenance . . . their dogs, their swine; their fish and their eggs . . . he has said what he said in the language of their lives.[33]

Jesus took the material of everyday life seriously in his teaching and theologizing, because he and the Godhead in which he participated took humanity seriously. For those who ascent to it, the mystery of the Incarnation is a startling, vulgar reality that insults every gnostic sensibility.[34] Distinct from romanticized nativity depictions, this foundational Christian belief first holds that God became fully human in Jesus. Beyond that singular embodiment, however, by this preemptive act of love, the God of Jesus Christ also wed divinity to all humanity. Consequently, the mystery of Incarnation—far beyond the singular birth of the Word made flesh—can and must continue. It continues in the ecclesial "body of Christ," as Paul (1 Cor 12:27) and Augustine (354–430 CE) after him asserted (*Sermo* 272). Yet, beyond Christianity and even the Abrahamic religions, the mystery of Incarnation from a Christian perspective continues in the birth of every child and in the living of every life.[35]

Theologizing that places this incarnational principle at the heart of the enterprise is fundamentally contextual. As Stephen Bevans explains, context is quite complex and represents a combination of several realities. These include (1) the experiences of a person's or a group's life, (2) culture, (3) an individual's or a community's social location, and (4) the dynamics of social change.[36] The category of social location is particularly rich, encompassing a galaxy of intertwining phenomena including age, gender, educational background, wealth, geographic location, and access to services such as the Internet or transportation.

Phronetic reasoning, the journey into practical wisdom, is by definition contextual. As Barry Schwartz and Kenneth Sharpe outlined it above, the first step in phronetic thinking is "our ability to *perceive* the situation";[37] that is, the ability to read the context. Forming future ministers to be self-consciously contextual in their serving and believing is a daunting task. It requires them to face their own presuppositions, to come to grips with

33. Goodier, *Good Galilean*, 64–65.

34. The Gnostic Mani (d. before 277 CE) is reported to have said that "a good God has nothing in common with the evil world." *Hegemonius*, 39.

35. From a Roman Catholic perspective, see Pope Francis, *Joy of the Gospel*, no. 179.

36. Bevans, *Models of Contextual Theology*, 5–6.

37. Schwartz and Sharpe, *Practical Wisdom*, 5.

their own social location and, in light of it, to be willing to honor and even live into the reality of the other—the different and especially the stranger. For that to occur, faculty, formation staff, and other personnel committed to accompanying students on this trek must embrace this integrative excursion as well. Consonant with the underlying concern to reimagine the integrating enterprise as one that marks the whole of our institutions, administrators and other personnel responsible for shaping both the public persona and the internal environment of our schools have a particular responsibility here. It is not only the courses, curricular design, and individual staff or faculty practices that need to reflect these incarnational-contextual instincts. There also needs to be sustained institutional self-reflection on the stories we promote, rituals we enact, personnel we hire, and missions we embrace in order to assess whether they and the agents who enact them are contributing to an integrating vision of education and ministry. Schools not only have to form students in their abilities to theologize and minister from an incarnational-contextual perspective; they also have to model a consonant and compelling incarnational-contextual commitment and praxis. This requires ongoing and integrative formation for staff, faculty, and administrators who never graduate but year after year bear a fundamental responsibility to read the context, face our own presuppositions, and embrace the stranger.

A Centrifugal-Communion Ecclesiology

Ecclesiology is theological reflection on what it means to be church. Every ecclesiology (like every theology) is contextual and often a form of apologetics about why one church believes it is more authentic than another. In an appreciative mode, ecclesiology could be considered theological reflection on how the baptized can be and even should be together in service of all humanity. This appreciative mode underscores the integrating contribution of ecclesiologies that spur our acting and reflecting upon the whole body with its many parts that can be united without being homogenized (1 Cor 12:12).

This communal lens is critical for Christianity, because our scriptures and traditions announce that revelation was never for the sake of an individual but always for a community of hearers. One central drumbeat throughout the First Testament is some variation on the revelation "I will take you as my people, and I will be your God" (cf. Exod 6:7). Revelation serves the shaping of this people. While the New Testament does not use the language of "people" (Hebrew, lə·'ām), there are emphases that underscore the priority of community over any individual. Linguistically, an analogous drumbeat throughout the New Testament is the emphasis on "one another" (allélón). Almost sixty times in the New Testament the community is instructed to pursue some action for "one another."[38]

There are many challenges to having such an appreciative and centrifugal perspective on "church" in an age when most mainline Christian denominations in the United States are experiencing a marked decline in membership. Juxtaposing this reality with the growing number of the unaffiliated as well as those who manifest multiple religious belongings could render a generous ecclesiological stance at least difficult, if not challenging.[39] One image from the ancient church that could be useful in the face of such ecclesiological anxiety is a communion of communions. As has been demonstrated by numerous biblical and patristic scholars, the early church was such a community of communities, distinctive in membership and even mission, yet bound together in a singular belief in Jesus as the Christ.

A modern recovery of this idea of church as a community of communities has emerged in the concept of communion ecclesiologies. While communion ecclesiology is a liquid term used by people at multiple, even contradictory, ecclesial positions, Dennis Doyle has suggested that it is possible to generalize about this ecclesiological perspective as one that emphasizes relationships over juridical or institutional understandings of church, with a strong emphasis on the mystical, sacramental, and historical. Furthermore, according to Doyle, authentic communion ecclesiologies embrace a healthy and dynamic interplay between unity and diversity, between the universal and local.[40]

While ecclesiologies focused on in-house apologetics or designed to defend the authenticity of a particular embodiment of church could actually be disintegrating, authentic communion ecclesiologies seem more resonant with the integrating vision promoted in this work. Their appreciative respect of other visions of community or church, marked by a notable degree of mutuality without jeopardizing anyone's personal ecclesial beliefs

38. See the useful enumeration of these at Exploring Christianity, http://www.christianity.co.nz/church5.htm.

39. See, for example, the overview of this phenomenon provided in Cornille, *Many Mansions?*

40. Doyle, *Communion Ecclesiology*, 12–13.

or commitments, is a promising and potentially productive theological model. For such a model to move a community toward a truly integrating journey, however, requires a decentralizing, even rhizomatic, vision of power and discourse.

French philosophers Gilles Deleuze and Félix Guattari utilized the category of plants known as rhizomes as a metaphor for thinking about contemporary culture and discourse. A rhizome such as ginger is a root that grows horizontally under the surface. Unlike trees whose roots generally grow deeper into the earth while branches shoot upward, rhizomes do not have a clear beginning and ending, top or a bottom. From a philosophical viewpoint, Deleuze and Guattari consider this a fruitful way to reimagine contemporary thought through a nonhierarchical framework that allows many avenues for entering and exiting a conversation. "A rhizome has no beginning or end; it is always in the middle, between things, interbeing, intermezzo."[41] A rhizome is an alliance—but often an alliance of the unexpected.

A rhizomatic-ecclesiological perspective might contribute to that integrating trajectory for which theological education and ministerial practice must strive. It is self-possessed without being defensive, inviting without being colonial, holistic but in a dynamic mode. It is an ecclesiology not embedded in a traditional rabbinic household but out on the road with Jesus, improvising responses to the subtleties of everyday life and the needs of the wider society.

Conclusion

Theological educators are invited to bring our distinctive theological gifts to bear in service of the educating vocation. For me that is best achieved by considering Jesus as a master pedagogue with a teaching style that was admittedly prophetic, provocative, and tuned to the transformation of individuals in community for the sake of God's mission. The point is not to say this is the only way to engage theology but to insist that theologizing is essential to the educating vocation, and to encourage theological educators and our schools to theologize in whatever mode is profitable. Such theologizing is a critical integrating element that prods us toward more holistic, dynamic, and wise ways of knowing and being. It is also a journey

41. Deleuze and Guattari, *Thousand Plateaus*, 23. See my *Theological Reflection across Religious Traditions*, 9–12 et passim.

that, from an eschatological perspective, is never finished. It is the already, not-yet unfolding of God's reign that we take up again in service of our institutions, our students, and the world that the Holy One loves from its foundations (John 3:16).

Bibliography

Anuarite Wasukundi, Francine. "Pedagogy of Jesus for Modern World Christian Teachers." *African Ecclesial Review* 54.3–4 (2012) 262–84.

Aslan, Reza. *Zealot: The Life and Times of Jesus of Nazareth.* New York: Random House, 2014.

Barclay, William. *The Daily Study Bible.* (1956). Rev. as *The New Daily Study Bible.* Vol. 1: *The Gospel of Matthew.* Edinburgh: Saint Andrew, 2001.

Bevans, Stephen B. *Models of Contextual Theology.* Rev. ed. Faith and Cultures Series. Maryknoll, NY: Orbis, 2002.

Cates, Benjamin. "Christianity and Communication: Kierkegaard, Hamann, and the Necessity of Indirect Communication." MA thesis, Liberty University, 2009.

Clapper, Gregory. "*Orthokardia:* The Practical Theology of John Wesley's Heart Religion." *Quarterly Review* 10 (1990) 49–66.

Cornille, Catherine, ed. *Many Mansions? Multiple Religious Belonging and Christianity.* Maryknoll, NY: Orbis, 2002.

Deleuze, Gilles, and Félix Guattari. *A Thousand Plateaus.* Translated by Brian Massumi. London: Continuum, 1988.

Doyle, Dennis. *Communion Ecclesiology: Vision and Versions.* Maryknoll, NY: Orbis, 2000.

Foley, Edward. *Theological Reflection across Religious Traditions: The Turn to Reflective Believing.* Lanham, MD: Rowman & Littlefield, 2015.

Freire, Paulo. *Pedagogy of the Oppressed.* New York: Continuum, 2000.

Goodier, Alban. *The Good Galilean: Lessons in Living from the Son of Man Himself.* 1928. Reprinted, Manchester, NH: Sophia Institute, 2009.

Graudin, Arthur F. "Jesus as Teacher in Mark." *Concordia Journal* 3 (1977).

Hegemonius: Acta Archelai. In *Die Griechischen Christlichen Schriftsteller der ersten Drei Jahrhunderte* 27. Edited by Charles Henry Beeson. Leipzig: Hinrichs, 1906. https://archive.org/stream/hegemoniusactaaroohege/hegemoniusactaaroohege_djvu.txt.

Jeremias, Joachim. *New Testament Theology.* Vol. 1. Translated by John Bowden. New York: Scribner, 1971.

Johnson, Elizabeth. *Quest for the Living God: Mapping Frontiers in the Theology of God.* New York: Continuum, 2008.

Kealy, Sean. "Jesus the Unqualified Teacher." *African Ecclesiastical Review* 19.4 (1977) 228–33.

Keller, Marie Noël. "Jesus the Teacher." *Currents in Theology and Mission* 25.6 (1998) 450–60.

Kitchenham, Andrew. "The Evolution of John Mezirow's Transformative Learning Theory." *Journal of Transformative Education* 6.2 (2008) 104–23, DOI: 10.1177/1541344608322678

Kling, Sheri D. "Wisdom Became Flesh: An Analysis of the Prologue to the Gospel of John." *Currents in Theology and Mission* 40.3 (2013) 179–87.

Lohfink, Gerhard. *Jesus of Nazareth: What He Wanted, Who He Was.* Translated by Linda Maloney. Collegeville, MN: Liturgical, 2012.

Mitchell, Margaret. "L'affaire Aslan: *Zealot*, the Media and the Academic Study of Religion." *Criterion* 51.1 (2015) 10–17.

Murphy, Roland. "Introduction to Wisdom Literature." In *New Jerome Biblical Commentary,* edited by Raymond Brown et al. Englewood Cliffs, NJ: Prentice Hall, 1990.

———. "Wisdom: Jesus as a Teacher of Wisdom." In *The Collegeville Pastoral Dictionary of Biblical Theology,* edited by Carroll Stuhlmueller. Collegeville, MN: Liturgical, 1996.

Palmer, Parker. *To Know as We Are Known: A Spirituality of Education.* New York: Harper & Row, 1983.

Perkins, Pheme. "Jesus: God's Wisdom." *Word and World* 7 (1987) 273–80.

Pope Francis. *The Joy of the Gospel: Evangelii Gaudium.* Washington, DC: USCCB, 2013.

Riley, George. "Words and Deeds: Jesus as Teacher and Jesus as Pattern of Life." *Harvard Theological Review* 90 (1997) 427–36.

Robbins, Vernon K. *Jesus the Teacher: A Socio-Rhetorical Interpretation of Mark.* Minneapolis: Fortress, 1984.

Schüssler Fiorenza, Elisabeth. *Jesus: Miriam's Child, Sophia's Prophet.* New York: Continuum, 1994.

Schwartz, Barry, and Kenneth Sharpe. *Practical Wisdom: The Right Way to Do the Right Thing.* New York: Riverhead, 2010.

Spear, Stephen. "The Transformation of Enculturated Consciousness in the Teachings of Jesus." *Journal of Transformative Education* 3.4 (2005) 354–73. DOI: 10.1177/1541344605278009.

Theissen, Gerd, and Annette Merz. *The Historical Jesus: A Comprehensive Guide.* Translated by John Bowden. Minneapolis: Fortress, 1998.

Troftgruben, Troy. "Lessons for Teaching from the Teacher: Matthew's Jesus on Teaching and Leading Today." *Currents in Mission and Theology* 40.6 (2013) 387–98.

Van Voorst, Robert. *Jesus Outside the New Testament: An Introduction to the Ancient Evidence.* Grand Rapids: Eerdmans, 2000.

Verhey, Allen. "Should Jesus Get Tenure? Jesus as a Moral Teacher and the Vocation of Teaching Christian Ethics." *Journal of the Society of Christian Ethics* 34.2 (2014) 3–25.

Walzer, Richard. *Galen on Jews and Christians.* Oxford Classical & Philosophical Monographs. London: Oxford University Press, 1949.

Wilder, Amos N. *Early Christian Rhetoric: The Language of the Gospel.* 1971. Reprinted, Amos Wilder Library. Eugene, OR: Wipf & Stock, 2014.

Index of Names

Aleshire, Daniel, 50, 52

Anderson, Herbert, 180

Anuarite Wasukundi, Francine, 223n12, 233

Aquinas, Thomas, *see* Thomas Aquinas

Aristotle, 79, 205–6, 217, 227

Aslan, Reza, 221n2, 233

Augustine, 93, 133, 138, 229

Baldwin, Christina, 39n16

Banks, Sarah, 31

Barclay, William, 225n20, 233

Bard, Elizabeth, 21–22

Basil of Caesarea, 199

Bass, Dorothy, 38, 40, 206n6, 207n8, 218

Benner, Patricia, 23n7, 31, 206, 213–15, 218

Bevans, Stephen, 229, 233

Bloom, Matt, 209n14, 212, 214, 218

Brebera, Pavel, 31

Brelsford, Theodore, 151n4, 157

Brookfield, Stephen, 184, 185, 209n16, 210n18, 210n20, 218

Brown, Warren, 37n10, 40

Brownel, 2n1

Browning, Don S., 4n7, 14, 77n7, 88, 206

Brownwell, Jayne E., 14

Calahan, Kathleen A., vii n2, xiii, 5n12, 81n18, 126n1, 207n10, 211n22, 216n39, 227n30, 14, 82n20, 83n22, 88, 126n1, 206n7, 207n10, 211n22, 216n39, 218, 227n30

Calhoun, Emily, 138

Calvin, John, 92

Campbell-Reed, Eileen R., 5–6, 15, 207n9, 219

Cannon, Lynn Weber, 173, 176

Cardoza-Orlandi, Carlos F., 176

Cates, Benjamin, 223n11, 233

Carroll, Jackson, 20n1, 31

Cassian, John, 211, 213, 218

Clapper, Gregory, 228n31, 233

Click, Emily, xiii, 13, 128, 136–37, 187, 189

Cochrane, James R., 154n9, 157

Coen, Joel, 170n5, 176

Colletta, Nat, 25, 27n39, 31

Coombs, Marie Theresa, 215, 217

Coombs, Philip, 23–24, 27, 31

Cornille, Catherine, 231n39

Index of Subjects

importance of faculty to, vii–viii , 33
and informal education, 24–26
and learner-centered curriculum
  designs, 78, 80
learning goals, 128
and the learning process, 160, 210–12
for online learners, 179–80
and the pastoral circle, 153
and promoting engagement, 187–88
showing respect for learners' previous
  experiences, 187
and the willingness to take risks, 187
Leviticus 19, 34
liberal arts education, viii
lifelong learning, pursuing, 43
linked, recognizing as part of integration,
  197–98
Louisville Seminary, "Senior Integrating
  Seminar," 85–86
love
  as action, 35
  as framework for integration, 30, 34,
    37, 67–68
  as God's commandment, 34–35
  modeling/practicing during faculty
    meetings, 38–40, 38nn14–15
Luke
  1:35, 10
  4:18-19, 10
  8:10, 223
  10:25-26, 34n2
Lutheran School of Theology at Chicago,
  senior interdisciplinary seminar,
  86

Mark
  1:21, 221
  4:38, 221
  8:27-29, 223
  12:18, 221
  12:28-29, 34n2
  comparison with gospel of Matthew,
    225
Matthew
  4:19-20, 222–23
  5:1-7:29, 225
  7:24-27, 225

8:20, 223
8:22, 222
22:34-35, 34n2
22:37-39, 34
comparison with gospel of Mark, 225
on loving one's enemy, 34–35
as the "teaching gospel," 225, 225n20
Wisdom theology, 227
Matthews, Rex, 111
McAfee School of Theology
  capstone course, 85
  community building, annual retreats,
    87
MDiv degree. See theological education;
  theological schools, seminaries
Mentored Ministries Office (Calvin
  Theological Seminary), 47–48,
  99–100
mentors, exemplars. See also practical
  wisdom/practical intelligence
  (phronesis)
  and Jesus's ministry, 226
  importance of, to novices, 209
  and modeling moral behaviors,
    37n10, 226
  as resource for guided practice,
    211–12
  and student's integrating work, 95–99
message area, Calvin Theological
  Seminary curriculum, 93
ministry work, ministerial practice. See
  also leadership; theologizing
  ministerial education
  academic/theoretical underpinnings,
    206
  acceptance/acknowledgement of
    calling, 212
  advanced beginners, 211–12
  bringing into classroom, 120–21
  and communally based theological
    reflection, 151n4, 184–85
  complexity of tasks involved in, 3
  and contextual education/service
    learning, vii, 49–51, 90–92,
    97–98, 102, 110, 112–16, 149,
    151–52, 171, 171n8, 216

self-love, integrating with love for God
and one's neighbor, 34–35. *See
also* love
semiformal (nonformal) education
definitions and examples, 24, 26–28,
55
as paradigm for integrative work, 29
types of learning and programs
associated with, 28–29, 28n43
within the educational ecosystem,
64–65
seminaries. *See* theological schools,
seminaries
sequencing, in curriculum design
and course-level integration tasks,
126n1
examples, 80–82
and the fourfold framework, 95–96
Sermon on the Mount (Matt 5:1-7:29),
225
silo effects, 2, 29–30, 45–46, 77, 113
sin, sinfulness, as form of disintegration,
9–10, 202
site visits, challenges associated with, 172
situated learning, 23, 206
situational factors, identifying during
course design, 159–60
small-group work, 44n3, 71, 83, 120, 143,
152, 171, 179, 182–83
social analysis activities (pastoral circle),
153–54
sociocentric *vs.* worldcentric perspective,
225
spiritual discernment, and practical
wisdom, 207, 211
students, theological. *See also* learning
communities/environments
cohort groups, 193–95
diversity among, vii–viii, 102–3
impact of faculty on, 37
and learner-centered curriculum
designs, 78
observations on engagement related
to space usage, 62–63
in online courses, developing
learning partnerships with,
179–80

preparedness, viii
role in developing integrative
communities, 70–71
subject-centered curriculum structure,
76–78
synthetic/synthesizing skills, 195. *See
also* integrating work, integrative
unity

technology as pedagogical tool,
understanding limits of, 179
thematic courses, 77
Theological Education as Formation for
Ministry course (CTS), 95–96
theological reflection (TR) (pastoral
circle), 96–97, 153
theological schools, seminaries. *See
also* ministry work, ministerial
practical
boards of directors, limited
perspectives, 21
as communities of practice, 20–21, 33
deans, challenges faced by, 37–38,
37n11
diagonally integrated curriculums,
83–84
dismissal of role of emotion and
intuition in learning, 35
diversity and preparedness of
students, vii–viii
as educational ecosystems, 22, 53,
54n2, 56–63
emphasis on scholarship over
practice, 35
faculty, vii–viii, 33
financial pressures, viii–ix
history and traditions, importance,
129
horizontally integrated curriculums,
82–83
informal and semiformal spaces,
learning in, 11–12
larger contexts and
interdependencies, 7, 19–20,
21n4
narrow views of integrating work,
ix–x, 19